THE INSIDE TRUTH
BOOK ONE: -

True life experiences from a former British Police Constable who was also a Coroners Officer.

This edition published 2018
by Copyright @ Howell Jackson LUNN

Cover design by Chris Williams
williamsgraphics.co.uk"

I write this book for my dear wife, three sons and in loving memory of my late mother and father and parents in law. I also wish to thank all the kind relatives and friends who have participated in helping formulate this book with their kind help and advice.

PREFACE OF BOOK

This is the first book I have ever written and in it I have portrayed all the hard work and interesting issues of everyday police work. It is a true story of me leaving school having no academic qualifications, coming from a basic background like most ordinary people of hard working parents. I have taken on life's challenges at every opportunity using my learning skills along the way, not knowing whether I would be successful or not. In addition I am most fortunate in having a good wife who has been the backbone of my career and has stood by me through thick and thin and never doubting me or any of my eventual decisions made. With sons who follow in our footsteps with whom I wished I had devoted more time to when young, as sometimes the job just had to come first. An offering not all dedicated staff would give.

One quality I recognise which is still with me today is that I see an inspiration to achieve which becomes an ultimate goal regardless of the obstacles. Being self-motivated with the utmost determination I have to think things out, either working on my feet, or through a planned strategy. I have to prepare for each manoeuvre and stand by my principles against the unseen enemy, as part of the journey on the road to success. I have always tried to be approachable, considerate and honest, a person who does not suffer fools gladly and who just gets on with the job. It is important to learn from mistakes on the way and advice at every opportunity. Hopefully having a wicked but naughty sense of humour without which life would be impossible.

The majority of my service I can say was the very best of the police force, where a large proportion of society treated you with respect and authority, and even included people you had arrested. Sadly this perception has deteriorated over the years but there are still very many officers who are not fully appreciated, who do still perform their duties to very excellent high standards, with brave dedication in a very dangerous and violent society. Sadly these officers are often overlooked, through bad publicity blighted by those of lower standards.

No locations of where I worked have been given, other than serving within the police service of the British Isles. Names appear in pseudonym of all colleagues mentioned including myself. This is to respect privacy for everyone. Any other person referred to, including victims witnesses or offenders have not been identified in complying with [The Official Secrets Act] and [The Human Rights Act]. Should any person bear any resemblance to anyone living or dead it is pure coincidence. In many chapters I have made comments on several issues which I have based on my own judgment and experience, all being in my view only and not wishing to cause any individual any offence. I understand other people may have other views or theories which is accepted and appreciated in a free democratic country.

In preparing the contents of this book I have re-lived all my true life experiences, some sad, some funny and unforgettable moments that will stay with me forever. Some people may consider my phrasing of sentences is not all within the full tradition of the perfect English language. I write how I speak after all we are individuals in life. The grammar in this edition has been corrected and I thank people for their comments and although I am not perfect, never has this ever stopped me in being successful. I suppose over the years there were far too many senior officers who would have made better English teachers as their main qualities in the police force appeared to be enforcing rigidly the scrutiny of reports. Just a pity some were not as highly qualified in detecting all crimes and bringing offenders to justice. No different to being gifted in solving serious problems within the community based on common sense, or being able to speak on the same level with all the people from so many walks of life you deal with every day in operational policing. Sadly far too many were far too pompous in their approach and manner being incapable of achieving this level of experience thus could not detect a smell yet alone a crime.

In these books I have told stories that actually happened in my career, no different to very similar stories that have appeared in the news in all forms of the media. In addition to stories of very similar police work in feature films and television dramas. In addition many instances of criminal behaviour is highlighted in numerous programmes showing the work of crime profilers in the United Kingdom and also the U.S.A, which are all part of highly informative television documentaries. Whist mindful of divulging any possible secrets of policing affecting any present day duties, no information is given that has not appeared in media previously, or aired before in these type of books or films. Many incidents or crimes detailed could not now however be committed in present day due to a change in police procedure or new legislation in various areas where the law has changed, in some cases definitely for the better.

In addition there a few examples in this book where bad language is typed, it is hoped this does not cause offence as it reflects the truth of what was said in all of the relevant circumstances. I fully realise that I have had a most rewarding and interesting career which has given me tremendous job satisfaction, most of which has been my own making following a path which has followed both good luck and judgment. This is reflected in the stories written of most of my experiences, some very sad, others interesting in all aspects of police work, good or bad memories that will stay with me forever.

Howell Jackson LUNN - Served 1970 – 1998

LIST OF CHAPTERS - BOOK ONE

CHAPTER 01

ERRATIC DRIVING RESULTING IN A 19 MILE CAR CHASE

I t was midweek, around early spring, in 1975 and I paraded for duty with the night shift, in a busy town centre situated within a Metropolitan Police district some ten miles from a large city. I took possession of a recently allocated brand new marked police vehicle for urban patrol, without realizing that within 4 hours I would be the instigator of a 19 mile car chase. This was to involve a police driver who would receive serious injuries, with damage being caused to three police vehicles, all being a total write off, and the subsequent arrest of two offenders.

As I went out on patrol I covered the busiest area close to the one side of the town centre. Like most evenings in the week there was plenty of activity, up until around 11.30pm, then things died down and it was a matter of looking out for the unusual and covering the places where most crime was likely to be committed. Back in 1975 the police vehicles had blue lights but no sirens, as only traffic vehicles mainly had that facility. I was in possession of a Pye radio transmitter and receiver, not one but two items of equipment. In addition in those days seat belts were not fitted in any vehicle, as there was no legislation on this kind of equipment. I was driving alone along one of the main roads when all of a sudden some 50 yards ahead, a car pulled out from a junction to my right. It was travelling extremely fast and swerved narrowly missing some stationary cars parked to the left of the road. I did what any other police officer would do, and started to follow, keeping observations from a distance.

It quickly became apparent that the car in front did not intend to slow down and his speed was increasing from 50 to 70 and 80 miles per hour whenever the opportunity arose.

Immediately I alerted the control room and it soon transpired I was in a car chase. I thought to myself, was I really ready for this? My driving abilities were only average and suitable for basic police duties and I was not up to advanced driver standard and so I realised exactly why the hairs on the back of my neck were standing up. I just had to stay with it and give it my best. I gave directions of the offending vehicle, which was a Ford Capri saloon with what appeared to have two people inside. I switched on the blue lights and continued maintaining my distance as our speed both increased well above 70 miles per hour in areas which were built up and subject to lower national speed limits. The vehicle was driving away from our sub-division and heading towards another town centre some five miles away, all the time speeding erratically along highways totally unsuitable for this type of road racing. Despite travelling at high speed with a brand new car which was performing well, I was also giving a running commentary using the transmitter and receiver alternatively.

Can you imagine this compared with today, driving at high speeds with the equivalent of two mobile phones taking it in turn to use whilst driving with one hand and without any seat belts in operation. How times have changed, but how dangerous things were then. We travelled along a dual carriageway, round a large five junction island and took an exit where the road was narrower. It was just after 2.00am and fortunately at this location the roads were reasonably quiet. The main thing was that the offenders were not making any diversions to areas so far unknown to me and staying on the main road towards the next town which was some six miles from a major city.

As we continued the Capri hit a humpback bridge at some 80 miles per hour and actually left the road travelling a short distance in the air until it slammed down back onto the road with several sparks. Undeterred the driver again built up speed. I also hit the same bridge, thinking God I am going to lose it. It was becoming extremely frightening and thankfully I managed to slow down sufficiently to avoid losing control, but as a result it slowed me down slightly and I had to accelerate hard to catch up. The vehicle continued towards the outskirts of the town where in the distance I saw that there was a road block created by a marked police vehicle with blue light flashing where the offender would have to stop. I managed to increase my position closer to the Capri when some thirty yards behind, I saw the Capri drive straight into the road block, causing severe damage and shunting the police vehicle to one side.

I maintained my speed in following the Capri still giving a running commentary to the Control room. As I looked through my rear mirror two or three other police vehicles with blue flashing lights were also behind and in immediate pursuit. At this point we were travelling along the main high street of the next town centre, speeds again increasing up to 90 to 100 miles per hour where I was still able to keep up with them. It just seemed to go on forever. Every traffic light on red was totally ignored and when I tried to overtake, the vehicle was deliberately swerving to the left and right sides of the road. Upon reaching the end of the high street close to a major football ground I saw in the distance another marked police vehicle with lights flashing which near to a junction had created a roadblock where the offending vehicle had nowhere to go. Again in those days there were no luxuries such as the presence of a Police Helicopter or any tyre piercing equipment which is today thrown into the path of speeding vehicles, which causes them to come to a halt or lose control.

Without any regard for anyone's safety the Capri crashed deliberately again into the police vehicle, hitting the vehicle head on travelling at least 80 miles per hour and ramming the vehicle into traffic bollards. It was obvious the driver in the police vehicle was injured and the chase had taken on a different sinister prospective, under no circumstances could I or my colleagues allow the offenders to escape. To witness this and have to continue on was absolutely nerve racking. It was later confirmed over the radio the police officer had sustained severe head injuries.

As the Capri headed towards the city, we approached areas where majority of night clubs were situated and although the road continued in a straight direction all the way, there were people all around and slight increases in traffic. The Capri had accident damage from two smashes, exposing various areas of the bodywork with jagged metal edges which would have had drastic consequences should any pedestrian had been struck down. Despite this, the driver was still managing speeds between 70 and 80 miles per hour. Along the road at intervals of every hundred yards or less traffic lights were in place. The Capri travelled through every set on red, swerving to miss people crossing the road, as at the time all the Night Clubs were closing and people were exiting the premises.

I was directly behind the Capri travelling also through every light on red, the chase was becoming hair raising and very frightening. What if he hit a pedestrian, or if I did, or if I smashed my car up, would I be hurt or killed, my wife, my children was all flashing through my mind. I thought to myself God they don't pay me enough for this. I was running high on adrenalin and in my mind I wondered where it was all going to end. Still I had to stay with it and I noticed other police vehicles still behind me for as far as the eye could see. As we approached the boundary of the city centre still travelling at the same speeds again another road block with a marked police vehicle was across the mouth of the junction to an island. Without any conscience it hit the side of the police vehicle ramming it out of its way where it continued towards an unknown outlying area of the city.

As I followed the Capri, the driver still reaching speeds of 60 miles per hour, prevented me from overtaking by again veering to each side of the road. He continued for approximately 2 miles when my opportunity came where I was able to overtake and ram him into a lamp post, where he finally came to a halt. I immediately got out of the vehicle and arrested the driver. Other officers stopped and the passenger was apprehended. Both men were in their mid-twenties, who during the previous journey had shown absolutely no regard for human life. With relief it was all over and a good result. I thanked God I had come through it safely, but I was still very concerned as to the condition of the injured policeman. His head had been badly split open when he hit the windscreen.

The prisoners were both taken back to the police station in the town where the injured policeman was stationed. Despite being hospitalised with severe head injuries he did eventually make a full recovery, but how it could have been just the opposite, possibly in death, resulting through reckless and dangerous driving. It is not until sometime after the event that you realise how lucky you were that you survived such an incident without serious injury.

Just imagine sadly, as with many other casualties who receive such life threatening spinal injuries and confined to a wheel chair for life all from road crashes that so easily could have happened to me all because of this persons irresponsible driving. You have to reflect on this because at the time all you think of is stopping the offenders at any cost, with nothing else coming into the equation and simply because of this reason alone, it must always be taken into consideration by the Courts in the sentence they receive. Yet in present day, some offenders who commit these kinds of offences get off very lightly indeed without any remorse whatsoever and possibly re-offend with a repeat performance.

No different to police officers killed or murdered in the execution of their duty, or indeed sadly our troops in heroic action during war. Quite rightly everyone at the time of such tragedy is filled with remorse and when it initially hits the headlines everyone always states - no one will ever forget our heroes, but sadly time does not heal the true reality when eventually the names disappear from our minds. It only adds credence to such theory of distant memories of our named brave ones being forgotten, so unintentionally whether accepted in life or not, it all adds up to the fact that we really are just an isolated number. For example PC JONES was a true hero why did he have to get killed and yet in reality sometime less than five years later, the same people will say - what was the name of that PC who got killed some years back he was a real hero. It is a sad indictment and without being disrespectful to anyone, this type of conversation does become a real fact of life. For several years there has been a National Police Memorial Day being on the 30th September each year. This is of tremendous value in supporting close relatives and friends of deceased serving officers mainly killed heroically in the line of duty and other officers who have also lost their lives in other sad associating circumstances when on duty.

Upon checking the vehicle evidence was found from several burglaries with various sets of number plates relating to other stolen vehicles. It was established the driver was disqualified and he was charged with this offence. In addition both men were charged with a host of offences of crime, criminal damage with intent to endanger life and other road traffic offences.

Upon pleading guilty they each received five years imprisonment which at that time had no remission. I received a commendation and as far as I can recall the men upon leaving prison never re-offended. I can say hand on my heart it was a good job done, with fortunately no civilian receiving injuries.

Again back then in those days there were no luxuries such as the presence of a police helicopter offering air surveillance, bring with it rich rewards of anticipating detours or finding alternative routes the offenders may have attempted to use. In addition any tyre piercing equipment which is today thrown into the path of speeding vehicles, which causes them to come to an abrupt halt, or where the driver is simply just loses control of the vehicle. In addition today police have the onboard luxury of Video Camera Recording equipment, where the whole incident in its entirety would be filmed. This would simplify completely the preparation of all evidence recorded live, merely transferred onto a disc for immediate prosecution, which hardly ever would be contested. Whereas with my car chase the whole of the area covered had to be revisited and the first opportunity and documented accordingly, which was extremely time consuming. With today's video evidence the whole scenario would be embedded into the hallmark of fame in a host of wide ranging television programmes and possibly shown throughout the world.

Car chases in present times are an everyday event but just as dangerous and frightening whereas back at the time of my involvement these kinds of incidents did not happen very often. At least the punishment given to the offenders back then was more of a deterrent, as today some sentences imposed by the courts are just plain ridiculous.

As a result of this for some time after I received compliments from many sources within the police station and all seemed genuine on face value. This was with exception of one person a long serving Detective John GLOVER. He was an unusual character, short and stocky, with spiky short grey hair and bushy eye brows. At this time he had about fifteen years' service and he was a man who always wanted to be the centre of attention. He worked in the local C.I.D. office at our station and stopped me one day in the corridor, shook my hand telling me, 'Very well done'.

It took a while for anything to materialise from this, but a few years later this man turned out to be my worst enemy as later in my career I found myself to be working with him, when in actual fact he was working against me. He proved to be extremely two faced very insincere, vindictive and jealous putting poison down against me behind my back whenever the opportunity arose. I could not understand any reason for him to behave this way towards me, after all as far as I was concerned I had done nothing wrong. This continued through the remaining 10 years of his service until he retired, but some of the damage was irreparable.

CHAPTER 02

THE GOOD AND BAD POINTS DEALING WITH TRAVELLERS

At a time when I joined the police we had problems with gypsies no different as today. In various circles these days many wish to be known as travellers or displaced persons and like people from all walks of life there are good and bad. The true Romany gypsies are honest clean and wealthy and rarely ever come to the notice of the police. They have true family values and in most cases settle down in their own built properties or magnificent caravans.

Then there are the other kinds of people, who just travel from place to place, who badly let down the true honest gypsy, being completely opposite in their character. I suppose these people were not as much gypsies but basically itinerants. Some of these were certain individuals who had undesirable backgrounds and survived on crime, avoiding tax at every opportunity and living most of the time on benefits. It is only a minority of these people who basically never settle down anywhere, even when offered a council home they still cannot adjust, I suppose travelling around the countryside is in their blood and is how they were brought up in the world.

We had one farmer who also experienced problems when travellers or gypsies camped on the highway adjoining his fields, especially in the height of the summer. There would be about twenty caravans parked to the side of the country lane for as far as the eye could see, with washing lines from caravan to caravan. Not a pretty sight, especially when they moved on with all their rubbish littering the countryside for which there is really no excuse for. I recall this farmer was spraying his field with foul muck, up to the hedgerow and by accident miss judged the control of high level spray. The whole of the area of caravans and washing were showered with foul muck in the extreme heat. They called the police and I advised them the farmer had accidently caused the damage. It did not take long before they soon moved on. The farmer was the type of person who would not suffer any kind of nuisance and one would have to ask themselves was it done deliberately or not. This I remember was most strenuously denied at the time and he was given the benefit of the doubt. I suppose in reality this practice could have taken place elsewhere throughout various locations in the country back then, but I was not aware of any similar incidents. I only ever came upon this one situation that had taken place, but if there had been any other repeat performances the same excuse could not be used twice. This kind of behaviour or such accidental excuses given would certainly not be tolerated today as civil redress for damages would most possibly follow against the farmer for using such a machine without proper control.

In another similar incident I remember reporting a traveller for camping on the highway with several others. With no fixed abode, I had to attend the Magistrates Court's office and lay an information covering the circumstances of the offence and then summonses would be issued for personal service against all offenders. I returned and to my surprise they were all still at the same location. I duly issued them all accordingly with the necessary documentation against the details given and registration of their vehicles, for them all to attend court the next day. I advised them failure to attend would result in warrants for their arrests for failing to appear which would make matters worse. In fairness they were all quite reasonable appreciating they had all committed an offence. I recall joking with this one likeable character that he possibly would fail to attend Court and move on but in fairness to him he proved me wrong. He completely shamed me, attended Court and paid his fine, so keeping an open mind they were not all bad or dishonest people.

We had an Official Gypsy Caravan Site within our beat area where the main person in charge was a main figurehead with the UK Gypsy Council and as police we had extremely good relations with this person who was always helpful and kind. In fairness this site was well run, except for occasions when there were disturbances and some occupants were fighting amongst themselves. If ever we received a call of that nature, it was wise to attend at the end of the fight and pick up the pieces, in any case no one ever made a complaint they would settle old scores in their own way and no policeman or civilian would be injured.

How true that was when one day I had been out most of the day busy with all kinds of matters, remember we had less staff in those times and larger areas to cover. Due to being busy for most of the morning, my wife gave me my dinner and just as I had sat down, the station door-bell rang. She stated that she would answer the door. She was pregnant with our third child and within a few moments she ran back into the kitchen screaming hysterically. I could not get any sense out of her and I returned immediately to the station when I saw a middle aged man lying on the floor with a knife embedded into his chest with blood all over the floor. He was rolling around in agony and I could see it was very serious and life threatening. Like with any emergency, I remember grabbing anything I could and I recall the wife shouting, "No not my best bath towels." I recalled later talking with the wife and smiling, but at that moment you could not pick and choose, time was of the essence. My colleague from next door joined me and we stemmed the bleeding the best way we could, but leaving the knife still stuck in his chest, as removing it could have caused further complications.

The nearest ambulance available was at a town in the force area some eight miles away, yet despite this, a mile down the road ambulances regularly passed a main traffic island in the area on the boundary of two adjoining police forces. We had no choice within moments we called out the auxiliary ambulance situated down the road manned by part time staff. Within minutes we were on route to the city and the Main Accident and Emergency Department of the nearest hospital. We radioed ahead and upon arrival he was taken straight into casualty. He began fighting with the staff and had to be restrained but I think it was just down to shock. He went into surgery and although it was a life or death situation he made a fully recovery.

The whole matter was treated as an attempted murder and I went into plain clothes together with a Detective Sergeant where we eventually traced, arrested and charged an offender. It appeared both men were gypsies and close friends, had spent the day thieving and had been involved in an argument over the proceeds, culminating in a fight with knives where the man was stabbed.

Needless to say, when the Court date came the offender appeared at the hearing at Quarter Sessions and pleaded not guilty. The injured party who had been stabbed failed to appear to give evidence and was never seen again. Can you imagine if we had done nothing and the man survived with possible severe disabilities, then there would have been possibly uproar from several parts of the traveller community, especially the UK Gypsy Council. No-one knows or do not appreciate when the justice system is abused. What a waste of time and trouble spent on this individual. I just hope someone at the hospital in the queue for surgery whilst waiting did not lose their life, as he could have easily done. To think of all the police time wasted on this enquiry, when efforts could have been put into other criminal matters, but that's what happens in society, life is never fair. I think any witness, from whatever walk in life, who demands a police investigation into any criminal case, but then fails to attend Court and give evidence without proper and justifiable reason should be placed before the Court to face the consequences. A charge for perverting the course of justice to act as future deterrent should be always considered.

A couple of years later working in a Metropolitan area, we had a large public house situated on a council estate, where the whole of the top floor was occupied by travellers who were celebrating a birthday event. There were more than a hundred in attendance and trouble was brewing with some of the locals due to the loud noise which resulted in missiles being thrown down to the people from the windows on the first floor. Naturally someone called the police who attended directly.

A uniform Inspector and a Constable arrived and went upstairs to sort the matter out. Both were hard working and efficient police officers who commanded respect but on that evening it was not to be, as both got assaulted before the arrival of police reinforcements. The duty Inspector was struck across the head with a heavy metal object and the other officer was kicked and punched. All offenders having left the scene before assistance had arrived. As for both officers they were taken to hospital for treatment. The Constable was later discharged but the Inspector remained unconscious for several days. His life was in peril as he was not expected to survive and if he did his future police service was in jeopardy. Fortunately he finally pulled through and several months later to his credit he returned to full police duties. It was a clear example of how dangerous police work can be, not only with those responsible celebrating a birthday bash, but with people from all walks of life who suddenly for no reason turn violent against the police and other emergency services. The worst part of this case was I believe the offenders responsible were never found. Today close circuit television is taken for granted, what an asset that would have been for that enquiry, but back then we could only rely on witnesses and information that might have been forthcoming.

It brings it all into perspective when less than a month before I was again in the station and a young man in his early twenties with long scruffy hair, tattoos and ripped clothing approached the desk. He stated he was in the area and gave the location of a traveller's caravan site where he was staying. In fairness from his appearance you would have thought he was signing on bail or high on drugs, but how wrong I was, as I soon discovered. I asked him the nature of his enquiries. He pulled a wallet from his clothing and immediately stated that he had found it on the pavement in the town. I took his details and upon checking the contents I saw it contained £50 in notes along with other cards and identification. It opens your eyes and reminds you always to keep an open mind. The criminal is always harder to find when he is dressed smart and plays the part of someone in authority. I thanked the man and later contacted the owner of the wallet who stated he was overwhelmed with the public spiritedness and asked for the details of the finder. He later called into the station to see me and I told him what had happened and he promptly gave me a twenty pound note asking this be handed to the finder as a reward for his honesty. I thought this was a superb gesture and forwarded it on against receipt.

Later in my service we would be more professional as when caravans parked collectively and settled down illegally, positive action was always taken. I remember one such incident after a period of observations where crime was suspected. Surveillance was completed without their knowledge and within a short period positive incriminating evidence was obtained implicating majority of those present as being active in criminal behaviour. This particular group of individuals clearly were not the good guys and rubbished any public scrutiny of the decent kind of gypsy.

As a result of this several search warrants relating to the caravan site were lawfully obtained. Then in conjunction with other enforcement agencies such as Inland Revenue and Benefit Fraud Officers they assisted us when we executed the warrants. Numerous items of stolen property were seized from various caravans and all identified from recent burglaries in the surrounding area where they had set up camp.

In addition the ancillary staff assisted us in rigorously checking out all occupants. In some cases persons were found to be wanted on warrant for nonpayment of fines, failing to appear at court, obtaining state benefits by deception, plus offences of theft and burglary. On that occasion two 4 x 4 vehicles were seized as a result of tax evasion. This was a successful joint police operation, which resulted in many arrests. All of those charged admitted their involvement in dishonesty and were punished by the courts. It was just so rewarding to have superb leadership at its very best with positive action taken without delay dealing with those responsible in clearing the crimes committed. However, it must be noted that most of the good travellers or gypsies in society have never offended and live honest working lives, being the complete opposite of those that we dealt with at that time.

Sadly for some reason this level of police professionalism does not always follow in every police area and that must be down to the different views or policies of senior officers and their level of experience. It is when successful operations like this are carried out, those who were all involved in the organising and executing of such positive action deserve full credit.

It is interesting to note that later in my service though positive police experience and procedures we looked closely into offences of sneak in burglary. This was part of an intelligence led inquiry and I was able to identify a team of gypsy itinerant travellers who were later found responsible. Throughout a twelve month period numerous offences of this kind of burglary were committed within our division and also neighbouring divisions, and bordering police force areas. The victims sadly were old and vulnerable who whilst being distracted by one offender using systematic excuses, allowed an accomplice to sneak inside and steal complete life savings and other valuables. Several thousands of pounds were stolen and although arrests were made and cash recovered it was not by any means a clear cut police operation. This was due to poor leadership in contrast to the previous story in failing to support initial police enquiries which are discussed more fully later.

CHAPTER 03

A SERIOUS CRIME INVESTIGATION CREATED FROM A ROAD ACCIDENT

Another lesson learning incident I attended on this beat that I recall, was at about 8.00pm, on a Saturday evening and I was alone on duty. My colleague next door and I each had separate beats each of significant size and population and when on duty alone we covered both areas.

A routine call came through to me from the Control Room at the Main Sub-Divisional Headquarters, for me to attend a road accident at a well-known black spot situated at crossroads at a rural country area. I arrived there within minutes of the call and to my surprise a neighbouring police officer from our same force, who covered an adjoining beat was also in attendance. I later realised this mature officer had contacted the control room requesting me to attend.

Although this officer was not going to deal with the accident, he briefed me on the circumstances and that he had taken a statement from a witness who resided at a cottage nearby. The driver had been breathalysed and the result negative. He left me to take charge, which I thought surely he could have done, but he pointed out it was my area. So why play any part at all or get involved in the first place. His presence at the scene and his actions made me very skeptical about the whole incident and it was not until later the reason why became crystal clear.

Two vehicles were involved, the offending motor car had entered the crossroads and failed to stop at the junction and had crashed directly into the path of the other vehicle that had precedence. Damage to both vehicles was extensive, especially at the front of the offending motor car. The driver of this vehicle stated he had pulled up correctly at the crossroads waiting to cross, when all of a sudden an unknown vehicle was travelling behind him too fast and had shunted the motor car he was in, out directly into the path of the other vehicle causing the accident. As a result the vehicle he alleged was responsible had reversed, turned around and had driven off, no other details other than a light coloured saloon car.

As the other police officer had shown me there was a towing bracket lying on the road which apparently had fallen from the rear of the offender's vehicle. However, there was a distinct lack of skid marks on the road which may have been present if the story was to have any credibility. The story just did not ring true. If I felt this, why didn't this other policeman or was there some ulterior motive for him it believe this other person. Did he know him, were they setting me up to treat this incident without any real question as to the truth of what actually took place? I had to keep an open mind but deep down I felt totally uncomfortable, the driver again reiterated that it was not his fault and this was confirmed by his girlfriend who was with him at the time. In addition the man stated there was a third witness to the accident, a man whom he knew who was walking in the nearby vicinity who would attend the Court if necessary to confirm what had taken place. It was all becoming very suspicious and instinct told me it needed a thorough investigation.

Full measurements were taken of the position of the vehicles and the drivers interviewed under caution. In addition a full statement was taken from his passenger. I saw that the police officer had taken an extremely short statement from the witness at the nearby cottage, which to me was a little suspicious especially when the same witness was able to give a much more thorough account totaling several pages. Although she saw the collision she did not have any view along the road the offending vehicle had travelled, or of the rear of the vehicle. I was aware the force had just implemented a Road Accident Reconstruction Squad who were fully trained in trigonometry calculations together with actual speeds and road markings from the accident. I thought if there was ever such a scenario to test these kinds of calculations, this was the perfect example.

The following day, the defendant cooperated and assisted the accident reconstruction team in confirming his story again. This together with noting the damage caused, they were able to accurately determine the actual speed of the vehicle at the time of collision. It was established through proved calculations the vehicle was travelling at 30 mph at the time of impact. In the meantime I took a statement from the independent witness who had been named. The more I delved into the circumstances

I was not at all happy with the initial police presence at the scene, it later transpired he knew all the parties involved with the offending vehicle, whether or not the officer came out as a result of an additional personal phone call could not be established.

With only the towing bracket on the road purporting to be evidence of a separate non-stop accident was called into question. Did this police officer advise the driver to place the item on the road which could easily be removed from the car, to add credence to the story put forward? With the taking of such a short statement from the other independent witness at the cottage, it made me suspect that this officer planted the seeds into the offender's mind to escape justice and this together with the reluctance to deal, had all the hall marks of conspiracy to pervert the course of justice. This was my first experience of any possible corruption involving another police officer, not wishing to draw the wrong conclusion and being completely fair and honest I just presented the facts to my superiors for them to consider what action if any should be taken.

It was decided the offender be prosecuted in the Magistrates Court for a straightforward case of due care and attention. In addition, I pointed out that in my view the driver, passenger and other witness would attend the Court and possibly commit perjury and how to be prepared to deal with this matter in the event it took place. As a result it was decided to have a shorthand C.I.D. dictation typist situated in an inconspicuous position within the court room and during the prosecution should any evidence come to light incriminating the actions of the initial officer at the scene then so be it.

So the hearing eventually took place with all witnesses giving evidence including myself and the other officers. Despite a rigorous defence the driver was found guilty. All parties involved with the offending vehicle gave a very dubious account of the circumstances which proved they were clearly lying, albeit no evidence was put forward to incriminate the other policeman and on that basis no action was taken against him. Not jumping to any conclusions but this was a man who in my view acted extremely suspiciously and if he was responsible in any way he would have put shame on the uniform in his role of Constable. All I know is I am sure he would never call me again to deal with his dirty work.

As a result all three were interviewed by C.I.D, which resulted in a prosecution at Crown Court where they each pleaded guilty to perjury and conspiracy to pervert the course of justice. They were each given two years imprisonment having no real previous convictions. I have nothing against them but what a price to pay for trying to cheat justice for such a trivial basic motoring offence. Even this kind of stupid behaviour goes on today, involving people from all walks of life, television celebrities, politicians, sadly some police officers, business people and so on. All risking everything in life to avoid a conviction for often a petty motoring offence when it would be easier to admit guilt pay a fine, to avoid disgrace, loss of freedom and losing your career.

The most recent example involved a high profile Member of Parliament who pleaded guilty to perverting the course of justice and his estranged wife who denied the offence but was found guilty of the same offence. They were both responsible for telling lies over a minor speeding offence in order to avoid penalty points on his licence. His downfall was not to come clean immediately and accept that he was speeding like any other law abiding citizen, but this man continually lied to the public and media about his involvement. To be in such a high profile position working in government where the laws of the land are made, it is quite disgusting behaviour and he should have set a better example for which I am sure he deeply regretted. He and his ex-wife both subsequently were sent to prison and he resigned as Member of Parliament. After all no one is above the law and no matter how the offence came to light, by revenge or in other ways, a figurehead such as this deserved to be found out and punished for the consequences of his actions. A hard lesson with so much to lose but he was the author of his own destiny, as was his wife.

I remember we had a uniform Chief Inspector working at one police station, who was always smart and a disciplinarian, who always gave his best and was a fine example of an honest and trustworthy policeman. He actually was driving his vehicle one day and was responsible for causing a minor damage road accident with another vehicle. To everyone's surprise he reported himself for driving without due care and attention and submitted all necessary paperwork. I do not think ever again I saw that in the whole of my police service and since. What a credit to the police service and a fine example to set, a lesson to be learned by all, including myself.

CHAPTER 04

UNABLE TO PREVENT A FAMILY TRAGEDY, SUCH A SAD STORY

One of the saddest cases I ever had to deal with was whilst working a little later in my career at a beat station, under the same sub- divisional area. At this location there was just me and another officer and we were close to the boundary of our force area and large city police force. I recall my colleague was on leave and at about 9.40pm, one evening in December, I received a call to visit a house in the street nearby, where there was a report of a man missing from home.

Upon arrival I saw a married woman in her mid-thirties, living in a large 4 bedroom detached house, having three young children of various ages up to about 10 years. As soon as I saw this lady instinct told me she was genuinely in distress and extremely worried.

She reported that her husband had returned home from work earlier that night at around 7.00pm. Everything appeared normal with him except that he was unusually quiet. As the evening proceeded she realised he was not his normal self, something was troubling him and he would not talk about it. Then suddenly at about 8-30pm her husband stated he was going out to the off licence to fetch a drink, there was nothing in this that appeared unusual as he had done this several times previously and was reasonably well known at these premises. She stated feeling some insecurities relating to his demeanour that she had thought to herself I don't know what's up but when he comes back and settles down he might talk over a drink about whatever problems he was experiencing.

Having explained that although he had only been gone for just over an hour there was no reason for him not to return as the off licence was only a couple of minutes away. Previous round trips he had undertaken were never any longer than to 10 to 15 minutes. Despite her telephoning these premises, no staff working there could recall her husband visiting as he was well known by them. There had been no other contact from him, as in those days mobile phones did not exist. She had received no communication from him via telephone or from any friends. She was genuinely concerned and distraught, as a wife and mother and desperate for any kind of action formally reported him missing.

With adults reported as missing things would have to take their normal course of events, especially with any history of drunkenness or domestic background, infidelity or similar behaviour. Details would be noted and the issue would be re-visited within 24 hours, when action to be taken would be re-considered depending on the circumstances.

Call it intuition on her part, but I shared her concerns, rightly or wrongly. If he was found within a short time safe and well, then so be it, I was prepared to face any criticism and at least my conscience would be clear in the knowledge I had tried my best to help. I took the view let's pull out all the stops and I immediately took a full description his appearance and dress, when last seen. Details were obtained of where he might go or visit and his wife was advised to ring friends or family and to keep me informed of any positive developments. As with any missing person enquiry, a routine but thorough search was made of the house, loft, garage and outbuildings just in case for any ulterior motive he had sneaked back onto the premises. It was appreciated his car was not present, but covering the basics in police work are an essential part of any investigation and can in certain circumstances save valuable time in case the missing person is found hiding. In this case he was not found. I advised her to have a friend or family member stay with her and advised what action I would be taking.

I immediately circulated him as missing giving all information and vehicle details to the Force Control Room and to all patrols within the surrounding areas. As we were close to the border of two other police forces, I requested they also be informed. As I had completed all the preliminary procedures I commenced a thorough patrol of the immediate area in the vicinity of the off licence and surrounding countryside. The search was meticulous, every isolated spot I could find and every road or lane in the area was covered. I drove round some locations more than once in case I had missed anything and within the next hour or so I had exhausted all avenues.

I returned to the address where I again saw the lady, who had calmed down but was still very distressed, she had no news despite making telephone calls as requested. Her parents had arrived by this time and I advised we would follow up enquiries next morning and to stay as positive as possible. In most cases these kinds of incidents resolve happily with the person returning safe and well, as the problems causing the unusual behaviour come to the surface, sadly with this man it did not happen.

At about 6.00am the following morning, I received a call that a local farmer had found the vehicle in question just inside the entrance to a field, out of public view. I drove to the location which was in the area I had previously searched, some two miles from the station. There was tubing leading from the exhaust into the inside of the car through a quarter light window. It was all over the poor man was dead and had apparently been there for some time. Other officers were present together with the duty sergeant. The car engine still running was finally switched off. Arrangements were made for the police surgeon to attend together with scenes of crime who also later took photographs. There were no signs of any alcoholic drink present in the vehicle or upon the deceased and no written note had been left at the scene or elsewhere. The police surgeon confirmed life extinct and as it was established nothing else appeared suspicious other than suicide, the body of the deceased was removed to the hospital mortuary.

Together with the police sergeant we had the task of breaking the dreadful news to the wife who had reported him missing, who had now lost her husband, the children, their father. There could not have been a worse scenario, but I had experienced death in my family several times unfortunately like most of us and there is no easy way in breaking bad news. All you can do is retain firmness at the same time being gentle and sympathetic but most important of all is to be genuine and sincere with every word you say.

With a family member, or close friend present it is more helpful, as when you have left the address after informing them of such tragic news, they are there to provide much needed love and support.

It was later that same morning when various checks had been made, it was discovered that the deceased had been arrested earlier that day, previous to going missing, by an adjoining police force. He had been interviewed in connection with a serious embezzlement of monies at his place of employment, totalling some several thousands of pounds. At some time in the future would have faced being charged, but had been released on bail pending ongoing police enquiries.

Formal identification was made by the deceased's father in law and a post mortem revealed death to be by carbon monoxide poisoning and at an Inquest later the formal verdict was suicide with police being absolved of any blame. I maintained contact with the family during this sad period, often thinking if only someone could have reached him before he made that fateful decision. Even if having to face up to the consequences of his actions he would have eventually rebuilt his life, as I am sure he would have had at some point the forgiveness of his family. Tragically not everyone can find the courage to overcome such an ordeal. No one knows why these things happen. So here I was in my early twenties with a family of my own, playing a major part in a tragedy which would affect people for the remainder of their lives.

CHAPTER 05

DUTIES OF A CORONERS OFFICER WORKING WITH OTHER SKILLED PROFESSIONALS

We had a small Cottage Hospital in the town where I was first stationed. When on duty if there had been a sudden death on the wards, or a dead on arrival at the main entrance, it was an unwritten rule that the local police were called to assist the nursing staff to remove the body to the mortuary, whilst the nurse waited outside to return the trolley. This was something I was totally unaware of before joining the police force, however it soon became a part of everyday work which you came to accept. For some officers this however was a task they would rather not have had to deal with as you can imagine they would find every excuse to be otherwise committed. Today this is a role normally performed by Hospital Porters and Mortuary Staff for which I have the greatest admiration.

I knew of occasions at night time where a body had been placed into the fridge and if there were more than one policeman, one would lie on the trolley covered with a sheet. He would be pushed back out to the waiting Nurse, who was told to go back to the ward as there was no room left. You can imagine the horror of the nurse whilst escorting the trolley back when the alleged deceased sat up on route.

Just imagine the screams bellowing out along the corridors and I am sure that happened several times between different staff. I can see the funny side but also that kind of behaviour could have had disastrous consequences, especially if the nursing staff got injured whilst fainting or falling down through shock. Not my kind of comedy not that I am boring, there must be dignity in death. I think today this would most certainly be a health and safety issue and looked at in a completely different view.

Being in a rural force a Police Constable was automatically a Coroners Officer and undertook the duties with compassion and empathy. This was especially true when breaking tragic news to loved ones and arranging for identification. It was something no training could prepare you for and it was there that your own upbringing taught you how to be dignified and respectful of the dead. It was always a nice touch and in good taste that when out on foot patrol should a funeral cortege appear along the roadside, a policeman in full uniform always stood to attention at the pavement edge and saluted as a mark of respect as it passed by. I also had to visit and observe post mortems which I did not realise on joining the police. This initially was very traumatic but also helpful to me in most aspects of police work where I would then have some knowledge of what to expect at the scene of any accident or sudden death.

In fact I recall back to attending my first post mortem I was with some other colleagues who had also recently joined and we were all advised to attend, being an important part of our probation and training. Two of the officers were taller and stockier than me and were ex-cadets and they were trying to be cavalier in their approach and wind me up on what I would have to do and see, even though I learned it was their first experience too. I smiled to myself that they were unaware of my pedigree of being a butcher and what I had seen and dealt with in that trade. When that moment came to witness the event I was not surprised one atom when one of them instantly fainted and the other screamed and threw up. They were amazed to see me standing close and asking questions and I can say that after their experience they looked at me in the future with a little more respect.

Still each death is sad, particularly so with children and young people. I always felt tremendous job satisfaction in helping and dealing with bereaved persons at the most tragic time of their lives. To me I felt for the deceased family, but it was just a body without the spirit, and not a person. After all, establishing the main cause of death was the primary target using the competent skills of the qualified Pathologist. The relatives would sometimes then have peace of mind and could make funeral arrangements.

Looking at various deceased persons especially those who had lived to a long age I just found it intriguing thinking about what they had done with their lives. What had they achieved, all the experiences of surviving possibly two World Wars. I would think they may have lived unique roles within society or were they eccentric in their behaviour or were they famous at any time and if so for what reason. All these unanswered questions from people now deceased who now could not answer.

In those days if you helped the undertaker remove a body to the mortuary he always gave you a drink against all the rules in the form of a small payment, after all you were saving him the costs of having extra staff accompany him. In some cases some staff couldn't do it anyway it just was not in them to deal with the deceased in that way. In addition in the mortuary if you assisted in weighing of the organs and taking down notes the pathologist would also equally reward you. Not many people wanted to swap these roles with you but I found it extremely interesting.

When out on patrol and you are sent to any incident where there is a report of a neighbour or person not being seen, with newspapers, post or milk bottles piling up, you always get that eerie, apprehensive feeling which are all clues to possible suspicious death or a person injured or seriously ill. You never know what to expect and you always hope you will find someone alive who you can help. More often than not sadly the person was deceased. To begin with it would be a sudden death, but initially the golden rule is to always treat as suspicious and preserve the scene and any evidence found, until you were positive of the circumstances. If in any doubt or any unanswered questions, you would always seek advice as there is never any shame in that. On most occasions you would have to make a forced entry and that's where your truncheon always played a major part, not just as a weapon of defence, but a useful item to help gain access into such kind of premises.

I recall a colleague, Monty THROWER, a good friend with whom I worked with for over 20 years as uniform constable and in C.I.D. He told me the amusing story when he was called to such an incident together with his Sergeant. It was before I knew him he was then still in his probation. The sergeant was from the old regime very strict, renowned for his strong disciplinary values. They arrived at a cottage with all the obvious signs that the lone occupant had not been seen for some considerable time. Not being able to gain access the sergeant had to stand on my colleagues shoulders. Unable to open any window the sergeant asked him to pass his truncheon. Knowing this question could arise and dreading the obvious, he had to come clean and tell him he had left it in his locker at the station. All the time he was thinking that he will report me under discipline for neglect of duty. The sergeant immediately challenged him demanding to know why this was so. He told him that he had just forgotten it which of course was no excuse.

All of a sudden he raised the obvious query, in those days you didn't question a senior officer's authority but in a subtle way told the sergeant perhaps he could use his truncheon. In a stern but comical reply the sergeant stated that he hadn't got his either and they both burst out laughing. This goes to show we are all human but sometimes there is one rule for one and another rule for the other. It was good it ended in laughter but one wonders what would have happened if the sergeant was in possession of his truncheon. Would Monty been subject to a fizzer? In those days this was commonly known as a disciplinary report.

In most cases the deceased was found after the autopsy to have died from natural causes and if they were old you can seek comfort in the fact that they had lived a long life, hopefully with good health, but that didn't make any easier for friends or relatives.

Then there were cases where the bodies were decomposed having not been found for long periods of time, or where someone had cut their throat or had hung themselves. Tablets were the main cause in most cases. Then of course mutilation through all kinds of tragic accidents, some involving severe damage to bodies caused by fire or drowning. You just hoped that they did not suffer and the end was quick for them. Then there is no comparison leading up to all the grisly scenes of murder which come in all various shapes and forms.

I always thought when you came across members of the public who were violent, abusive, anti-police or those just totally ignorant of our real role in society. If they had any insight of this kind of police work I am sure they would see us in a different light, especially those who kill through drink, reckless or dangerous driving, or are responsible for stabbing anyone without any regards for the value of human life. Only a close experience to death involving a friend or member of the family brings this kind of person down to earth, or basic reality. I often think that self-centered people who think the world owes them something or those who bully, abuse or are just plainly disrespectful to disabled, elderly and infirm, or just violent to others, should be made to do a tour of the Children's Wards and other Hospital Departments and see those poor patients less lucky in life, to make them appreciate how lucky they are to have healthy lives and learn to improve to help others.

Working in a Metropolitan Police area, all sudden deaths became the responsibility of Coroners Officers who were professional in their field. We covered all four towns each with their own mortuary within the division, so it was sadly very busy. Having over five year's experience of police work and previous skills in that role I was seconded for a six month period. I was privileged to have been chosen and I thought this was a good way of making contacts, in working in the hospitals, attending identifications and post mortems. In addition to arranging Inquests together with members of the public appearing as Jurors, and of course, meeting with the Coroner or his Deputy and fostering good relations.

With winter as in summer it can reflect different cases. In very hot weather people who are elderly with health problems, sometimes have difficulty surviving in extreme heat conditions. In the winter it is the complete opposite. One of the most dangerous activities where people are sometimes elderly and unfit is to participate in shoveling snow or pushing motor vehicles, as the sudden exertion can sometimes result in a fatal heart attack. Some reports of sudden death involve the autopsy to be carried out by a Home Office Pathologist who is independent to the normal appointed hospital Pathologist. This can be for various reasons, but most common include death by alleged medical negligence, or death of a prisoner in custody.

We had a Locum Doctor visit an ill patient at a home visit, the patient was extremely ill and he rang one of the local hospitals during the night. One of the young doctors initially refused immediate admission, which caused a delay. A further request was made some 30 minutes later and it was agreed the patient could be admitted. However, upon arrival at the hospital the patient died. The family made a formal complaint alleging the doctor was to blame.

As a result of this the young Doctor had to attend the post mortem, undertaken by the Home Office Pathologist. To his relief it was established death was due to natural causes and he was absolved of blame. I am sure he gained experience from this and he later qualified and became an excellent G.P. We all learn from our experiences.

No different from when I was in C.I.D. and I was called out to a report of a suspicious death. It was a force policy at the time and although I didn't mind anytime, I couldn't help thinking it was because some of the staff were not experienced or were unsure what action to take. I remember the deceased was a young man in his twenties who apparently had taken an overdose, as tablets were lying all around. Still there was no note left. A Police Surgeon had already attended and certified death. The uniform Inspector present was very young in service, who asked if the body could be removed. I asked if scenes of crime had visited and because not I arranged this to establish if there was any unlawful entry or signs of foul play. I asked the Inspector if photographic had been contacted to attend, the answer was no, so I arranged this. The Inspector asked if all was okay after when both these parties had attended could the body then be removed. I asked him if the body had been examined and it had not. I had to explain the reason why, in that if the deceased was later taken to the mortuary and found to have had a stab wound in his back or other injury not found, we would all have egg on our faces.

This Inspector was very inexperienced and either a graduate entry or very educated, but his police expertise in my view was very restricted. I am sure he went on to become a good supervising officer. If only we all had that privilege of receiving specialist treatment in rank and wages, we could then all qualify, but it is all about getting the balance right. I don't believe in putting people into circumstances where they have to learn by mistakes, as you cannot put an old head onto young shoulders.

This situation is an increasing issue in the modern world of today, as knowing your trade and being qualified by exams, shows there is no accounting for experience which should take precedence in promotion of any kind. After all the people who have worked hard and obtained degrees I have never yet met a person who has any similar degree awarded for common sense. This includes people from all walks of life and all areas of society, whether in high positions of authority or not. Without prejudice against any individual there would be a long wait for some people if they had to achieve this kind of award and virtually impossible for some.

One important role of the police is to identify the deceased so relatives can be informed. This can sometimes be a difficult task which may involve a forensic Odontologist who can examine the teeth of the deceased and trace the identity from medical records. Scenes of Crime and the Forensic Science Laboratory working jointly together were all extremely skillful. They were all highly trained and often engaged in the most pain staking work. Their diligence and perseverance essential in looking for clues, today D.N.A samples plus evidence of wrong doing in leading to the detection of all serious offences, mainly involving murder, terrorism and suicide. Professional fingerprinting of the deceased can sometimes help identify the person, but tattoos, birthmarks and known scars together with property can assist the investigation. This is particularly useful where the deceased is badly decomposed or a victim of fire. All records of missing persons are always looked into and compared with unidentified bodies.

Surprisingly there were several occasions when a deceased person was found in unbelievable situations, normally where some sexual deviance had occurred shortly before death. In most cases they had asphyxiated prior to some kind of self-inflicted sexual act where they were found in uncompromising situations inside dustbins, or polythene bags, dressed as women or pretending to be a fetus inside the womb. We had one man who died of a heart attack whilst masturbating with the use of a ladies hat pin.

The deceased was usually a male person living alone and his death would not always be discovered immediately and often several days or weeks later. Majority of these incidents the behaviour was found to be completely alien to the deceased's wife or family. In all these cases strict discretion was most important in dealing with all relatives and friends, who were given the dignity and support they deserved as in all such cases of sudden death. Following full investigation majority of the causes were found to be accidental death or misadventure with no suspicious circumstances.

Within a week of going back on the shifts, I was on uniform foot patrol and came across a fatal road accident where a middle aged man had walked out into the path of an articulated vehicle which was travelling down a hill. With a good background to my skills I was able to thoroughly investigate the accident from start to finish as a uniform constable being such a rare achievement compared to today. This involved notifying the relatives and arranging the identification of the deceased, to attending the autopsy and organizing the Inquest.

No foul play was established and no intention of suicide, just a simple accident where he walked out with not really looking. As sad as it all was, it was good to have the opportunity to deal with something from beginning to end, whereas today the role would possibly involve several officers.

CHAPTER 06

FROM CIVILIAN LIFE TO BECOMING A POLICE PROBATIONER

I was born shortly after World War 2 and grew up in State Schools, leaving at the age of 15 years without any qualifications. However my time was not exactly wasted my father introduced me to the butchery trade when I was 12 years old. I learned every cut of meat and my dad taught me how to be a professional Butcher tradesman. How sad it is today in 2017 hardly any of our younger adults have ever had the opportunity to find a part-time job in almost every part of life. The opportunities lost in developing confidence and customer service skills in learning to talk with people from all walks of life, whilst complimenting this valuable addition to life with combined studies in education. This in many ways can be a real backward step in future careers for many but sadly many colleges and universities dismiss this challenge as an affront to education which in their view should be a full-time position.

Dealing everyday with members of the public, I developed a rapport which would serve me well in the future and upon leaving school I was more than well qualified for my role. I was taken on by a local and well established butcher, who had several shops and I moved around learning different skills. When I was 17 years sadly I lost my father who died of a heart attack and despite spending several more years managing my own butchers shop, my interest in the meat trade was waning and an earlier concept of a career with the police force was becoming increasingly more tempting. I began to improve my education in Maths, English and General Knowledge until I felt confident in taking the police entrance exam in which I was successful.

This followed an interview with a local police force within the British Isles, before an Assistant Chief Constable and two Chief Superintendents. Although stringent and daunting my performance was impressive and in late 1970, I was appointed as a Probationary Constable, pending a medical which I passed. What a career change, I knew I had a lot to learn and achieve and I was handed a definition book with over 100 subjects on law that I had to learn word by word, plus criminal justice procedures and criminal law relating to general police duties, traffic, evidence and criminal offences. I had my work cut out because at this time I was married with a child with another on the way. I thought to myself what an achievement as I had taken quite a reduction in pay. In those days I earned more wages working as a butcher, than as a police officer. I just had to succeed, there was so much at stake for me to lose everything, but I also thought what a challenge. Initially I attended a local Force Training School, where I was handed a police uniform, pocket book, truncheon, whistle, life was becoming to be completely different extremely interesting, but it was never boring.

The uniform I received, well that was something else. In those days we had a full summer uniform and a separate winter uniform. It was October and cold and you could understand the reasoning behind the dress change. Only problem was my uniform was like a hand me down, something off the set of a Norman Wisdom movie. Always taking pride in my appearance, it was totally impossible to retain creases in the trousers and the tunic hung over me like an old overcoat. In those days you just put up and shut up, the bonus being, all my measurements had been taken and at the end of my training, I could look forward to two brand new made to measure uniforms of winter and summer issue.

Discipline and respect to all colleagues was the backbone of the police service in those days and before long I was making new friends, learning by my mistakes. I was becoming more confident but there was still a very long way to go and just took it one step at a time.

We soon got into a regular routine, having periods of drill and parade every morning, not quite dads army but it was obvious we were new recruits and as green as grass. In addition physical training and self defence were a must. I doubt today if I would have met the skills required for joining the police, as fitness is a priority in line with the armed forces and to some extent more severe. We had lectures on what to expect when we started our 10 week course at a Regional Police Training Centre, where officers of several forces were each completing against each other.

As each day we got accustomed to the role, it was then down to the local Magistrates Court one morning, all to be sworn in under oath as Constables. It was the first time I had seen the inside of any court, but it was impressive and I felt proud to be in a job where I could serve the community.

In those times we were up against a high percentage of police cadets who had been working alongside regular police officers on operational duties. They had a significant advantage against us and their manner, attitude and behaviour appeared above us. Thinking about it today I believe they were led into a false sense of security. They had been institutionalised with nothing other than one side of life, seeing everything from the police outlook and not a true reflection of the real world. I felt not being a Cadet and seeing early life outside of the police force was an asset and this became more evident as I continued to gain experience in my role. Basic skills when first working part-time at an after school job did indeed prove valuable for me in mixing and circulating with all these new people.

No one in life is perfect including me and that means everyone whether it is just simple things or the very serious. Some people are a danger, very sinister and evil, whereas some people are greedy and jealous and obsessive. Others easily led, down trodden and lazy, thankfully there are a tremendous amount of people who are kind, helpful, caring, hard-working and supportive.

Every valid piece of law essential to policing was taught, together with practical situations relative to everyday policing from road accidents to sudden deaths, crime scenes to assaults, traffic offences, domestic incidents and crimes of all kinds. It included preparing make belief cases for prosecution and obtaining of all evidence available. Insight into all the famous murders that had taken place over recent years was introduced and proved extremely interesting, with film clips shown of many murder scenes and atrocities involving bombings on the mainland which involved the IRA and other international terrorists. We had lectures showing different methods of detection which had taken place including various techniques used at that time. Even back in those days forensic science had a major part to play and you learned the importance of being completely thorough in all aspects of investigation.

It was also my very first experience of theft, where in this case I was the victim. What a laugh but not so funny at the time still that's life. Within the first week of training, I needed to send my wife some money, so I purchased a good wish card placed in a £5 note, which compared to today would have been a quarter of my weeks wages and posted it to an address where she was staying. This she never received. Who, I thought could be responsible was it staff employed by the Post Office, or staff employed by the police, either way it was disturbing and a bitter pill to swallow. All outgoing mail at the police centre went into a post box in the Administration office for later collection by the Royal Mail. Not an easy matter to detect, unless there was some pattern to follow, but I am sure later in my experience I would have found ways to clear up these nasty types of crime. I suppose to put money inside post was not a wise thing to do on reflection, but in those times I thought people would be more trusting how things change. Lesson learned I did not make that mistake again.

The weeks soon moved on and the reality of the wealth of knowledge I had learned was forever increasing, regular taking of exams was a shock to the system, but putting theory into practice was another learning curve for me to overcome. We had smartened up with exercise and drill was an everyday event. Finally we all donned monkey suits and toasted the Queen, followed with a passing out parade the following morning. Our performance was almost perfect, with a sense of pride marching to the sound of brass bands and the regimental movements including traffic signals all blended in, right up to the final inspection by a local Chief Constable.

It's really sad those days have now gone forever as today police training is at individual police stations within the force area where stationed. No memories of friends from other forces some of whom became useful contacts later in my service. No passing out parades and no drill, all were for a reason to instill pride and discipline a basic essential for a British Police Officer.

As we move into modern times some police forces are considering privatisation involving many roles performed by operational police officers to be undertaken by civilians. As there is now a Police Complaints Authority will they too be responsible for this new venture. Some people will argue that big business is not in the public interest after all you only have to look at the buses and rail networks where there is no service whatsoever in some areas. It may be that with these new incentives it will work, but at what cost to service provided to the public, only time will tell if it is a good or bad move.

After the 10 weeks of regional training was over, I had a further 2 weeks of learning involving local procedures, the day to stepping out on patrol for the first time was becoming increasingly closer. By this time my new uniforms had arrived and I finally felt like the bees knees, I felt smart and looked the part. It was a point of putting everything learned into practice as I was frequently told there was nothing to distinguish me on appearance to that of a well experienced Officer. Members of the public at all times can see your good points, but also any bad points would be easily remembered. This is a statement that still stands true today and is more fully documented later to reflect present day policing.

CHAPTER 07

A TESTING TIME FIRST STEPS OUT WALKING ON THE BEAT

So the time I had been waiting for finally arrived, my first official day on duty facing the public as a fully-fledged Police Constable. Would I be accepted, was I forceful enough, positive and confident as well as being fair minded. Most of all was I knowledgeable to a sufficient standard, only time would tell. With all these qualities to be tested, I had a lot to live up to, yet the most important ingredient combining all qualities was just plain common sense, listening and learning. I had already met my colleagues on a previous meeting all were friendly, helpful and each full of character. The Sergeant was an old fashioned and wise individual, always very approachable and able to give good advice which to a new recruit was a lifeline. I just knew with hard work and determination, plus a push in the right direction I would succeed, but there was a long road ahead and the future looked intriguing.

I remember my first tour of duty was 0600am until 2.00pm and we had to attend some 15 minutes before for a formal parade which I believe is still normal practice today. This was important as you were briefed regarding any serious crime or incident that had earlier taken place, noted national or local wanted criminals, suspicious or stolen vehicles or any other item of valuable interest. In addition every officer was required to produce his appointments in the form of a whistle, truncheon, notebook and a torch if on evening or night duty. Handcuffs at that time had been withdrawn as they were not practical to fit on a person when struggling owing to poor design and were only used in transferring prisoners already in custody.

I was stationed in a small but busy market town with an overspill area well into the countryside of people moving from a local city, not all unfortunately of the best character. This with a large surrounding rural area gave a thorough mix of work from almost every offence in the book and nearly every crime imaginable. We all paraded for duty with a shift of some six constables and the duty sergeant. He was the man in control full of real experience, approachable, confident, sometimes a disciplinarian and equivalent in present day rank to a police Inspector. He was certainly a leader and a man that had earned full respect. Promotion later became instant for those who met the criteria upon completion of probation, due to the ever changing role of the police force, but as I gained experience I found this was not always the best move forward. At that time I joined it was unknown for a sergeant to have less than 10 years' service except for rare exceptions. At the time I left the service just prior to the year 2000, in most stations there are normally four sergeants to every shift, in some cases, all collectively having less than ten year's experience. This would not include the Inspector who normally had over five years plus service.

Today this fluctuates depending on the population and in larger police areas there are more staff, but sadly in today's society there are far less police officers and operational police station. As we move into 2017 this must be very daunting for the police who do a very difficult job in areas where there are people from many races. Violence and public disorder an everyday event sadly with ever increasing offences involving the use of firearms and knives, with no real deterrent in sight. What an extremely dangerous country we have become, the role of a police officer is now more unsafe than ever and at times extremely risky and hazardous.

Back at the time when I joined each police station had several police women but they worked independent to shifts, they played a unique role, where they dealt mainly with indecency against women and children, missing persons and school liaison. Complementing our role was the dog branch and traffic division and CID short for Criminal Investigation Department. Later in my service we had the horse section and the wonderful luxury of the police helicopter.

So there I was out on patrol for the first time in full view of the public. For the first six weeks I was assigned to work with an experienced police officer, but in reality I was basically on my own after two weeks. I had moved to a town which was completely alien to me, so in addition to putting into practice things I had been trained for, I had to learn all the local areas and every street within the town, places and buildings where people would hide and where I could gain access to every building.

One of my very first arrests I was on foot patrol round the back streets of the town. It was mid-morning when I saw a young boy who looked around the age of 13 years actually I later discovered he was just 10. Instinct told me he was up to no good and he seemed to panic as I approached him. He looked scared to death and I think he may have been with someone else who was not to be seen. He was a short distance away from the rear of a public house. I stopped him asked him where he had been, his reply was plausible so I asked him to empty his pockets making sure he could not escape. I found £50 in his pocket, equivalent to approximately £200 - £300 today. Having called for assistance other officers arrived and he was placed into a police vehicle. I made enquiries at the public house and established the monies had been taken from the private quarters, which were part of the weekly takings. He was dealt with for burglary and implicated his older brother. Both later appeared at the Juvenile court where they received supervision orders. It was sad to say that both went on to be career criminals committing serious and quite violent crime. You cannot win them all.

At night time every part of lock up business premises within the town area had to be physically checked at least once and if any premises found insecure the named key holder would be immediately contacted. This was particularly important if there was any sign of unlawful entry. If you had failed to identify any insecure premises on your tour of night duty, they would demand your presence at the police station immediately. This happened, even if it meant awakening you from your sleep and getting you out of bed following your night shift. You would have to give realistic explanations as to why these premises were not discovered, with the potential for discipline.

I recall early in my service checking out the rear of some premises which I found insecure. I opened the door and as I walked inside I was fiddling with my torch which was not working properly. When I finally produced the light what I saw before me was something like straight from a horror movie. All I could see were bodies all laying on various tables, with 3 or 4 in coffins. I was alone and no one was speaking, I thought my God somebody tell a joke. I checked the remainder of the premises as quickly as I could and there appeared to be no break in. I just could not wait to get out and as soon as I could, did I exit from those premises quickly. I realised the building was the local undertakers and the back door had been left open. Trust it to be me to be the one person to have to find these premises insecure. We had not received any reports of bodysnatching and when the key holder arrived all deceased was present and correct and the premises secured. That was it I had passed the test, if I can walk around the local undertakers alone at night I could venture anywhere, so all in all a good lesson received.

In those days we wore steel tips boots in the daytime with shiny helmets, night time was rubber soles with a night helmet showing a black badge. In the daytime the public could hear us walking, whereas at night we could see members of the public, but we remained inconspicuous and made our presence known when essential to do so. I later realised this was beneficial in detecting offences. In present day police officers appear to walk around at all times in yellow florescent jackets and perhaps this is in line with health and safety. This can have good points where law abiding citizens need to see the visibility of a police presence, but this certainly makes it harder to catch criminals committing offences.

Police behaviour was extremely important in those days as it is today. Any lateness, drunkenness or untidiness would not be tolerated and in some more serious cases involving discipline, would mean transfer to another station where your family would have to up root and move home. In some police forces officers who had drink problems would end up being posted to towns with well-established breweries and if the temptation to drink on duty became too much they were easily discovered re-offending and dismissed.

A condition of joining the police force was that you lived in their accommodation. How things have changed. Today you can live in another county, have no involvement with the community outside police work and be much older or any reasonable height. Some of these things are very practical and sensible, as your family can be vulnerable to known criminals whereas at the time I joined there were dangers but also full respect for the local police officer.

In present policing rules you can have shorter people who do as equally as good a job as being police officers. The only problem I have discovered is they sometimes deliberately put the shortest with the tallest, which I suppose is funny. You can imagine supervision referring to them as little and large. At least someone is retaining a sense of humour. The same applies to officers from all ethnic backgrounds providing their standards are equal they can be invaluable and over the years I would work with many who adapted well who integrated into the service and became a serious asset to the job.

Another change is the requirement of all women police officers to do the equal job as men, however many male officers were found to be extremely bias. Equally so there were some women who did not want this change, but with a changing world equal rights and pay, it forced these decisions to take place. Some were able to adapt some not, but like any rule there is an exception, for over the years I was able to work with some women who were equally as good as or better than some men themselves. The only danger which is accepted, women in some cases are not all built as physical as men and cannot give the same restraint but equally so there are always encouraging stories of bravery involving police women as well as men.

I had joined soon after the implementation of unit beat policing and the introduction of the panda car, gone were the old police boxes and in came two way radios. We were each issued with a Pye police radio and transmitter which proved to be an essential tool in all aspects of police work. Not so good when involved in a car chase, as told in a previous chapter, where you regularly had to use both items when driving and on patrol. The golden rule was to be brief, accurate and professional at all times. Any improper slang words, garbage or crudeness would not be entertained at any cost as only the Queen's English over the radio was to be spoken. The radio communication was invaluable for directions and police checks and circulations of missing persons, descriptions of offenders and most importantly calling for back up and assistance. In those days we patrolled alone, whereas in present day most police officers are doubled up basically for safety and corroborative reasons.

It was a time when all police dress codes had to be consistent throughout the force, all drivers of police vehicles in uniform were required to wear a flat police helmets at all times, as some of the legislation required the police officer to be in uniform and that included the helmet, otherwise case law could result in any prosecution being dismissed.

We wore the police flat caps for about 4 years, before being introduced nationally to the chequered band as worn by the London metropolitan police to distinguish police drivers from prison officers, ambulance and fire brigade officers. I remember some city police forces where motor cycle riders on small bikes had a crash helmet incorporated into a police helmet, not like in the television series Heartbeat, but an actual police helmet beat officers would wear, designed as a crash helmet specifically for riding motor bikes. I must say they looked utterly ridiculous and this dress code was eventually phased out. Can you imagine wearing something so heavy in middle of summer, it would be like having your head in a hairdryer which you would not be able to switch off, or riding around with a Noddy helmet on. Then at one time they considered having torches incorporated into night helmets. Can you imagine that, police officers walking round as if they were part time coalminers, trouble is people who come up with these fantastic ideas never have to wear such ludicrous inventions.

Dress code in the summer was always different to winter. This also included shirt sleeve order, in summer months this was ideal, winter was always with tunic and raincoat with helmet, but with no in between they would not tolerate some Officers in shirt sleeve and others in just tunics. Police in uniform always wore some kind of police helmet, unlike today we regularly see police in various forms of uniform and without helmets. I appreciate it is not always practical to be in full police uniform for everyday policing duties which is a shame, as there is nothing better than a smart appearance when dealing with members of the public. In my view I always feel this gives the impression of an undisciplined workforce, the only exception being in an emergency situation where action is immediate and necessary. In these circumstances dress becomes less important and safety a priority, but as this is not all the time on duty. A poor excuse in my book for not dressing smart when able to do so.

Yet within a short time of working and parading for duty with my shift, there was always the odd colleague who showed character, or was it just plain thoughtlessness. A police officer who had two years more service than me who turned up for parade in full uniform, only to be seen wearing pink florescent socks instead of black, needless to say he was sent home immediately to change. We had one police officer return from annual leave and needless to say he had grown a beard which was un-trimmed and looked very untidy which was against the rules. He was required to smarten up or shave the beard off completely.

Then another policeman, who paraded for duty and instead of having a police whistle on his chain, actually produced a bottle opener, amusing he was obviously drinking at times whist on duty, mainly on nights. It created a laugh on the shift back then, but really he was showing his true colours in addition to making himself vulnerable in relation to any future discipline. Surprisingly if he ever did have a drink from any licensee, upon leaving a public house he would mostly go unchecked and get away with it. He was a person with unbelievable good fortune if that if he was being called on the radio as he hadn't been seen or heard of for a period of time he would fall out of the premises right into the path of a burglar or someone who was wanted. This was not exactly engaging investigative police work but sheer luck. It's amazing he had never been detected drinking on duty. That's how it was in those times, he took the risks knowing the full consequences of his actions in a strict disciplined environment and made a laugh of it, but easily could have got moved or lost his job. Despite his faults he was a good and likeable character with a good a sense of humour which was essential then as it is today.

Like the time I walked out of the station early one cold but bright sunny morning. I had not walked more than half a dozen steps and there it happened. I slid on black ice wearing steel capped boots and collapsed in a heap on the floor. Not so bad you may not think, but I was on the floor directly alongside at least a dozen people waiting at a bus stop, who immediately became hysterical with laughter at my expense. But I was down on the floor and had to deal with it. I just stood up immediately repositioned my helmet, dusted off each shoulder with my gloves and with a small bemused smile said, "Morning all" and carried on walking up the street. I could still hear them sniggering some fifty yards on, until I turned the corner. That's something I will never forget, I could never have planned it, it just happened. I am sure that has been their individual topic for conversation for many years. Now I know how the politician Neil Kinnock felt when he slipped on the sands at Blackpool and fell to his knees as the tide came in.

That story went all around the world, but my embarrassment was certainly no different but at least when I reminisce I can still see the funny side without blushing like I did on that eventful cold and icy morning.

So there I was out each day on foot patrol, having been briefed on any items of interest, local stolen vehicles, recent crime, missing persons and wanted persons. What we did not have in those days was the Police National Computer. Any vehicle or person checks were long winded as enquiries by office staff had to be made by telephone to Scotland Yard or force headquarters where records were held in a conventional filing system. This was ultimately a very time consuming procedure. During the daytime I would walk regularly around the town centre being conspicuous when needed and checking alleyways always looking for the unusual and learning the area in readiness for night duty. It did not take long to build up a rapport with local people, as this was a priority in learning about what was going on in the community. In those times the public were extremely good in coming forward as witnesses and were always more than ready to help giving assistance in apprehending people and assisting the police with their enquiries. Generally speaking even up to present day, majority of the public are still very law abiding and very helpful, but need more protection than ever against a very violent society.

Within a short time of my probation, I was present in the Magistrates court which in those days were normally adjacent to the police station. I had been seconded there, as a young man was ready to be sentenced, which was to be custodial for the offence of taking and driving away a motor vehicle to which he had pleaded guilty. He was given six months imprisonment and taken to the police cells in the station. Whilst waiting for a later transfer to the nearest adult prison, he was allowed to see his girlfriend. In those days 6 months meant 6 months. I felt so sorry for him, but he knew the consequences of his actions and the old saying truer than ever if you can't do the time, don't do the crime. I remember him telling me as we later took him to prison that he would never offend again. I think he learned his lesson. Today this would be a slap on the wrist and that's if the matter went to court and was not dealt with by way of a warning.

As stated today people who commit crime are normally given a chance before they are sentenced to imprisonment. Only when the circumstances are so serious that prison can be the only decision. In most cases it is after they have committed numerous offences where alternative methods of punishment have failed. They are under their civil rights given every luxury imaginable, radio, television, iPod, IPad and mobile phone, food of their choice, swimming pool and gym. Even naughty children have to earn respect from bad behaviour and are not given all their toys at once. I can never understand why these facilities are not first earned by prisoners, where they are not given everything at once and taken away at the first sign of misbehaviour. Then prison without being barbaric, would be a deterrent and instill discipline and encourage reform and education and not a luxury taken for granted. In other words imprisonment would be a sentence which the criminal would most definitely not like to receive. However today discipline in prisons has become a joke, they have lost control mainly due to interference from the powers that be, anything not to cause upset, or not to reflect on the running of the prison that could downgrade it in the point's league. This would seriously affect the governor's bonus into the bargain, or to relax the rules, anything for an easy life and it does not take long for the inmate to treat the officer as the prisoner.

When you were on probation you had limited discretion only and were duty bound to report accordingly all offenders no matter what the offence. It was the decision of the chief officer of police as to whether any action was taken or not. Today the Crown Prosecution Service has taken over that role. During my first two years I could be dismissed at any time without appeal, for failing to become an efficient police officer and that also applies today.

There was a time when we had a young lad nearing his teens reported as being missing from home. This was always treated seriously as potentially it could be the beginning of a murder enquiry, or suicide or a cry for help. More often than not thankfully it usually was the latter, bullying at school, or parents being two strict, jealousy in the family home or being found out being dishonest. So many reasons but all investigated rigorously, starting at first by making a thorough search of the house including the loft, cellar and outhouses, anywhere where a child could hide had to be checked. Details of time last seen and who by, together with a description of the person and clothing worn were all essential details with accuracy of major importance. Details of any vehicle used or persons who they associate with are also important. Whether or not they had gone missing before and results of where last being found, all positive factors to consider.

I recall passing the description out we had various clues to where he may have gone and different haunts where he would hide. I was joined by a dog handler and we went across fields. It was a rainy evening and he knew all the tracks. He was adequately dressed with wellingtons and waterproofs whereas I was in normal uniform. He took me up this steep embankment, he knew exactly what he was doing as the ground was wet due to it raining earlier, as I kept slipping down in the wet mud and grass. He intended me to look as if I had been in the outback or the wilderness because I was covered in thick mud all over my boots and all down the front of my uniform. They all had a good laugh when we got back to the station, but it was all part of the comradeship. Main issue was the missing child was found safe and well. He had lost his money for the shopping and was frightened of his parents. I definitely would not go out with a dog handler again in that way, lesson learned.

Police women also played an important role especially when the child was found, in recording debriefing notes as to where they had been and who with, if they had been any offences committed especially involving indecency which sadly was sometimes the case. In those days offenders were dealt with straight across the board by uniform and plain clothes officers, the word pedophile was not a label we were familiar with at those times.

The weeks soon turned into months and I was well into my probation I had dealt with a variety of matters, crime was always there, but back then there was a real deterrent, as explained with the person convicted of take and drive away and his sentence. Whilst on probation we were privileged to have been allowed to perform Assize and Quarter Sessions duty normally every 3 to 6 months. We were required to be in full smart uniform, without any helmet and it was essential white gloves were worn. Our role in those days before the system changed to crown courts was to perform the duties of the court ushers.

We would be in charge of calling witnesses and escorting them to the witness box, where we would hand them the bible, or a similar religious book personal to them. They would then read from the card they held and they related the oath, or affirmation to tell the truth, the whole truth and nothing but the truth. When the jury went out to consider their verdict, two of us would be sworn in by the clerk of the court to keep them safe, whilst they deliberated their findings in full privacy of the Jury Room. Not to have any contact with them other than to pass messages for the information of the judge. These were a wealth of experiences which were invaluable for a young officer as you learned court protocol and how to conduct yourself. How to prepare for cross examination and to get your answers across in a way the evidence became clear and unchallenging and to ensure you left no stone unturned in the presentation of your file of evidence.

The Officer in Charge of the case always went into the witness box under oath, after the finding of guilt and gave evidence of antecedence and if other offences were to be taken into consideration. It was of vital importance to have an accurate and up to date list of previous convictions before the Judge passed sentence. Barristers in those days always complimented the officer in charge of the case for excellent paperwork and I was always proud when this happened. Especially as later in my career when complex and complicated files produced for court, became a very regular event.

When out on patrol I soon learned that you find what you set out to look for. If you are looking for no tax on a vehicle you will undoubtedly find it, same for looking for a thief or a burglar but it takes longer but you get there. You learn to look for the unusual things that are out of place within a normal crowd of people. Thus identifying an opportunist thief looking around furtively waiting for the exposed handbag or purse just waiting to be snatch either discreetly, or by using force. This was a skill I found later in my service that does not come easy to some officers.

It was during the early hours of the morning that I pulled up the police vehicle and I was in the vicinity of some multi- story flats. A car with three men pulled up which looked dubious. I did a quick vehicle check. Whilst I was waiting for a reply I approached the driver and spoke with both passengers. I gave the impression I was not interested and asked them if they had had a good night and where they had been. I had a call over the radio and told them to excuse me for a moment. Quietly I was told the car was stolen so I just answered with two words, location and assistance. I went back to the car and started continuing my chat with the three men, cracking a joke and talking about their night out. Within a short time they were surrounded and all arrested. Inside the vehicle I found evidence relating to several burglaries. Just imagine how far I would have got if I had been alone and said to them, 'Right you are all under arrest this cars stolen'. They would have scarpered in all directions so you had to be as cunning as them.

My first taste of plain clothes work came when I had locked up a young man for burglaries and he started to confess all crimes committed by him to clear his slate. I had been on uniform patrol and investigating factory burglaries and my actions led to an arrest and the recovery of stolen property. Altogether I cleared over forty offences of theft and burglary and I had assistance from CID in dealing with him and others implicated. In those days if your enquiries produced sound evidence the accused when confronted mostly made full admissions and wanted to show that he was cooperative with the police.

In addition priority was always given to the recovery of stolen property, all these issues going in the favour of the defendant when facing a future court appearance. Whenever a person was arrested, especially when performing uniform shift duties, if three offenders were implicated, all were to be arrested. If one person was in custody, it was an unwritten rule every effort must to be made to trace, locate and arrest the others responsible, even if this meant staying well into the next shift. This was extremely important, as it would restrict collusion between offenders and prevent evidence being lost and in most cases assist in the recovery of stolen property. This was always the priority at that time and for the whole of my career, being dedicated to a job that gave you good standing within the community.

Throughout the whole of my probation I had regular training weeks locally and towards the end of the second year it was time to return to the same initial training centre for a two week refresher course. What a difference, a uniform that fitted no exams or drill, just a good overhaul of training issues to which confidence was as high as it could be. We all felt we had achieved our ultimate goal, acceptance was guaranteed otherwise we would not have been sent, as we had all successfully passed our period of probation and were each confirmed in our appointments. We were fully fledged police officers, still with a lot to learn but also a force to be reckoned with.

I returned back to my station and was later informed I had been put forward for the probationer's police cup for that year. One candidate per division within the force area and I had been chosen. What an achievement, sadly I did not win, but the competition was strong. I am sure someone much worthier than me was the prize winner. In any case my wife and I now had two children and a pay rise bringing me level to my wages as a butcher even if I had to wait two years for this it was very welcome indeed.

CHAPTER 08

A NEW EXPERIENCE DRIVING POLICE VEHICLES

Within a few months of occupational duties, I undertook police driving techniques and became qualified in driving the police panda cars. This gave more variation to my duties as I was now attending roads accidents and other incidents more or less one after the other. I became to realise that you always saw something suspicious when being sent to other jobs and one had to prioritise which was more important. Following your instincts and checking out suspicious characters, whilst advising someone else to attend the other calls including domestics or burglar alarms. It was a fine line, but some of my best arrests over many years came by adopting this practice.

During a busy night shift, I stopped to check a young man who was walking away from a factory estate and although I could not prove anything about him doing wrong, he was a known offender. He was allowed to go on his way, but later arrested when we discovered a stolen double decker bus had been found abandoned in the area where he was originally seen. He was later charged when we found vital evidence on the bus connecting him to the offence. It just proves the importance of checking people seen at night, otherwise this crime may not have been detected. Naturally no person wishes to be inconvenienced especially if an innocent person is quietly walking home minding their own business, but any person stopped could later be established as being an important witness should any crime or incident later come to light. Providing courtesy and politeness is at the forefront of any routine conversation with any person, coupled with firmness should the character change behaviour or appears acting suspiciously, then more appropriate action can be taken.

Working another night shift, we had a call come from a witness who had seen a neighbour break into a motor car removing property which he had taken into his house. It was about 1.30am in the morning and being on nights we only had limited staff on duty as all neighouring beat officers had finished working. Having attended the scene and verified the witness's actions, I went to the house in question. As I knocked the door a man answered fitting the description. He was some 6ft 4ins tall, very well built, extremely fit and muscular. He smelt slightly of drink and you couldn't help notice that he was either into boxing or weight training and had hands as big as plates. He was either way a force to be reckoned with. From his attitude it was obvious he was angry at my presence and his aggression soon surfaced. It would have been suicidal for me alone to have made any attempt to have tackled him single handedly. Before I said a word he shouted, "Fuck off "and slammed the door.

This was the first time ever in my service that I needed to call for assistance. I thought logically that there was nothing else that I could do and within moments my Sergeant arrived. I reiterated what had taken place and although I sensed the sergeant was thinking why I could not have sorted this little matter out myself. I waited in anticipation for his reaction as he too knocked the door to see what this man's behaviour would be. I need not have worried as the sergeant faced exactly the same response that I had witnessed. He also swore and slammed the door in the face of the sergeant and I recall saying to him, "See what I mean sarge." On that basis I realised then and there I had been completely exonerated for calling for help.

It was obvious this man would be a serious threat to both of us and was far more than we could handle together and he then called for further assistance. The duty Inspector was called out who arrived with another constable who was driving the Black Maria, a slang term for a police van used to transport prisoners. Originally these were horse drawn but that was many years previous. When we finally went to the house it took all four of us to restrain him and take him into custody. As we grabbed him and started to explain he was under arrest he immediately commenced fighting swinging out with punches where we each went for a limb. He kicked the other constable away in the struggle, but he regained control. I just held his one arm down as did the Inspector who held the other arm. The sergeant had the other leg. We held him for several minutes until he calmed down and then lifted him together to get him into the police van. His wife was shouting and screaming hysterically.

A search of his home was made and the stolen property was recovered. All this commotion and violence just for stealing a car radio why get into such a situation in the first place. The following morning the man had sobered up and apologised for his behaviour. He admitted the theft and assault on police and was later charged. How easily things could have turned out more sinister and without the correct amount of staff we could easily have received nasty injuries.

Then there was the 09.00 o'clock policeman, the first time I had experienced someone after the event criticise the action taken at the time. He was a new detective officer at the station who was stating the offender should have been left alone and arrested later the following day. Common sense always dictated to me strike whilst the iron was hot, if we had left it until the next day the offender or accomplices could have got rid of the property then the same source would criticise for taking no action. In any case it was a matter of principal that he should not have gotten away with such bad and vile behaviour. Over the years I always had to fight the negative person no matter what rank and there were always plenty of them around.

When on patrol either in a marked police vehicles or on foot patrol at various stages during our 8 hours shift, I could be called upon anytime, providing I was not committed, to have an official meet with the duty sergeant. He would arrange the location and give a time and you had to be there, it was part of his supervision to do this and to sign your pocket book accordingly with the time and location. Periodically a meet would also take place between yourself and a senior officer being anyone from an Inspector to a Chief Superintendent the latter being fairly rare. One significant point of interest would be all these officers above the rank of sergeant would never wear police helmets only flat caps, with brown gloves and a walking cane which had a small silver crest at the top. A salute was always required which was promptly returned. This stemmed from mainly the earlier days of policing when there were less cars and more officers on the beat, all being before my time. Most of the meeting places would be at the old blue police boxes, situated in every force at various points of a sub division.

At the station where I worked we had a police sergeant living in a house just across the court yard, appropriately named believe it or not 'Handcuff House' This particular sergeant was as eccentric as the name of his property, in fact he was extremely efficient at his job and well liked. He would play opera very loud, most nights well into the early and late hours of the morning. Fortunately his house was far enough away from anyone else living nearby, to be disturbed, apart from his loyal wife, who must have worn ear plugs or suffered from deafness. Whenever he was in charge of the shift he really tested your knowledge, not only did he arrange to meet in certain streets or roads, sometimes the only clue would be the name of the property. This would be in the most inconspicuous of places concealed by shrubbery or hidden out of view. Fellow colleagues would pre-warn you over most of his favourite spots and this really tested you. When you arrived at the place in question without having to repeatedly ask directions he was always duly impressed. However sometimes it was impossible not to ask, as you had no choice, all good fun which you grew to respect.

Official meets carried on for several years until they were virtually fizzled out, today a sergeant will normally examine uniform constables pocket books after parade. However this is still good practice as it shows entries are regularly made, that the pocket book is fully kept up to date and in court cases can help to support the accuracy of the evidence recorded. I always thought of the pocket book being the policeman's bible. Keeping it up to date continually was essential and right up towards the end of my service it was a practice I always maintained and proved invaluable to me. Records made shortly after arrest or following a conversation under caution were important, especially when the accused was invited to sign the entry. Whether he agreed or not, the offer was there and weeks later in court your credibility was at the highest in showing honesty and fairness. This practice was keeping an up to date pocket book especially as a detective, was no more essential as when you least expected it. Suddenly arriving at a crime scene, or at hospital, visiting a victim close to death, where the person made a dying declaration. To make a record directly into your pocket book at the immediate time, would all go to supporting the honesty and accuracy of any statement made. Under the Police and Criminal Evidence Act, this later became law if any reply was made it would not be allowed unless this procedure was fully put into practice. It was hard work documenting all that happened each and every day directly into writing as soon as the opportunity arose, but a practice I always encouraged especially with younger keener officers who soon learned to appreciate this. Where I have seen some officers fall a couple of days behind and this could leave you open to all kinds of problems missing important details and severe criticism.

Like most towns and built up areas all experience the menace of sneak in thefts. This technically is burglary, as quite often the area where the theft takes place is part of a building where the offender enters without permission and as a trespasser. As we all know there is nothing worse than being the victim of a pick pocket or a sneak in thief, when you are suddenly without your purse or wallet which normally contain personal and private

71

information, keys or jewellery and of course cash. This happened well before the introduction of plastic debit or credit cards, so even in current times this is still very much a despicable offence and well- practiced by low life criminals, druggies and immigrant gangs from many parts of Europe. The worst part is that without detection everyone in an office, canteen, factory or wherever the offence has taken place, all staff feel themselves under suspicion and no one can trust anyone. That is why it is so rewarding when these kind of offences are detected. I recall one morning shift I was driving the police car patrolling the town centre area when I attended such a report of an offence. I took all the details and obtained a partial description of a young man seen acting suspiciously close to the office premises, although no one could say he was responsible for the actual theft.

Taking a full interest back at the station, I obtained all the crime reports which related to similar thefts through the previous six to twelve months. Again there were some sightings of the offender with partial descriptions and staff at receptions in most buildings all reported a similar story where the man was looking for employment, as an excuse to enter the building. I actually under my own volition developed a profile of the person I was looking for, which was of tremendous value in this enquiry and used by me on numerous occasions in the future.

This was a practice I always completed throughout my uniform career and more than ever during my C.I.D. years. Today it is called a cold case review looking back over old cases filed as the old saying which is completely true – out of sight out of mind. Even detected crimes or none detected crimes files all containing similar offences. Some reports with partial sightings of offenders helping build a picture of the current offender or previous workings of a past offender and his method of working, habits and accomplices. All extremely useful in the detection of crime and knowing what to look for in tracing those responsible for actively committing crime.

This particular offender believing he had not been noticed whilst staff were busy answering the phones, would choose his opportunity to enter empty offices riffle through drawers and clothing in cloak rooms and steal property. Having a picture in my mind of the potential criminal, I continued with my patrolling duties driving and walking in all the areas of the town where most offences had been committed. Although out in a panda car it was just as important to park up and walk around, staying within a reasonable distance of the vehicle in case an urgent job came in for an area elsewhere. As I walked the town area I was asking questions at every opportunity, I established that on some occasions a pushbike was used. With this in mind I was given a name. Checking against this man's description he did fit the bill and found out that years earlier he had worked a paper round delivering to most of the addresses which were now scenes of some of the crimes.

This one day a little later in that same week whilst walking through the town I suddenly saw him alone and went up to him. I told him I was investigating a number of offences and that I had reason to believe he was responsible. I arrested him on suspicion of theft and took him into custody. I explained most of the methods used to enter premises the plausible stories put forward which resulted in sneak in thefts from all parts of various buildings and that he fitted the description. Eventually he admitted being responsible initially for two or three thefts and as the morning went on he admitted close up to fifty separate offences.

With another officer I made a search of his home and he was driven throughout the town centre area and other areas where he showed me all the places where he had been thieving. In addition he showed me some places where he discarded purses and wallets, some of which were recovered. Others had been thrown down drains which the council later assisted in retrieving. He was later charged with several of the thefts and subsequently bailed. Paperwork was to be prepared for all other offences to be taken into consideration.

It was during this exercise that I looked at one crime report to which he had identified premises resulting in him stealing a purse. Looking at the original report, I saw that it had been amended with additional property stolen. I could not believe my eyes when I saw that there was a ladies engagement ring which was inside the purse which he had stolen. It was valued on the crime report as over £3000. Straight away I went to see this man again and demanded an explanation for the missing property. Thinking he would deny all knowledge, I was utterly taken back when he told me what had happened. He stated he had sold the ring for a one pound note to his brother, who had given it to his wife. I just couldn't catch my breath, I was totally flabbergasted. Just a pound paid for such a valuable item of property, fortunately in this case crime certainly did not pay. I explained this must be recovered if he was to have the respect of the Magistrates.

We both then went to the home address of his brother and sister in law. In the kitchen at the address I asked them about the ring and they admitted that they suspected it was dodgy and should not have taken it. The lady removed the ring which she was wearing and I took possession of it. Both were arrested and all attended the police station. Later in formal interview they each admitted knowing he had been stealing and all they could afford between them was one pound in monies. Although I felt sorry for them I had no choice they had to be charged. Both were treated leniently at court for at least being honest about what they had done. As for the main thief he got a total of 12 months imprisonment. Prior to this I took the stolen ring for identification by the owner. The lady described it perfectly and curious over the value I asked her how much it was worth. She stated the ring had been valued sometime previously for the house insurance at £680 so it was still fairly valuable back then, whereas today it would have been in access of £10,000. The lady showed me documentation to support this valuation which also contained a drawing of the ring itself. I took a statement to that effect.

I later saw the female police Officer who had completed the amended crime report showing the ring being valued at over £3000. I showed the officer the statement which I had taken from this witness and just asked for a simple explanation as to the subsequent identification of the recovered property which was correctly valued at £680. Suddenly realising her error made, the officer stated that the crime number 3000 had also been mistaken for the value. You just could not make it up. I was just hysterical with laughter and so was she. As for the owner of the jewellery, I had not got the heart to upset her by informing her of the price paid by those receiving the stolen property, or the fact that the crime report the recorded value was £3000. Some things are just left better unsaid. Most of all I experienced the most wonderful job satisfaction in recovering for this lady an item of jewellery which to her was of esteem sentimental value and irreplaceable.

It is sad today that majority of police Officers, solicitor's magistrates and judges dealing with such crimes, have to accept the offender's story that they sold the stolen property to an unknown person whom they met. In most cases it is obvious they are not being completely truthful. Many items of sentimental stolen property remain outstanding and if not recovered, can have devastating consequences for victims. Such as irreplaceable photos of loved ones who are now deceased, today this includes videos and photographs held on mobile devices and similar recordings on other stolen equipment. This includes all sentimental property which the offender really knows of the whereabouts but fails to help recover any items outstanding. In cases of serious crime, orders can be now made under the Proceeds of Crime Act legislation where large amounts of money and possibly other goods, if not recovered, can result in severe penalties with the offenders receiving additional sentences of imprisonment. It would be good if similar orders could be made for smaller items where it is believed the offender is not being completely truthful, in assisting in the recovery of other sentimental items of stolen property.

As time went by many solicitors just come to accept these well-established lies as if it was a criminals right not to have to explain when questioned over the whereabouts of stolen property. Indeed they are interviewed under caution so they are not obliged to say anything, but giving ridiculous answers, such as," I sold it to a bloke I met in the pub", or simply, " No Comment". Defence staff would have doubts, but all of us knew the accused was possibly lying but that bought no comfort to the victims. In many cases they would lose out, with having no insurance to cover them, or had to accept poor reduced settlements from inadequate insurance claims. This is why when the person is found guilty of the theft or burglary, these lies and failure to recover stolen property, especially sentimental items should carry the threat of doubling the sentence, in the event it fell on deaf ears. This would be a definite threat to those who commit similar crimes in future cases, where the property is deliberately not recovered.

On a lighter note covering an unforgettable experience, I recall during the early hours one morning whilst on patrol with the sergeant it was quiet and all town centre premises had been checked and he drove out into the country. Whilst out on patrol he chose to investigate business premises where caravans were for sale. He obviously had some private interest and I recall out in the sticks in the middle of the countryside, there was this very large yard where about fifty caravans were situated. We climbed over the six foot gates and started to walk around, perhaps on a crime prevention exercise you could call it, but to him it was window shopping. It did not go all to plan, as within a very short time I saw the sergeant climb back over the gates, he was leaving and shouted me to join him quickly. It was not long before I knew the reason why, as two large ferocious Alsatian dogs roaming free in the yard had their sights on just one target – Me. They were fast approaching and extremely close running directly towards me. I just had to move and my God that meant fast. I ran to the gates and vaulted them completely falling into a heap on the ground, with the dogs growling and barking the other side, tearing my trousers and tunic into the bargain still that was better that being ripped apart. What a scrape, my former P.E. Teacher would have been proud of me. This was another subject for laughter back at the station and another mistake that I did not anticipate making again.

On one Sunday in the summer months at our town we had a carnival parade which was fairly well attended. There were several lorries converted into floats, all addressing various themes, with army cadets, salvation army bands, boy scouts and girl guides all which formed a lengthy procession of about half a mile. It was to be paraded through most of the town streets finishing up on the local park where there was a fairground, pig roast and horse riding and jumping competitions. It was a very well turned out event with no public disorder taking place. Naturally policing was important and officers were drafted in from surrounding beats to increase numbers with all the members of the special constabulary of all ranks in attendance.

Surprisingly a decision was taken that all senior officers in the special constabulary were to have the same powers of supervision to that of all regular officers and were allowed to command all those under their rank. This allowed part-time unpaid specials to give orders to regular officers, below their rank. With regular officers having far more experience and service this did not go down at all well and it was not before long serious questions were being raised at very high levels, involving the Chief Constable and indeed the Police Federation.

We never found out who gave the permission for this to happen but all of a sudden later that day the order was countermanded and we reverted to normal supervision, with the special constabulary being responsible for their own staff. What a serious misjudgment of staff policing, I later discovered along with other officers that it did not happen elsewhere in the force area, that someone in charge of our station possibly the Superintendent made a serious judgement of error. This was never to happen again as it was totally against all the rules and could have resulted in severe consequences if any other wrong orders or decisions involving staff had been given.

There was another uniform sergeant at the same police station who I thought was possibly a former army sergeant major. Many police personal with any service all had military backgrounds from the army, navy or air force having joined sometime after the end of World War 2 and had many talents being full of experiences of life. This particular sergeant was unique in character, a master of his craft and highly professional, as well as being a calm, friendly, and reserved person. However make no mistake at the other end of the scale, he was a disciplinarian who would also stand no nonsense. He truly was a force to be reckoned with not an easy touch or pushover as one annoying member of the public discovered to his detriment. The man had entered the police station and sought advice over a dispute which had taken place some moments before in the town with a local shop keeper. Having told his story the sergeant listened intently before he fully explained the law to the man relating to the issue, which clearly was a civil matter. Not accepting this the man started ranting and raving, hurling abuse back to the sergeant showing his aggression.

The sergeant some six feet tall leaned over to the man telling him to calm down and behave. It had the opposite effect whereby the man started shouting obscenities and was banging his fist on the low level counter in temper and making violent threats towards the officer. He was told by the sergeant the advice was correct and he gave him a final warning to control his behaviour. Other members of the public were also in the station waiting at the same side of the counter and they too were concerned at the man's threatening attitude and possible further violent action by him.

This man just would not give up and in continuing to display his dis-approval of the advice given, continued shouting and swearing. The sergeant firmly told him that he had been given enough warnings about his conduct and told him that he was arresting him for disorderly behaviour in a police station. The man was some 6 inches shorter and of stocky build, who then attempted to swing a punch towards the sergeant. He was then grabbed at both lapels of his coat and lifted up off the floor and the sergeant dragged him over the station counter. He was taken directly to the cells and placed into custody, where he remained for a couple of hours, until his demeanour became calm and subdued. The man was charged and later appeared that same day at the Magistrates Court next door, where he pleaded guilty and was fined. All because of his own stupidity in failing to take sound advice and accepting it. What a performance throughout the whole disturbance the sergeant was fair, yet uncompromising resilient and showed the man exactly who was in charge and that his kind of behaviour was not to be tolerated under any circumstances.

It just proves the point there is one place where if you have any common sense to behave yourself at all times it is definitely in the police station. The very same applies elsewhere in all government and court buildings, where misbehaviour of any kind will not be tolerated and the same laws apply. Can you imagine this today, certain people in society would be up in arms criticising the police action then taken, whereas some members of society would just love to see more examples of positive policing, especially where justified as given by people believing they are above the law.

CHAPTER 09

MOVING TO A BUSY RURAL BEAT WITH DISCRETIONAL DUTIES

We had been in our home then for two years, we had made new friends and we were beginning to feel comfortable. Things were looking up and I was in a job that I loved. However all this was to be short lived, as I had obviously impressed my bosses and I was offered a new role as a resident beat officer, a rare experience in the force back then for an officer with only two year's service. It meant uprooting and moving some 6 miles away to the northern part of the sub division, close to the boundary of two other police forces and within 6 miles of a large city centre.

So I had to break the news to my dear wife who could not understand but accepted the move from a modern brand new police house to a police sub-station with police houses adjoining at both sides. However when we moved in we were in for a cultural shock when we discovered the whole kitchen from walls, doors, skirting boards and ceiling were painted in a deep orange and apart from being a disgusting colour was completely filthy. Exactly the complete opposite of the property we were leaving. I later established the Inspector with his secretary visited our home after we had vacated, to ensure no damage had been caused, which I was advised was routine practice. How naïve I was back then, when no one ever visited this second police home, perhaps on reflection they were already well aware of the pedigree of the constable who was the previous tenant, but still double standards. If they had inspected this police house I am sure it would have been condemned or an order made for it to be fumigated. In addition the gardens at the rear were completely overgrown and the size of nearly two football pitches. So apart from my D.I.Y. skills, I also had to become a professional gardener.

Still enough of that again I was faced with a tremendous challenge it was the busiest operational sub-station in the force area, having 24 hour cover. With my new colleague next door we worked discretional duties working any 8 hours within the working day, taking alternative duties with night cover between midnight and 09.00am. However it was also a privilege being trusted to work alone without total supervision and also very unusual for an officer having such short service in an area with average crime with nearly every kind of offence imaginable. I soon got accustomed to working my own discretional hours I had a good mature friendly colleague next door and we worked well together. When we were out our wives would answer the telephone and the station door, can you imagine this today, I don't believe it would ever happen. Like I said we had everything in the book to police, from poaching to shotgun offences, licensing, straying cattle, offences of every kind and some involving gypsies or travellers as they prefer to be known today. In addition, we also dealt with swine vesicular disease which involved the monitoring the movement of livestock and the issue of licenses. This together with everyday road accidents, sadly many fatal and sudden deaths of every kind and domestic disturbances it was busy and I was still learning from all these experiences. In addition to this we had a selection of various crimes, although in 1972 there were not too many serious offences at that time.

One interesting complaint was made to me from a local farmer where the owner's wife had a horse located in a field next to their stables. She complained that a stallion in a neighbouring farm had jumped the fence and had served her prize mare which resulted in the mare expecting an unwanted foal. That was a test for my knowledge, so I took the details and returning to the station out came the law books and there it was -The Horse Breeding Act 1827. There was an offence of keeping an un-licensed stallion over the age of two years, the only exception being the stallion had to be castrated and if not, a license was required. I interviewed the owner a pleasant young lady who admitted the offence and was duly reported. When I submitted the paperwork I had to smile because senior officers were bewildered in what to do about it, they asked for my comments and being up on the subject I informed them The Ministry of Agriculture was the prosecuting authority. Off went the paperwork and within 3 months it came back with a decision for the offender to be cautioned. All were happy and I found this incident so rare an event and to me just an unusual offence and very unique in itself plus very interesting that was dealt with according to the law.

Sunday mornings were nearly always busy as people would visit the countryside and trespassing with firearms was a regular occurrence. On one occasion another farmer complained there were trespassers on his land, I took descriptions and went out on patrol. When I reached the location I found two people at opposite ends of the field, a man and a woman both with shotguns. I approached the man, who signaled for the woman to join him, who I established was his girlfriend. She had borrowed the shotgun and because she was not in his immediate supervision technically she had no shotgun certificate and both were trespassing with a firearm. The weapons were seized and they were both reported for offences and later fined. However the man was later allowed to keep the weapons after an appeal and as far as I knew did not re-offend.

When dealing with members of the public it was just my job to detect and report offences and I never mistreated anyone I was always polite and professional. It's a small world and you never know where you will meet them next, they could be a potential witness or an acquaintance of another person I would have to deal with, a situation that is still true today. You soon got a reputation for being fair and honest and gained respect from the public and this was a main priority for working and achieving job satisfaction.

So much so to prove this point, the mother of the man I had reported for the shotgun offences telephoned me at the station some two months later. She was extremely annoyed and had genuine cause to be, immediately outside her country cottage for a distance of some 30 yards the total area of the lane, household rubbish had been strewn. There were the equivalent contents of up to twenty dustbins so you can imagine the mess. It was as if a tipper lorry had just pulled up and dropped its load whilst driving away. Apart from everything you would find in dustbins there were numerous items of paper and books. As I commenced going through the mess, I realised why she was so annoyed, it was not just the rubbish but it was apparent the offender was possibly a police officer and quite rightly she wanted justice and was out for blood.

She need not have worried because there was no excuse for such disgraceful behaviour unless someone had set him up, but from the evidence I did not think so. All together I discovered 15 official police documents including pocket books and other confidential police information in addition to personal and private information of the person responsible. Three vehicle registration books also in the same name were found. The incident was serious and I arranged for photographic in those days, a role undertaken by a scenes of crime officer to attend who took pictures to show the incriminating evidence. A full report was prepared for senior officers and the constable from an adjoining force was investigated. He was prosecuted for litter and failing to notify change of vehicle ownership for three motor cars and fined. Unbelievably he kept his job despite being on probation. In my force even out of probation for something this serious, you would have been required to resign. A few months later I heard a whisper through the grapevine he had been sacked anyway for failing to stop at the scene of a road accident and drink driving. Just a bad apple, like there are in all organisations and all walks of life.

Most city police officers would probably joke about having to deal with horses or cows on the road something most people do not experience, but very annoying for those that do. Most of these incidents can be very dangerous depending on the location especially during the hours of darkness. It was no fun during a cold winter night being contacted from the main sub-division being interrupted from a night's sleep, to have to get into the police car scrape off the ice and drive out into the country on roads covered heavily with snow. It was however all part of the job. In most cases it was the same offender, he always allowed his cattle to roam as his fields were unfenced and when prosecuted he never paid the fines, so things were getting out of control. The cows would roam over people's front gardens eat shrubbery and in some cases create havoc. Then they would be allowed to roam into other farmers fields. The same applies to horses where the owners are neglectful and normally in colder weather are too lazy to get out and leave feed for them. Then there are people entering fields and leaving gates open where cattle or horses eventually escape, again in search for food. This can be particularly dangerous especially at night if they wander down country lanes where the unsuspecting motorist is driving way too fast, or where they roam onto busy roads carrying traffic such as, dual carriageways and motorways. Looking back it reminds me very much of the television series Heartbeat, our patch was no different we had our fair share of comical characters like all police areas throughout the country.

I spoke to one farmer who had the perfect solution. On the last occasion the same cattle roamed he allowed them onto his land. He had transport laid on and took them all away and impounded them against a civil redress for damage caused to his land and fencing. On instigation they would not be released until the farmer paid all damages and costs incurred. As a result he duly paid up to get his cattle back and fenced his land to prevent similar offences occurring again. This was a common sense and practical solution which solved the problem once and for all. The offender even later paid all his fines. Whether or not this would be allowed today I do not know, but it certainly worked for us back then.

With two small children and one on the way and it was early one morning around 7.00am when a neighbour across the road telephoned the station. I took the call in our bedroom. He stated that he did not wish to alarm us but our two boys were sitting on the window ledge with their feet dangling out of the open window. The windows were of metal design and not too secure. I had to think quick on my feet and suddenly shouted from the landing "Come on breakfasts ready", rather than burst in and frighten them possibly causing them to lose balance and fall out. Thank God they just climbed back inside as normal and came out of their room. The windows were tied together from that time, lesson learned. With older police property the windows were not exactly top of the range, whereas today majority of homes have secure double glazing.

One other incident not funny at the time, with the one boy nearly two and his brother a year older, I went down into the station office which we could not lock properly from our residence. To my horror I discovered we had had intruders, yes the two little boys again. They were not always naughty and most times very good, after all they were only young and still a short existence from being babies, but this time they had excelled themselves. A report half complete in the typewriter had been destroyed with some kind of practice and over typing. Drawings and pictures were found in the general occurrence book where official police entries were made, together with other police documentation scribbled on. Being such a young age we only told them what they did was wrong, but I certainly had some explaining to do when the divisional Superintendent visited a short time later. He had not even got the same sense of humour, after all without being able to lock the office door I was not able to predict their actions. All part of life again another lesson learned.

Interestingly enough, although high in rank, in later service I established he was not a very nice man and was very vindictive against other first class officers of different ranks, at the same time definitely not a person of integrity. This arrogant behaviour continued well into his retirement. He still thought of his own self- importance in not allowing anyone to sit in his chosen seat in the local police social club and if anyone did, they were expected to move so he and his dear wife could occupy the spot. Not in my book I would sooner give the seating to anyone else rather than bow down to his whims and whams. One day I was in his so called royal throne with some guests and I refused to move much to his annoyance. I told him what right had he to behave so selfishly and that he should be ashamed, after all it was 10 years into his retirement and he had abused members longer enough. The practice ceased thereafter and I thought long overdue. Many other colleagues I met over the years of all ranks would never have behaved like that and later I was complimented for my actions, so I was extremely pleased he had been finally put in his place.

In the police, like many other professions, there is always the saying that you are never off duty and that is still true up until this day. I had tried to master the garden in between work hours and I was mowing the front lawn to our house one morning. All of a sudden along the main road in front of the house I heard police sirens, I looked up and saw a van travelling erratically with several men inside. As it passed the rear doors burst open and a man with a shotgun fired it at one of the police cars in pursuit. It missed but as they all travelled past and down the road I heard further shots being discharged. I immediately got the keys to the police vehicle and went onto the force radio, at that time I stated red call which gave me radio priority and gave full circumstances of the incident.

With the boundary of two police forces in close proximity information was automatically circulated to them as well. I drove off with the police cars involved in the chase well in the distance, giving a running commentary over the force radio. I don't think I had ever seen so many police vehicles attending one incident so quickly in my whole experience. The offending van drove into a field followed by police vehicles including land rovers and vans with police dogs onboard. The field was circulated and all men arrested. They had committed an armed robbery at a post office just across the police boundary in one of the city suburbs. It was so good to see such a quick response by so many officers, something I was to experience many times as I went through my police career.

Another interesting little tale was when I received a call from the local airport, which today is one of the largest international airports in the country. A telephone call was directed to the senior management team from a young hoax caller to the effect that one of the planes due to take off later that day had a bomb on board. As serious as the situation sounded the member of staff that I was speaking to, provided me with a full detailed account of the person making the call and a breakdown of everything that was spoken. Adding the voice appeared to be that of a young person and in the background, the giggling of other similar young persons could be heard. The telephone kiosk phone number was given plus its location from where the call was made, which was in the vicinity of one of the local senior schools on my area. Having all the facts I visited the area in question and made house to house enquiries at several addresses. I established three pupils from the school had been causing a general nuisance in the area in they were knocking doors, ringing door bells and running off. At some gardens pulling up house plants, kicking over freshly delivered bottles of milk, throwing mud at windows, in addition to making telephone calls to a couple of people in the same road. It was not long before I could put a name to one teenager and soon established who he was associating with, and it became apparent these were possibly the guilty suspects.

With sufficient evidence to commence enquiries with the named individuals, I arranged to attend the school premises where I interviewed those implicated in the presence of a parent and a member of the school staff. As I started to chip away at the truth the main culprits admitted being responsible for all the nuisance incidents reported. The phone call that was made to the airport was then discussed and I eventually established the truth identifying the three were all present with the actual juvenile who made the call. They were all reported for various offences committed including the juvenile making a malicious telephone call under the Telecommunications Act for consideration of prosecution. Due to no previous criminal behaviour a caution was issued against the main offender and the others were warned as to their future conduct.

As for the complaints of nuisance in the nearby area the group of pupils responsible, with a member of school staff had to visit the house owners individually living in the road, to apologise formerly. All had been named and shamed in school assembly and given detention. A couple of months later it was Christmas and my wife was visited at the police station and given a bottle of homemade wine by one of the ladies who had been a victim to the nuisances. She did not leave her name but left a message thanking me for my help in sorting out the petty but annoying problems which had since ceased occurring. That was so kind and thoughtful. This was one of the many examples where the local policeman was fully appreciated for just doing his job.

The most tragic part of police work involved the investigation of sudden death, you may state as police officers we become hardened or immune to dealing with these sad cases, but being human you cannot help feeling sad for relatives or loved ones. This is even more traumatic when you have actually spoken with someone who has taken an overdose in an apparent suicide bid. At the time of arrival they are coherent and explain what they did and tablets taken. Even though they are rushed to hospital, they did not arrive in time to prevent major organs from shutting down due to the toxic substance already entering the blood stream, when people who have been desperate take an overdose.

I recall a woman in her mid-thirties who had three young children had taken several tablets. Despite being conscious at the time of arrival and telling me what she had taken, the damage was done with liver failure you just don't survive. Just so sad, these children were without a mother she had left it too late in contacting anyone. The Father who was separated regained custody of his children. No different to speaking to a person involved in a road accident, who apparently has just suffered from shock and required to be taken to hospital a short time later, but dies from effects of their condition. It is always totally unexpected. When someone is suffering shock they must always be treated seriously and be cared for hoping they calm down through reassurance.

Then the case of a woman in her late twenties who had bequeathed her eyes sadly not surviving a serious illness, how I felt for her husband and family. The eyes were successfully used to help another person's sight, even in those days there was real success in surgery by the medical profession.

Another incident involved the sad death of a middle aged man, who lived alone in a caravan situated on the edge of a field rented from the local farmer. Apparently having no electric or gas supply he always had wooden fires mainly in cold climates in a make shift fireplace, where the chimney was incorporated into the roof. He had fallen asleep it was believed with a large wood fire to keep warm, where either a cinder or log must have fallen away causing the fire to spread throughout the caravan. The man eventually became engulfed in dangerous fumes according to the autopsy, causing him to stop breathing, before he was aware of the seriousness of the situation, well hopefully that is what happened.

He was a likeable man, well-built but grossly overweight at some 20 plus stone and was a regular at the local off licence where his favourite drink was cheap rough cider. The fire completely engulfed the whole of the caravan leaving just the chassis and debris together with twisted and melted metal. I recall attending the scene with other officers, the fire brigade were in attendance and through the remains we saw just the torso of the deceased, as the remainder of his body had been cremated. He was identified by dental records. The coroner recorded an open verdict, pending any other evidence coming to light, as no witnesses to the death or circumstances leading up to it could be found.

On a lighter note, there was the time a man was due out of prison after having served two complete years for theft, he lived a short distance from the station. His arrest and sentence was in those days the talk of the neighbourhood as he was a rogue and lived on crime which funded his previous lifestyle. Prior to his release the neighbours tied a yellow ribbon round the old oak tree, across the road, as made famous by the pop group Dawn. Neighbours in those days were less forgiving than today and everyone knew he had been dishonest. No matter what he had paid for his crime and later he moved out of the area. Perhaps the embarrassment was too much for him and his family. I just hope he learned from his mistake.

One of the happier times was an International Golfing Tournament held on an adjoining beat, where all the world famous golfers were playing together. This event lasted several days. I remember the Spanish golfer Severiano Ballesteros and Tony Jacklin being present, who were both famous international stars. The latter stopped driving one morning and pulled alongside me asking me for directions. He cracked a joke with me and smiled and was completely down to earth. I saw all the golf for nothing which was televised worldwide. What a privilege to enjoy whilst still getting paid for it. That was something the butchery trade did not provide.

Well I had been in the job for three and a half years and my wife gave birth to our third child at home. During the time the youngest had his leg in plaster with the eldest was down with flu and the wife suddenly going into labour there was no way of going to work. This was time for me to take annual leave with no exceptions.

Our young baby was 7lb and within 4 days was not putting on weight. The doctor believed it was gastroenteritis and advised sugar and water, my wife had different ideas and so we went to the Children's hospital in the city. So much for the doctor but he only acted in good faith, thank god for a mother's intuition which saved his life. My wife had come into contact with a woman who she found out was badly infected with German measles and it caused our baby to have serious life threatening illnesses and was at several times not expected to survive. The following day our doctor paid a visit and was talking to my wife where he apologised and stated it was always hard to detect illness in young babies. He stated there was nothing better than a mother's intuition.

A few years after retirement I was working the hospitals and I worked with a man who lived on this country beat where I was stationed. He was not in the best of health as he suffered with Cronin's disease, affecting the digestive system. Talking about his problem it became apparent his illness was detected around the time I was stationed in the village and we had the same doctor, as he clearly remembered his name. He stated for 18 months he went to see his doctor and he was losing weight and at various times extremely ill. All the time he was being palmed off with silly advice and needless prescriptions not sorting the problem. This colleague with his wife decided to go to the main hospital casualty department, where it was fully investigated and later the Cronin's disease was detected. As soon as the hospital advised the doctor of his patient's condition, the doctor paid a visit to see my colleague and his wife. Surprisingly again to apologise, stating it was his wife's intuition that possibly saved his life by referring him to the hospital. How coincidental, I wonder how many more times throughout his career this doctor had done this, he was clearly not a very thorough medical practitioner and basically extremely negligent. A small world but in those days what a frightening one. Sadly we still have problems today even with huge advances in medical science.

It was ironic only a few months earlier my sister had a 9 month baby also suffering from chronic gastroenteritis and took the baby to her family doctor. She lived a few miles away from us and her GP gave the same advice and advised sugar and water. My sister returned back to the surgery a couple of hours later to see the same doctor stating there was no change and she was worried and concerned about her baby's health. She explained she was continually throwing up and not keeping anything down and believed the baby was becoming dehydrated and were very worried. Even this did not work with him, it became apparent that this doctor was clearly a professional who back then 'Can't cut the mustard' as it did not raise any warning signs with him that more serious action was needed. To my sister and her husband's surprise, the attitude of the male doctor was abrupt, very rude and un-sympathetic in telling them not to waste his time he had given advice and follow it and stop pestering him. They both left the surgery but when they got home the baby had stopped breathing and returned immediately back to the surgery and to the same doctor. He kept out the way and had another doctor examine the baby who sadly certified death. All that was needed to save the babies life even in those days was the child to be fed intravenously with some kind of glucose or saline drip, just as simple as that. Back in those times no-one ever sued a medical professional it was unheard of, he did not even apologise how disgusting.

Life of course still had to go on I was still an operational policeman doing the job I enjoyed with all the pressures that brings against the background of our youngest child's ongoing health problems. As for my wife she was wonderful in that she looked after our other two demanding children, whilst visiting the main city hospital on a daily basis facing and confronting all of the problems associated with his illness. Our child remained in hospital for 12 months and thanks to the wonderful medical profession he made a complete recovery. Sadly our niece had to lose her life so tragically that we were able to benefit in addressing the illness of our own child.

CHAPTER 10

A DIFERRENT STYLE OF POLICING WITHIN A METROPOLITAN POLICE FORCE

Our young baby had been in hospital for nearly 3 months, and working discretional duties was proving difficult. Part of our force was amalgamating into a Metropolitan police area and had four large towns in one mainly built up divisional area, with pay and overtime a huge plus. So it was goodbye to four years of splendid comradeship with a well-established family police force, to areas that were again alien with completely different work practices.

I was back on shifts and the down side was the sub- division I was posted to, covered not only one but two town centres. This was obviously a cost cutting exercise as a result of government planning, but in my view disastrous for everyday policing. It was bad enough learning new areas but for two towns, as each day you were posted walking or driving at both sides of the police area. I suggested to the powers that be, working the same patch on a regular basis to build up knowledge, but this just fell on deaf ears. How naive. They just did not realise that it was just impossible to build up any rapport with the public or to easily identify known offenders or work out patterns of crime. Today the situation I imagine is even worse.

I continually raised all these issues which were then preventing positive police work but nothing materialised. I couldn't believe it, we had a large newly formed police area with new ideas, but just no interest from those in leadership to support those frustrated officers working on the front line. In my view they had just got it so wrong, but who was I to make such comments. It was to be several years before any realistic changes were made at that sub-division. This was the only time so far in my police service that I became disillusioned I was just a number, going from job to job, where I could not follow anything up, as the next day I would be 6 miles away working a different area. To me I just found it all so depressing, in reality I was just one of the troops with less than 5 year's service working on the front line. It did not stop me doing my job as I was always self-motivating and extremely keen, but given the opportunity or the correct environment I knew I would be able to do my job so much more professionally. The larger areas to cover and no regular pattern of policing I found so demoralising. If only they had implemented some practical changes to create a more positive approach to improve the areas mentioned would have been good for morale, but we were short staffed and this added to the problem.

In the initial few days we went out with other officers who had previously worked the area. I recall on one session of nights this one officer, although a likeable chap he would park up and get his head down for an hour or so. I thought why on earth join a job where you had no interest. The job was only as good as you made it and like in any career or workforce or team, surviving was all about interest and motivation. He later got promoted to the rank of sergeant, but it certainly was not based on merit or his impressive work rate. Absolute rubbish, good for skivers but not for me I had to move on. I found this utterly frustrating and had seriously thought of resigning. I did not wish to leave the job I loved but something had to happen, so I sought another move to a busier station at divisional headquarters in a town I grew up in.

As it turned out over a period of time I was to enjoy excellent satisfaction for several years patrolling in uniform and becoming a first class thief taker, making good friends, these were to become some of the best days of my police career. For once although I had to travel further to work I did not have to disrupt my family by moving home again I remained in the same police house.

For the first few months I patrolled the town centre, where there was always plenty of action with many incidents of crime all varying between robbery, burglary and theft to assault and public order. We had a multi-racial society and this crafted new ideas and methods in policing and a welcome change to previous experiences. In addition some areas of society were more violent with regular fights taking place where we all relied heavily on assistance from colleagues. Shoplifters and cases of begging and drunkenness were an everyday occurrence.

We had a regular drunk whom we initially took pity on and the Chief Inspector at the time always advised discretion before arrest. We were allowed in some cases to take him home or move him on if he did not create any scene. It's the old story if you give a person more rope they will hang themselves. This is precisely what happened, he began to believe he was above the law, the softly, softly approach was simply not working. He became a total nuisance despite any compassion as he was forever begging in the street when sober and when drunk was an utter embarrassment. He would always be at the central bus stop drunk swearing and falling over. He only had one leg and whenever this happened his artificial leg would become detached and roll down the street. This followed with him urinating in full view of members of the public.

To lose a limb for anyone must be traumatic, but so many carry on with their lives regardless and indeed are an inspiration. Just look at the young victims of cancer and other life threatening illnesses, plus serious accidents, where people from all walks of life lose limbs. This is especially true with regards to our troops who have sustained dreadful injuries and lost limbs and have artificial limbs fitted with some even returning to active service. How admirable. As for this drunken person who really had never achieved anything in his life and had no intention of wanting to improve or change his role in society, just became a burden to the taxpayer for the remainder of his pathetic life. Whenever he was arrested he would give his name. When you asked him where he lived the answer would always be, "Down by the cut, why don't you drop in sometime". Amusing for the spectators but it was wearing a bit thin for the boys in blue, so every occasion we met this behaviour he was taken off the streets.

I remember at the same location being a busy main bus station later in the summer. Walking the town on foot patrol I recall being sent to an incident involving a black man on a bus which was stationary in between destinations. Apparently it was normal practice for the bus to remain at this location with the engine running and this was the main problem. People who had already travelled to the town would normally alight if they wished or remain in their seats to travel on. Not this passenger. All of a sudden he could not stand the heat no more so he went berserk throwing property about and threatening the driver and conductor. It was quite surprising because he was well dressed in a very smart suit with shirt and tie and appeared to be out of character with his appearance. He was well over 6ft tall and well-built and looked the sort of person who was quite capable of handling himself.

Despite our presence and the offer to stand outside the bus he just would not listen or cooperate in any way. Whether or not the heat played some kind of problem or he suffered with claustrophobia was hard to judge and despite being sympathetic he would not calm down and his behaviour was aggravating the situation and causing a public nuisance. He was duly arrested for a public order offence. Assistance arrived and he was taken to the police station. It was established the man had a large amount of money in his possession, together with plane tickets, passport and hand luggage to catch a flight the following morning at Heathrow. The man was returning to Kingston in Jamaica to see his priest as he was not replying to his letters or returning his phone calls. He calmed down and apologised. His identity was checked and he was not wanted for any offence. As a result of a practical decision with our Inspector, because the man would not accept a formal caution, it was decided to report him for summons rather than keep him in custody. If he ever returned we could follow up any further action accordingly.

Problem solved, you might think. You do things based on common sense, but life is not always like that as the issue came right back to punch us in the face. The man eventually left the station and was no further trouble. Then later the following morning our Inspector had a call from Scotland Yard and had to answer some embarrassing questions. In those days it was not policy to report someone for summons where there was no prospect of dealing with him properly.

The man had made it to the airport and within four minutes after takeoff, again he could not stand the heat on the plane and started a disturbance putting other passengers at risk. So much so it was necessary to bring the plane down where he was again taken into custody. That's when all the questions were asked about why release a man who was about to leave the country where justice could not be seen to be done. I believe a few white lies were told over the property in his possession and the matter was forgotten. I think even if you had a crystal ball there was no way you could have anticipated this incident happening again especially on a plane.

Then there was the occasion I arrested a 74 years old lady for shoplifting from one of the town centre stores. She was well dressed for her age and reasonably smart and although pleasant she seemed shy and embarrassed for being in such a predicament. However she admitted responsibility and could not stop apologising for her actions. As with normal practice I would take the female prisoner to the sergeant relate the facts in everyone's presence. When the formalities were over and all signatures made, to cover myself I would always relate to the sergeant whoever it was, I was leaving the prisoner in their care whilst I went to the main reporting room to complete my pocket book entry, as soon as possible whilst the full facts were clear in my mind.

On this occasion it was no exception. I completed my entry and returned to the custody block to interview the prisoner. The sergeant was at the desk round the corner and I could not see the prisoner in the charge room so entered the cell passage. Apparently this lady had been left alone unsupervised for only a short time and when I walked down the cell passage round the corner I saw that she was trying to hang herself with the cord from the metal window. She had managed to stand on a chair and having climbed onto the radiator just below to give her some height. Another moment and it would have been all over, as she just dropped down in front of me daggling with the cord round her neck. I immediately shouted out at the top of my voice calling the sergeant whilst I stood holding her and as she was well built and fairly heavy I supporting her weight the best I could preventing her from harming herself, but it was touch or go she could easily have succeeded in killing herself. Assistance came and the sergeant and other staff rushed in. The woman was released away from further harm and a doctor called. She finally received a caution and was released into the care of a relative. What an experience, I think I was suffering from shock myself but saving her from harm bought me back to reality. In any case just having to deal with the consequences if she had been successful would have been even more unbearable.

You can smile and joke about it later, but you would not need this kind of incident to have to happen very often, still we are all human and anyone can make a mistake. I am sure we all learned from that experience. And joke about I did. I will never forget about a week later I was in the station and saw the sergeant alone when I said to him," Have you seen Mrs. Smith hanging around lately Sarge." This name of Mrs Smith is a false name in order to protect the ladies identity. With a broken smile he muttered "You bastard" but still appreciated how bad things could have turned out. I never judged him but you could never forgot such an experience as that happening.

In fact some twenty years later I met the same sergeant who was then Inspector, I am sure well deserved as he was a pleasant and likeable man. It was at an award ceremony for long service and good conduct recognition and I recall saying "Do you still see Mrs Smith hanging around Inspector" He retorted "You don't forget a bloody thing do you" We just burst out laughing and we have remained good friends ever since.

As time went on I alternated foot patrol with unit beat policing and drove a marked police panda car. It was mid- week and early evening when I was sent to local public house some two miles from the main town centre, in a busy built up area. The lady, wife of the licensee served three young men in their late teens, who had called in the bar for a drink soon after opening. They appeared to be behaving themselves and she left them alone to have their drinks. They stayed some twenty minutes and left. It was not until an hour later that her husband went under the counter to get some change that he discovered a bank bag containing £500 was missing, which basically amounted to the whole weekend takings. Back in those days the average weekly wage was about £20, so it was a huge amount to lose. The matter was subsequently reported to the police as an alleged theft. I obtained all details and noted the descriptions of the young men. It may have been they were involved or just innocent victims either way they needed eliminating from the enquiry as soon as possible. It was difficult as they were not known to the licensee or his wife or any other customers.

As the evening continued I was sent to various other jobs and during my travels I was constantly looking for the three men from the descriptions given. I was sent to a burglar alarm and whilst on route there they were in the distance walking along the pavement some 100 yards in front of me. I informed control I had become committed to the annoyance of the radio operator as he then had to find someone else to continue my last job.

These were the times when you always saw the unusual whilst going from one job to another, an experience I could not emphasize enough and when this was highlighted by me in briefings it just fell against unjustifiable criticism, with some stating if your sent to a job you must stick with that and not diverse. I used to think What are we robots? If you were on route to a life or death situation, yes I would agree, other than that nonsense, as instincts of criminal behaviour became part of a thief takers pedigree. I stopped the vehicle and they were cooperative. Whilst talking asking where they had been, I saw the one young man throw something into the hedgerow which he thought I had missed. I asked them to take a seat in the rear of the police vehicle and called for assistance. I asked them to empty their pockets and recovered several hundreds of pounds between them.

Upon arrival of other officers in the presence of all three men I retrieved an empty blue cash bag from the hedgerow. All the evidence was seized and they were all arrested and taken into custody. Under caution they verbally admitted being responsible for the sneaky theft of monies from the public house by leaning over the counter, when staff were not looking. It was near to the end of my shift and unknown to me the station sergeant had already contacted the C.I.D who covered that area, as coincidently they were in the main police station at that time.

I was told by the senior detective sergeant who was with his constable colleague, "Okay we will take it from here ". No suggestion we will give you a hand if you want it, they just grabbed the prisoners and I later discovered why, they had an ulterior motive free drinking at the pub where the theft took place on the basis of their brilliant detective work. I discovered through sources they had taken the glory for my actions purporting they had cleared the matter up.

Feeling pretty miffed by the whole affair I vowed there and then if ever I went into CID I would never behave towards any colleague like that, especially claiming glory for hard dedicated work that they had not done. It would be the opposite as you will read further on in this book. However fortunately at that time there are many detective officers who were a credit to the service, with whom I had the greatest respect. Officers, who would put these two undeserving clowns when it comes to real police work, to complete shame.

A few weeks later, I was not quite so lucky when on patrol in the early hours I stopped a motor vehicle in one of the streets close to the town centre. It contained five middle aged men who from my instincts had all the ingredients of being an active criminal gang. I remained positive but let them think I was a naive kind of policeman and on that basis they all provided me with full details of their identity. We now had access to the police national computer, known more commonly as the PNC, which had not long been launched and was a tremendous success in the vital fight against crime. Immediate identity of stolen and all owner vehicles, missing and wanted persons and of course criminal convictions.

I checked them against the police national computer and I recognised some of the names which had been branded around the station, as being professional villains. Collectively between them all they had accumulated a total of some 40 years imprisonment over their joint criminal career, but discovered none of them were wanted. To say they were cooperative was an understatement, something did not ring true and I just knew they were up to no good but had no evidence of any offence being committed. They allowed me to search thoroughly the complete inside of the car and the boot and with the vehicle not coming back with any other notifications I had no choice but to be polite and thank them for their assistance, so having secured all their details they were allowed to continue their journey. They must have been smirking behind their faces because whatever they may or not have done it was with the full believe they had gotten away with it. When I returned to duty the following night, I received a compliment from the detective Inspector based on my actions and recording full details of my stop and search which included descriptions of all clothing worn. The five men in question were subsequently arrested later that day. They were taken into custody on suspicion of a jewellery shop smash and grab in one of the other towns on the division. The address where they were all staying was the place of arrest and the location where all the stolen jewellery was found. They all had been charged and I could not work out how during the search of the vehicle I had not discovered the stolen property. I was told they had hidden all the jewellery which had been wrapped in newspaper inside each of the four wheel trims, when stopping at an isolated spot away from the attacked premises. We never stop learning but perhaps it was a blessing I did not find the property at that time. I was alone with all of them, as with their pedigree I would have most certainly been the victim of a good hiding. The main thing was the crime was detected as a result of stopping the vehicle and placing them all together which was recorded back at the station before I went off duty.

This was one of the cases Dc Glover was involved with and whatever you thought of him character wise, this was certainly good work by him and his colleagues on this occasion, proving completely cooperation between uniform and CID was an essential ingredient towards the fight against crime. It was so sad later in his service Dc Glover refused to adapt to the many changes within the police force. From being a detective with many obvious qualities his downfall over the years was due to him becoming so very bitter and twisted for which there was no justifiable reason. Over the years you always took the view to catch a criminal you clearly learned to think like a criminal. However as you will read later on this subject this ideology changed to a more forward way of thinking.

Another occasion was a Sunday morning at about 11.00am, a very quiet kind of a day, we as a shift had all been called in for a brief meeting and a cuppa. This would normally have been frowned upon with so many officers on duty all in the station together and with no one out on patrol. I am afraid this appears to be the norm today with so many officers tied up with paperwork, but from when I joined up until the 1980's, we would just go onto the tape recorder fitted into the telephone system within the station and dial a tape. We would then dictate all our reports for typing, whereas up until the day I left and I believe to present day, all paperwork in the main is written out in long hand. Can you imagine businesses running in this way obviously the powers that be thought a policeman's time engaged writing reports is cheaper than other dictated methods of paperwork. Some would argue at that time that the file which had to be completely typed may not lead to prosecution and therefore a waste of time, but experience always taught you that if you had sufficient evidence and the circumstances warranted it, that it would go to court.

So there we were all the shift members together in the police station, but what a benefit that turned out to be. Within a short while of being there, before we had time to finish a drink, a call came in involving a serious incident having taken place within half a mile of the station. An enormous fight was taking place between rival gangs of Asian men of all ages, so we all made our way immediately to the given location. I am proud to say within ten minutes eighteen men were in custody some covered in blood and all kinds of weapons and knives recovered. In addition ten other men had been taken to hospital with serious injuries. CID became involved and jointly we all helped out. All were charged with affray and serious offences of wounding and grievous bodily harm.

If we had not have been altogether at that particular time, I am sure some of the main offenders would have driven off or may have left the scene altogether. Sometimes these things happen for a reason and this gave the perfect excuse for calling into the station for a hot drink on occasions when time allowed the facility.

My first Christmas working with this shift will always remain memorable for the wrong reasons. It was regular practice to call round the hospitals as in those days they did not have security like there is today. In the early hours of Christmas morning the shift would take their break in relays to ensure adequate cover and we had all paid to have a Christmas meal at a local hospital canteen. I was due to have my break at 1.00am, and about 45 minutes earlier I was out on mobile patrol. It was snowing very heavily. As I drove along one of the main roads being a dual carriageway, I saw the figure of what appeared to be a body with a small covering of snow lying on the central reservation. Another 30 minutes it would have been missed because of the snow and some of my colleagues later wished that had been the case.

I pulled the vehicle to a halt close by and saw that the body was lying face down which I turned to its side and saw that it was a man. When I checked, he had a pulse, but then I immediately established that he was heavily drunk and stunk completely of booze. He was small in build of average height. I searched him and found no identity so I had no choice but to take him into custody for his own safety. It was easy to get him into the back of the police car as he was a bit like a rubber doll. At the station they were aware of my arrival and with help the man was taken directly to the cells and place in a recovery position on the cell floor. He received constant visits from thereon.

As the time of our meal was fast approaching, I collected the Inspector and two other members of the shift and drove to the hospital. We were walking along the corridor and to my horror I saw that the two officers who had been seated in the rear of the vehicle were covered with human excrement all over the back of their clothing having sat where the drunken prisoner had been placed. What a present for Christmas I hadn't got the heart to tell them, but I could not let them enter any further into the hospital without explaining to them what had taken place. They were not exactly pleased and in fairness neither would I have been, they just had to leave. You can image how popular I was as their meal was temporary cancelled whilst they changed into other clothing. The vehicle was taken off the road and had to be fumigated. Later we could all see the funny side of things and it soon was the talk of the station.

We went off duty and when returning at 10.00pm Christmas night the same prisoner was still drunk and unable to stand, even after nearly 24 hours. When sober he was made to clean up his mess, his identity obtained and released after being charged with being drunk and incapable. Lucky for him he was found as he quite easily could have perished under the frozen snow so undoubtedly he had clearly used up one of his extra lives. I don't think I ever saw a man so intoxicated in my whole life and I have seen a few.

Christmas must have been a jinx as far as I was concerned as a few years later I was working the Christmas day shift as the cells were full with prisoners mainly there due to prison disputes. The Home office supplied frozen Christmas meals. I put them all in the ovens as the instructions, but someone distracted me and when I served the food I realised the food was all dried up and not at its best when I handed it to each of the prisoners. Worse still there were no replacements, so I conveniently left as soon as the opportunity arose. I did not like playing the role of a coward as it was not within my nature, so I never knew whether they were eaten or not. Can you imagine this happening today? They would have sued us under their Human rights and got free legal aid for consulting a solicitor with compensation into the bargain. How times have changed.

It was whilst working on this same shift that I first met Monty and together we dealt with several incidents together which involved the whole team. I recall Monty worked an adjoining police panda area and one mid-week evening during the hours of darkness when he was involved in the investigation involving theft of numerous charity boxes. These had been stolen by sneak in thieves at various licensed premises within the town centre area. Apart from being an utterly despicable and selfish crime, the identity of the offenders was even more horrific as it involved members of an entire family. Apart from the mother and father being responsible, they had taken along their three teenage children who were indoctrinated as willing accomplices.

It was established that they had been going round the town visiting different public houses and other establishments under the control of their mother and father, where each young person took it in turn to enter and sneak out with charity containers from open display which they gave to their parents. Altogether several tins were stolen with all offenders making good their escape. As a result of enquiries made by Monty the offenders were suspected to be from the same family and were traced to their home address. Upon visiting this location he made a forcible entry where he caught them all red handed, counting and sharing out all the contents between them, which were tipped across the lounge floor.

They were all arrested and with assistance taken to the police station, together with the recovered stolen property. Every member of this family were subsequently convicted of theft and dealt with accordingly by the criminal justice system. The parents really should have hanged their heads in shame and care proceedings should have been implemented with regards to their children. However, in that respect I believe any action would have come too late as it was already a troublesome family, with two of the older boys already carving out criminal careers. Over the years they were arrested several times by various officers, until eventually one of the brothers was fatally stabbed during his involvement in crime which I later had dealings with, which is referred to in full detail in another of my stories.

During my time working this busy market town industry was thriving and employment was high. Weekend shopping attracted huge shopping crowds, this was well before the arrival of out of town supermarkets and retail shopping malls and of course the internet was still just an idea in some inventor's head. One disturbing trend would involve groups of teenagers totalling a minimum of a hundred who collectively created havoc in running in mass altogether through shopping precincts and other areas. They would have no regards for anyone especially the very young, elderly and disabled people, who bore the brunt of such action and always came off the worse. As they stampeded their way through the crowds, people would be deliberately knocked over and pushed with some having items snatched and thrown away creating a very frightening public order experience for the innocent shoppers.

Something had to be done as it was the second time this kind of occurrence had taken place, with no particular pattern established as it did not follow on from week to week. All we could do was be prepared in the event it cracked off again and take positive action. Finally one weekend shortly after it all materialised unknown to the trouble makers some officers were in plain clothes and different areas cordoned off. In addition we also had a large contingent of uniform officers behind the scenes. We monitored the activities of these youngsters, who again were congregating into groups when they all joined together and ran through the crowds on mass causing their normal chaos in upsetting shoppers in pushing and knocking people over. Fortunately no-one was seriously hurt although many were shaken up. As this group filtered into the distance they made their way to end of the precinct where we were able to suddenly show our presence and surround them and prevent any further trouble. In relays groups of these individuals were arrested and transported to the police station having been arrested for public order offences. Majority were aged from 15 to 18 years respectively and naturally we had the task of informing all the parents to attend, as well over a hundred offenders had been apprehended and were in custody. The main objective of this exercise was to stop any similar behaviour occurring in the future.

All were charged with public order offences which upon conviction carried a fine, with an alternative offence of committing a breach of the peace. This is not a conviction in itself but where a person can be taken before the magistrates and be bound over to keep the peace for a period of 12 months. All were processed and summoned to appear with their parents before the local Juvenile court. With so many offenders we had to have two separate days to deal with them all at court. I recall spending two whole days personally issuing summons to all the parents of the offenders visiting each and every one of them at their home addresses, which were scattered all over our division and neighbouring police areas. That believe it or not was hard work in itself to ensure all were formally notified to attend prior to the date of the hearing. No one escaped court action and for those that pleaded not guilty, rather accept a bind over were convicted of a public order offence. Some might say because of ill advice received, involving some parents who thought their kids had done no wrong. No matter what, it was a positive way of preventing future problems and dealing immediately with the issues as in those days that sort of behaviour would not be tolerated under any circumstances. In present day lots of shopping malls are patrolled extremely efficiently by independent security staff without the same resources, but at least they can remove such trouble makers from the premises banning future entry.

On a lighter and more entertaining note, nothing ever compensated the fantastic occasions that the Grenadier Guards in their official dress uniforms complete with bear sklns, and Royal Air Force and other military bands kindly visited our market town. On those days in soring summer heat I was able to witness firsthand whilst on duty in full uniform the presence of such a rare sight of marching bands playing nostalgic music, marching directly into the delight of large crowds, before doing an about turn to march in an opposite direction. These amazing displays lasted for a good 30 minutes with two different intervals taking place. We had several well-known regimental bands scheduled to appear in the town all in that same summer. It was just everything that was so good about being British. I was just disappointed I had no video memories of these special treats, or indeed the council as we did not freely have that kind of technology, but these were some experiences that I will never forget.

I remember another time I had been on duty and after 8 hours of walking the cold streets in freezing weather conditions, I was so pleased the night shift had come to an end. It was a non-eventful night, even the burglars and thieves had taken a night off. Of course the hours just dragged on and on, but on a different patch the vandals had been working overtime. The ice was cleared from my vehicle and by the time I had started to thaw out, I had arrived at home. All I was thinking about was sleep and more sleep, whilst it was still dark. If I did not get off to sleep whilst it was still dark it would never happen and I would be awake all day until it was time to return to work for the next night shift.

Upon opening the front door I was in for the biggest shock anyone could anticipate. I had discovered the vandals and they were in my house. I switched the light on and all I could see throughout the hall, kitchen and lounge were two sets of footprints and hand prints in the form of a reddish orange colour of emulsion paint all over the carpets, doors and walls. We had been in the police house for about a year and I had fitted carpets throughout, but major decorating was a priority. As I started to walk upstairs the mess was consistent if not worse. I went into the small bedroom and there they were, our two boys, one aged 2 years the other a year older. They had managed to tip over a five litre can of emulsion paint and as I looked at them, both said, spontaneously, "It's not me daddy." Normally I would give them the benefit of the doubt, but the evidence was overwhelming. The paint was all over their pajamas, hands, feet and faces and they were standing in the centre of a large pool of paint which was all over the carpet, with both of them each jumping up and down.

My wife and other baby son were both fast asleep unaware of this horrendous mess and impending predicament. I quietly broke the news to my wife. With a change of clothes, sleeves rolled up I had the task of scrubbing and wiping the mess up from all affected places. At the same time both offenders were promptly thrown by their mother into a warm bath and washed of their sins. Within a couple of hours order was restored, although one carpet was completely ruined. I finally went to bed even though it was daylight by then and guess what against nature, I dropped off to sleep. I can assure you there was no repeat performance of this again, one of life's memories that still make us laugh that even with time never fades.

CHAPTER 11

VARIOUS CHARACTERS INVOLVING UNUSUAL EXPERIENCES

Walking the beat you come across many characters. Such as this one man who used to walk around the town going into different butchers shops. I remembered him back when I was in the trade at one such shop and he used to call in regularly most days and ask if we had any chawl. This was a cooked meat popular back in those days. If we had sold out he would ask for the scrapings off the cooked meat machine which we would give him free. It consisted solely of fat, completely 100% free from any lean meat. He knew that but would lick the contents off the greaseproof paper until it was all gone. Not for the faint hearted as it just made you feel completely sick still that's just how he lived. Sometimes feeling sorry for him I would occasionally give him the odd small pork pie.

This particular man now was in his sixties and as I patrolled the streets during my career in the police, I often saw him around the town and would speak to him. I am sure he did not recognise me from my earlier days and I noticed he was always keeping guard at car parks protecting owner's cars from possible theft or damage. This would either be at the rear of different bingo establishments or cinemas and for a charge of 50p for every car he had a reputation for being honest and dedicated to his work. He certainly weathered all storms and whether or not it was freezing windy, raining or boiling hot he was always there. I believe this man had done this type of thing for most of his life and he gave the impression he had lived rough. There were never any incidents when he was around he gave complete cover throughout his period of security. The local people just loved him, as this was some crime prevention which was pretty much guaranteed. A few years later when I had moved on I read in the local paper he had passed away and had left £200.000 to charity. What a decent and honest, but very bizarre person he was.

I stated when I first got Monty transferred as a resident beat officer to the area adjacent to my beat, he had to get permission from high rank in order for him to move. Whilst working with him I recall the story he told me that when on traffic duties at various times they had to have officers who were close to completing their probation, for an attachment period of two weeks to give a different outlook to their experiences of everyday policing. On this one occasion he was covering a very busy division of the force area well away from where I was stationed. Working with him for such period was a young polite black officer who was friendly, super fit, and intelligent. To his credit was as keen as mustard, who had performed well during his earlier service. His probation was soon drawing to an end where undoubtedly he was soon to become a fully-fledged police officer confirmed in his appointment.

Both officers had been out most of the shift on patrol duties and decided to call into the main town central police station for their break. With force radio installed in the vehicle both were in possession of independent radios which they took with them so they could monitor ongoing police activities taking place. During their break they were listening to an ongoing car chase some twenty odd miles away and the younger officer kept edging Monty to interrupt their break and join in. He explained that at the current location the stolen vehicle could end up in any area and that it was futile at that point to intervene.

Nevertheless this officer was persistent in his thirst for action but the vehicle was still too far away for any realistic involvement. As they left the police station returning to the traffic patrol car the stolen vehicle which was engaged in the car chase had escaped from the path of pursuing police vehicles and its location at that time was unknown, as it could have travelled in virtually any direction. Within a relatively short period of time Monty and this officer pulled out to travel along the town's ring road system, when his younger colleague pointed out they were directly behind the offending stolen vehicle. They immediately began pursuit of this vehicle activating sirens and flashing lights where Monty followed the vehicle a short distance being able to overtake and block it to the side of the road and prevent it travelling any further. Two men quickly alighted the stolen car in moments and were seen running away in the opposite direction. They were quickly chased by the young officer who had tackled the one car thief and bought him to the ground. As Monty joined him, the other offender was well away and not to be seen. The man detained was arrested and later taken to the police station and dealt with for various offences.

It just seemed surreal, who could have predicted such a turn of events, to be at one moment twenty odd miles away from the incident to have it descend immediately on your doorstep and directly in front of you just goes to prove nothing is impossible in police work. As Monty stated the young officer proved his tenacity and industrious approach to operational police work who with luck would go far in his career, such a refreshing sight to see.

Having been at this Station for a couple of years, one of my neighbours near the police houses where I lived transferred and ended up working on our shift. He was a pleasant chap but I felt too laid back for a busy industrious police area. Despite this he got on well with all our colleagues. We used to share travelling alternating each week. On the late shift we had to parade at 1.45pm prompt. When I called at 1.30pm his wife would say he was just sitting down for dinner, this became irritating because it always meant we would be late for work totally against my principals. For two days running this happened and the Inspector warned we would be disciplined if it happened again. I had to lay the law down and tell him to leave for work earlier.

The day after this, I called round, and could not believe it. Despite still being late, his wife had given him dinner. My vehicle was at the garage and we were again late starting out. We travelled to work and when we reached the outskirts of the town I told him to stop. I rushed out and grabbed this juvenile who I knew was on the run. He was wanted for burglaries and failing to appear at court. I arrested him and placed him In the back of our vehicle taking him direct to the custody block upon arrival at the station. As we both walked along the corridor all officers were walking out of the parade Room, followed by the Inspector. He clearly was showing his authority and demanded we go into his office. He was very annoyed we were again late and about to take disciplinary action. However when I explained the genuine reason for being late and the facts of the arrest he took a different view. Thank God that saved our bacon. Stuff having lifts in cars from colleagues, I made my own way to work after that.

We were experiencing a large amount of thefts from vehicles in one area of the town and it was decided each officer perform two shifts working plain clothes during the dark evenings and nights. The colleague I used to travel to work with was first to undertake these duties, but was unsuccessful. The next shift it was my turn. Whether or not I had a lucky streak I do not know, but there in the early hours of the morning I saw two men park up and walk over to a line of unattended vehicles. I was then in possession of a new ratchet style of handcuffs which had been restored to general police use in replacement of an older unsuitable version. As they both forced open a car and got inside I pounced, cuffing one straight away to the steering wheel and took hold of the other. Both were in their late teens and did not struggle. I identified myself and made the arrest calling for assistance. As for my neighbour colleague it was plain to see that he was pig sick with jealousy, why I can't imagine, but he was out for promotion having recently passed his exams. The prisoner's home addresses were searched and in excess of 200 car accessories were recovered. Both families were respectable having never come to our notice. The offenders were sneaking out without knowledge of their parents and hiding the property in garages and sheds. With assistance of CID we interviewed both prisoners the following day. Majority of the goods could not be identified even though serial numbers of radios had been checked through our system so only a quarter of the items were restored to their lawful owners. This was despite a press release in local papers inviting members of the public to visit the station if they had been victims of this kind of offence. In addition enquiries were made with various manufacturers against some with serial numbers but to identify any owners was a task too difficult for them to perform as it was too time consuming and still could not guarantee any result. Whereas today with computer technology it would have been a simple task with loads of victims if reported being listed at once. Charges were formulated with over 150 offences asked to be taken into consideration by the court.

I was not amused when the Juvenile Magistrate made damning criticism, over the preparation of the evidence presented, relating to the non-identification of the property as over half of the items of property could only be associated as belonging to persons unknown. We had tried our best in my view to the highest standard, that's all you can expect of anyone. If people fail to report such crimes involving theft from vehicles then it is harder to trace such owners when stolen property is recovered. Needless to say the offenders were treated with kid gloves and received only minor sentences, pity they did not get a stricter bench of Magistrates given the offender's involvement in all these crimes.

In those times we had industrial action by bakers and on top of that due to a very hot summer causing a drought through most of the country we ended up with a potato shortage. The true nature of some people certainly comes to the surface when food shortages occur, some with very amusing consequences. With most of the bakers out on strike the only means of getting a loaf of bread was at shops where it was actually baked on the premises. In present day all supermarkets of any standing all bake their own bread each day on their business premises thus stopping any future industrial action as back then by bakery Staff. When I say queues you would have thought the Beatles were in town, but this was for purchasing a loaf of bread. They were as far as the eye could see. There was one problem public enemy number one, the old age pensioner. As part of our duties we had to be sent to the location of these small bakeries to quell disturbances caused mainly by the pensioners who were constantly arguing and shuffling other people in the queues. You would have thought they would have known better at their age, no arrests were necessary, just strong warnings given. Fortunately there were some other people in the same age group who were a credit to themselves and well behaved, but it did not excuse the others who behaved badly and extremely immaturely.

However with the potato shortage there were a series of offences involving men who were conning gullible trades people in the green grocery profession. We had various offences committed in different parts of the force area. Basically a trader would be telephoned by these offenders purporting they had available imported stocks of potato, albeit the price was high but a possible solution to their problems and still a bargain where shortage demanded higher retail pricing. Delivery was to be made at an appointed place and time due to demand. The arrangement would normally take place at a venue either at a public house or licensed restaurant when the sales person of the team would invite the prospective buyer to attend. In this one case that was reported you could not make it up. The buyer met the seller at the venue being a public house providing meals. They were unsure the time of arrival so they commenced a meal, during which the driver of the goods would arrive. He would state to the buyer you sit there enjoy your meal, he gave the man the keys to his wagon to have a load of potatoes transferred onto his vehicle. Later the man returned with his keys and stated all done and the buyer handed over £500 in cash, a large amount of money back then for the long awaited goods.

Shortly after the man entertaining finished his meal and drink making excuses he had his next call to make as he was busy. He told the buyer to remain there and finish his meal which he did, leaving his bogus contact number for further orders in the future and left the scene. Surprise, surprise when the buyer finally went out to his motor vehicle there it was completely empty with not even a potato present. They just did not exist in the first place. You have to say sucker because this kind of crime was preventable and greed is always the main ingredient for victims of deception. If that was not enough with all the humiliation caused, the trader even had to foot the bill for the restaurant, what an expensive meal that had turned out to be. A mistake he would not make again. The golden rule is in life when something is too good to be true, there is always a catch. A bargain not to be missed, something so tempting it is hard to refuse a once in a lifetime opportunity, these are some examples which should be warning signals to all that there may be a con trick or some kind of deception. It is that moment when we could all be tempted, when in fact we should really be firm and refuse to get involved. Unfortunately this practice still goes on today with deception committed involving people from all walks of life. If unsure or having doubts it is for a reason best to avoid at all costs as you will not regret it.

We had a well-known barmaid who had worked in most of the town's public houses. This one night she chose to shack up with a chap she had met and stay over in a room at one of the main hotels in town. Needless to say he left before her and she was caught sneaking out where the bill had not been paid. She was arrested for bilking as she had done it previously, along with her boyfriend who was later traced.

No police woman was available at that time so she was not photographed or fingerprinted. She agreed to call back the following day to assist in this respect. She kept her word and arrived shortly before midday the following morning. She was dressed in a full length fur coat and stated she was on her way to work in the city. As the police woman took her fingerprints I completed other paperwork. She said, "You haven't seen my work outfit". She then opened her coat completely revealing tousles to her breasts and scantily clad knickers, stating she was a stripper at the City Man Club. With her peroxide blonde hair pillar-box red lipstick and thick heavy makeup she really looked the part and should have come with a danger warning 'Avoid at all costs'. Thank God the police woman was present. Despite all this she was friendly and bubbly just another character you met in the line of duty.

Whilst working in uniform at this same police station we had a good liaison with all detective officers within the CID, especially whilst I was working in the Coroners department. I recall there was a mature officer who came from another station working a 6 months attachment in CID who had a reputation as a good thief taker, but clearly had an extremely bad drink problem. In fact I do not think there was a time of day that he hadn't had a tipple of one kind or another. He always concealed it well but his giveaway was being always red faced with high blood pressure. He always seemed to carry out his duties satisfactorily and you could not ever state that he was not a likeable character.

During his attachment it was close to Christmas and with him having a certain connection with a local butcher, he started taking orders for Christmas poultry and legs of pork which were competitively priced and attracted a huge response from officers and civilian staff alike. I believe he told me he had well over one hundred orders altogether. A couple of days before he was off duty, but attended the station to deliver some of the orders which was fine and those in receipt were indeed very happy with their purchase.

However on Christmas Eve he drove with the remaining part of his orders which were all packed into his vehicle and left on the car park. Well over sixty staff were waiting to collect their orders. What happened next was nothing short of a disaster. As stated this chap was off duty went on the town and met a load of buddies and went on the pop. He had so much to drink he became paralytic and later collapsed. With him being in such a bad state it was believed he had suffered some kind of suspected heart attack. An ambulance had been called for and later he was taken to hospital. The keys went missing to his vehicle and panic set in with all the customers at the station arriving to collect their Christmas goodies. I think I would have smashed the one window or have gotten into his vehicle somehow, even if had to receive expert advice from one of our expert criminal present in the cells, but it was not that clear. No one knew his vehicle or even where he had left it.

Fortunately being a former butcher I had made my own arrangements, but I know many of his customers were without their Christmas fair and had to purchase replacements from butchers in the town, having already paid out for items of meat and poultry which could not be found. Either way his name was mud and I am sure he was the source of at least one or two family domestics. Some of the other staff un-affected were more than highly amused at the whole scenario. Those that were not able to replenish their order did get their poultry and meat eventually, as he had sobered up Christmas morning and was discharged from hospital. Friends and relatives of this disgraced officer found the keys to his vehicle tracing back the man's footsteps for the previous few hours, eventually finding his vehicle still intact. Not the best Father Christmas in the world and his reputation was in tatters, needless to say he never made it into CID. A few years later he faced discipline for drinking on duty and resigned.

We had a shooting incident resulting in murder committed near the outskirts of town, this was linked with a series of murders throughout various locations of the country involving several police forces and a highly profiled offender who was later caught and was serving life, up until his recent death in prison. This was of national interest and it was decided to have a press conference at the time. I was appointed together with another uniform constable to stand at the entrance to the building where it was being held. It was being televised so I telephoned my wife and there I was in the background for nearly all the News at Ten program, of course being on my best behaviour.

What I did not realise at the time of this enquiry was the lack of communication between the various police forces, which basically stemmed from old style policing methods involving some of the older senior detective officers. Each police force wanted the credibility for catching and convicting such a ruthless murderer and so were extremely reluctant to show all their cards, for fear of giving away too may clues. In keeping evidence to themselves, hoping they would be the successful apprehenders, but how naive that was when such a dangerous criminal was at large. At the end of the day no one can argue how the individual officers had many talents and skills, but sadly found it hard to share the intelligence gained. Eventually information was exchanged but this could have taken place much earlier in the enquiry.

All criminals, especially the serious offenders have no boundaries committing crime. All these individual police forces should have thought on a similar basis where pooling information is a priority, which they eventually did, a massive change from the past. It does not matter which police force catches the terrorist or serial killer, as long as he is caught and bought to justice as quickly as possible. This national case had enormous influence and changed completely bad practices of not sharing information, resulting in new policies on inter-force relations and openness with all major criminal investigations. These days communication between police forces has never been better. With integration with Europe good policing skills and cooperation are an absolute must.

Back on patrol I will never forget being sent to the home of an astute elderly woman who lived alone. Her daughter was present and I could see from the attitude of both ladies they were of high standing and good character. The daughter was concerned that her mother had about £2000 missing from her savings and although about the same amount was still in place, she advised her that it must go into the bank. She admitted her mother had not looked at the money for several weeks, which was kept inside a cake tin under the bed.

The only person having access to her home during this period was a neighbour down the street who was described as polite 50 year old woman. She used to go in and clean for her, but had to cease helping when her health allegedly deteriorated and she had returned a key which she had been given. No one else had been to the home during this period, but they just could not believe she was in any way responsible. I took full details and paid a visit to the neighbours address. Keeping an open mind I thought I would just have fact gathering enquiry. As the door was answered I was invited into the home and went into the kitchen, it was late afternoon and the lady was cooking the evening meal in readiness for her husband. Looking at the lady she was fairly presentable and could have been on face value, anyone's Mother. She was very polite and offered me a drink, but I am sure she knew the reason for my visit.

As I went into conversation and she confirmed her previous role at the old ladies home, instinct told me she was hiding something. It was not a nice thing to do, but instincts told me I had no choice. I told her she would have to switch off the cooker and leave a note for her husband and that she would have to attend the police station. She was later arrested on suspicion of theft. It certainly was not a pleasant experience for the old lady either, who foolishly kept such a large amount of money inside her home. Eventually the lady confessed to the theft. She stated she had made an additional duplicate key before returning the original back to the family and that when the old lady was out, she would go inside and help herself. The temptation of seeing so much money was too great to resist. Half of the money was recovered and she was charged. She received a Probation Order, but the shame of being caught was her real punishment and breaching the position of trust that had been placed upon her.

Later in my service we had a similar case were the offender entered a former lodging address using a duplicate key, which like the above case really is burglary. On this occasion the offender was a man and the lady of the house suddenly returned without warning and disturbed him rifling through her private possessions. Upon recognising him as being a previous tenant the callous fiend brutally murdered her in cold blood and left without a penny. This story is told more fully in a later chapter and goes to show how a simple theft or burglary can turn into something more grotesque and sinister.

CHAPTER 12

THE BEST DAYS OF MY UNIFORM POLICING BACK ON THE BEAT

Having become well established working in my home town now in a metropolitan police area I began to look for new challenges. I had served four years in a rural force and moving to an area where I grew up I found my credibility as an experienced police officer with various friends and acquaintances well received. Those who were not so friendly looked at me from a different perspective. With majority of supervision at that time from a background of practical policing combined with excellent management skills, I was offered again in my career the role of working my own resident beat, under the direct supervision a well- established police Superintendent.

My beat this time was completely urban being a large busy town centre, combined with a residential area. I suppose you could say it was multi-cultural, although that wording was not used at that time. It had a large percentage of all ethnic groups, white English, Asian, Jamaican and Chinese and many others. One very noticeable issue was that many people integrated far more than today and at least tried to speak the English language, some fluently. Good and bad people from all races. During that time it was an area buzzing with crime.

I had the privilege of alternating from plain clothes and back into uniform whenever the situation demanded. The shifts worked by other uniformed officers, were to not trouble me with normal basic town centre issues which would derive me from my objectives, priority being catching criminals. In fairness I always kept the fine balance and helped out where I could, but was able in most cases to choose my jobs. It gave me a sense of independence where I could target some of the main issues occurring on my beat. I was chosen to replace my predecessor, who initially was well respected officer but had become a bigoted uncouth, lazy policeman with some service who to his superiors had hung his boots up. Although to himself he was a legend in his own mind. This officer did not take too kindly to this enforced action against him, so although I had done nothing personally to orchestrate this action, I had to watch my back and keep my enemies close. So there you are in a job where teamwork is of the essence, having enough enemies in the criminal fraternity was bad enough but in reality you had them in the job as well. I had to deal with extreme jealousy for most of the remainder of my career, but I knew exactly who my enemies were. I just continued doing my job keeping them at arm's length, the conduct of some materialise in the coming chapters.

One absolute must was to have a working colleague on the same level as myself. I pointed out this important issue to the Superintendent and asked for Pc Monty Thrower to be allowed to work on the adjoining beat. A vacancy became available as a beat officer in an area adjacent to mine, as the previous officer had been moved to another job. Monty's boss was initially reluctant but finally agreed after a lot of haggling and my friend was transferred from the traffic division. He was by then a fully trained traffic officer having expertise in driving on motorways and all major roads within the force area, where he would mainly target dangerous speeding and reckless driving. They would also be fully trained in vehicle examinations for roadworthiness, having all necessary equipment on board their vehicles for dealing with serious pile ups involving accidents with several vehicles and serious injuries. In addition experience in chasing vehicles and dealing with fatal road accidents, so it was obvious they did not wish to lose such a valued officer.

Although an important job Monty was just a damn good thief taker and his talent was wasted in that area of police work. To be fair understanding our role the boss did not expect immediate results as it takes time to settle down, build a rapport and cultivate informants within such an intense area. It did not take long we both worked well and to some degree covered each other working both beats. When we came across a useful snippet of information we just pulled together and took immediate action ourselves. In other words when it was necessary we would always strike whilst the iron was hot. These days some police officers put a short report into the intelligence system never to be seen again. We were not nine to five policemen and often worked during the night through to early morning and other very irregular hours, something some shift officers would prefer not to do.

We had a burglary at the main offices to a local factory and although there was no forensic evidence found, various items of expensive office equipment including a new computer and a photostat machine to a value exceeding £5000 were stolen. The persons responsible even took the carpeting which covered the total floor area. During our enquiries we obtained a sample of the carpet. Through their greediness it led us to the doorway in detecting the crime.

Monty and I each had a small sample with us as we went on patrol in the area and it was not long when we were together round the back of some old council maisonettes that we found some of the carpeting. It was an unusual colour and pattern. Odd pieces were found in the bins with a long piece just placed hanging over the staircase railings directly opposite the front door to one of the addresses. As we knocked on the door a young woman opened. We made an excuse that we were looking into some nuisance problems on the estate and were invited inside. The lounge door was open and we saw the carpet had been crudely cut and fitted. We wound up the initial story and concentrated on enquiries relating to the carpet. It did not take long before she told the truth and was arrested. She implicated a gang of some three men and they too were arrested. A few other items of property stolen during the burglary were also found, as for the larger equipment it went off in a van the next day, to the main city area where it was sold on. The main burglars were all charged and received prison sentences. The girl was cautioned for handling stolen property. If they had not taken the carpeting they probably would not have been caught. This is where most criminals slip up, over the simple things.

This was the first arrest of many between us and that was in less than the first 3 to 4 weeks. We came across a gang of vehicle thieves all from one informant. If you could put up with the stench of visiting this man his home was just utter filthy just like in the television series grime busters and I am not joking. As good as his information was you would have been insane to accept a drink, but he was a mine of information. Can you believe it as well his wife had just started working as an Auxiliary Nurse on the wards, at one of the main hospitals. Pity they didn't see her for interview by a visit to her home address.

We had information this man was driving out and about in a stolen Ford Capri on false plates. If you were sensible and did not go mad and drive stupid, travelled only in the day and early evening and dressed respectably the likelihood was that you would not get stopped by the police. We went into plain clothes and located a garage where the vehicle was being kept and maintained observations. After a short period of time the new owner turned up and got into the car. We were able to stop him just before he started to drive. He was arrested and the vehicle was seized for examination, which was found to have been stolen from the city some three months previous. Naturally it was bearing false plates and a fraudulent excise licence disguising its true identity.

This man was charged and bailed to court. He had only previous for petty offences and we treated him fair and he was cooperative. He told us the location of where another six stolen cars were and taking him out in a plain car he showed us all the locations where they were kept. He named all people responsible and included those persons who had stolen them in the first place and had sold them on. Subsequently we arrested all of the offenders in turn and recovered the stolen vehicles out of which two of them were virtually brand new. This was serious crime back in the late seventies. All were charged and dealt with all over the country at the places where the initial theft took place.

As for our man due to his help and information that had been forthcoming in clearing up all these other crimes, I decided to speak up for him at his hearing. The court was held in camera for this, meaning no one who was not involved could be present. The Magistrates thanked me for enlightening them to this man's cooperativeness. As he had no previous convictions I thought the magistrates would go easy with him, to my surprise they just hammered him. Although they did not send him to prison, he received a suspended sentence with fines way above anything we expected. I was not to ever trust them again after all I requested leniency and think they were a little naïve in the sentence given out, compared to other defendants I had dealt with for similar charges. Despite this, the defendant was still okay with us realising it was not our fault. It's a fine line between upholding the law and cultivating informants, but a reliable well tested source of information is irreplaceable. This is especially true in reducing the necessary time spent on enquiries and spadework to build up a file of evidence.

As for the man whose wife was a Nurse, it was not long before we had several reports of theft at the hospital where other staff, patients and visitors were victims of what they believed was a sneak in thief. It got to the stage where it was embarrassing for the hospital and a colleague who worked the beat that covered this location had not got a clue. In fact his arrest rate was pretty limited. Not wanting to spoil the relationship of this informant, I passed on all my suspicions to this officer and told him to do a spot check whilst she was at work in the presence of senior staff and to ensure he searched her locker. This he did and bingo, inside numerous purses wallets belonging to the victims were found. At least he acted on my instructions and the woman was arrested and charged. She was given probation, but more irritating than that was for the next six months all we heard from this officer was the success of this last arrest. No one else in the job had any idea how he came by his information, he just took the glory that he had cleared it all up. I suppose while he was gloating in the publicity he wasn't boring us with other topics.

I recall Monty was on leave and I reaped the rewards of sowing seeds in cultivating informants. This one girl was having trouble in her relationship and wanted her boyfriend out, but he kept going back. There had been domestic incidents and over a period of time a pattern emerged every time the boyfriend left her flat.

During the early hours a car was stolen from the nearby area and this had happened at least two or three times each week. I retrieved all the crime reports and found the common denominator. He was using stolen vehicles in his journeys backwards and forwards and upon checking records some stolen vehicles from the location of his home area were being found abandoned on our patch. Armed with this I also had feedback from his girlfriend about other jobs he had bragged about. As soon as the opportunity arose, I was out to arrest him. I established he was appearing at court for failing to pay fines and his case was adjourned for reports. I seized the moment and took him into custody before he could leave the building.

Sometimes interrogation can be difficult especially if they are anti- police, but treating them firm but with respect giving various facts relating to their suspected behaviour was always a good start. He admitted one offence which led to others and before long he cleared up all the vehicle thefts. When I investigated further, on his way home across the boundary to another division he used the vehicles to commit factory burglaries. Unaware I would dig even deeper it was not long before he was admitting well over 15 burglaries together with a similar amount of theft of cars. He was charged and kept in custody and eventually given a prison sentence. The girl was finally rid of him and had started a new relationship.

We had continual offences involving crime as soon as we cleared one set of crimes, others would be committed and this became pretty normal whilst walking the beat. It did not take long to build up patterns and get established with our fingers continually in different pies all with potential results for clearing crime. We also assisted CID whenever there was a serious crime committed such as robbery, rape or attempted murder. I recall our services were invaluable in completing house to house enquiries, a very time consuming exercise but extremely essential in positive policing. This often resulted in gleaning positive information from newly found witnesses to such an events where we would obtain thorough statements of evidence. Majority of these enquiries would be in plain clothes where we teamed up with CID officers and attended regular briefings of all kinds of serious offences.

I recall one occasion we were with our beat sergeant, who was well experienced having been a former detective who transferred to our station on promotion. Monty was with him and both together doing house to house enquiries in the same street as myself and other officers. The sergeant knocked on the door which was answered by a polite middle aged housewife. The sergeant introduced himself and showed the lady his warrant card for identification when she suddenly burst in hysterical laughter. He could not understand what was happening and when he looked at his warrant card instead of his police photograph, to his amazement he had forgotten some time back he had inserted a family beach picture of himself, his wife and children and suddenly coloured up with total embarrassment. He removed the picture and showed his proper identification which was well received and definitely broke the ice, where they all had a good laugh. I am sure he did not make that mistake again, but after all it just showed the character of the sergeant being a happily married family man, sadly a rare event with so many other members of the police force.

We had various lodging houses at different locations on the beat, some owned by the same people usually from all walks of life including immigrants. Some of these owners were honest and had fair principles, with others from dubious backgrounds, where they were unscrupulous at every opportunity. In those days there was probably some kind of tax fiddle, with them charging unjustifiable weekly rents should have been a crime itself. Some rooms left a lot to be desired with rubbish electrical installations and dangerous gas fittings. I remember one such owner being present at one property where a flat roof extension was having a crude refurbishment. They had a gas ring which was being used to cook food whilst three others were working. It was a summer's day very warm, which for them got even hotter because there was a massive explosion and fortunately no one was seriously hurt. The fire brigade was in attendance, the cause being the piping connecting the gas ring to the mains was just a plastic hose pipe. Can you believe it and these people were responsible for ensuring repairs were professionally completed in majority of lodging houses in the area. With such properties where these people lived it was a frightening thought, but you had to feel sorry for decent people without a proper home where having no choice but to rent such rooms. This still goes on today but over the years the law has tightened its grip on such bad workmanship, but there is always room for continual improvement. If only they could today also tighten up and sort out all the scams involving highly inflated rent claims. Where benefit is paid and there is a fraud between the tenant and the owner with cash being given back as a reward for participating, where both profit from the deal at the tax payers' expense.

One old lady who acted as a rent collector for several properties knew all the good and bad families and she used to have a form which she created as a questionnaire for insurance purposes. I asked her to include a few extra points in giving details of any vehicle owned, previous addresses and date of birth. Most people in those days did not have telephones and mobile phones were not yet invented. She would give the forms back to me updating her records for every new tenant. It was interesting every time a form was half completed or unreadable to some degree as subsequent checks either turned up people wanted on warrant, failing to appear at court or just simply wanted for criminal offences. Those people who had never done any wrong had nothing to fear, which is true in all lines of police enquiries. However in today's modern world and with the implementation of The Human Rights Act this useful source of obtaining information would not be allowed.

Having part of the town centre incorporated into my beat it was helpful to visit the magistrates court also on my area, most days either in plain clothes or uniform so basically I could fit a name to a face, which is essential in positive policing. Even more important if they were living on my patch. It was beneficial to keep a running profile as to who was committing what type of crime, which offenders were currently on bail. In addition get to know all the indecency offenders that were living or visiting various locations. Identification of all disqualified drivers especially those associated with crime who regularly drove motor vehicles, many of these characters would continue to offend and in any case it made every day policing just so much more interesting.

To arrest a disqualified driver a police constable had to be in full uniform at the time of my service, so when on foot patrol it was essential knowing the identity of such people. It was also important to learn where they lived and frequented, together having the knowledge of different vehicles used and where located. I would keep a book with all these pointers recorded for my own benefit, all being tools of the trade. There were occasions when I would see them driving and stop the vehicle. This would result in their subsequent arrest where assistance would be given by colleagues in taking the offender into custody and impounding the vehicle. This would happen also when I was on duty in plain clothes. Knowing a disqualified driver was active in driving illegally I would wait in locations such as junctions where they would have to pull to a halt and were restricted to the next move especially when traffic was very busy. I would speak to the driver pointing out I was aware of his disqualification and that if I had been in uniform he or she would have been arrested. I often talked them into leaving the vehicle voluntarily having secured the vehicle safely and seizing the keys. Prosecution would follow by summons instead of being charged, in any case in those days, prison was always the punishment dished out, as they were driving without insurance. In addition with some cases enquiries went down the path leading to the investigation of other criminal offences. Just by following my instincts and profiling the activities of these persons I would average sometimes catching two disqualified drivers using vehicles on the road every month.

We were encouraged to build good relations with all parts of the community. I remember we had a well-known business man who was asked to produce his driving documents. He was worried as his jaguar vehicle being just over three years old, he had forgotten to obtain an MOT certificate. I was in the station and he produced all the other documents which were found to be in order. I duly reported him for the offence of having no MOT certificate. I included recommendations in my report and he received an official caution which would have been normal practice for any person in the same circumstances. However he was grateful and appreciated my help.

I never had any other feedback from him or any information materialising in the arrest of any person. I was surprised about six months later when this same man who always dressed smartly and appeared respectable, sought my advice again. He was telling me he had been arrested and charged with criminal deception. He was asking if I could get the case quashed and advised he had denied all knowledge of the offence. He had arranged to have his motor vehicle stolen by friends and then made a false claim against the insurance company. I told him to go and see his solicitor and tell him the truth, plead guilty and expect the worst. I made a pocket book entry concerning the conversation and eventually spoke to the officer in the case who was in another division of the same force. I advised him of what had happened. He later contacted me when the case was over and told me the man had pleaded guilty and had been sent to prison. It's incredible what some people will do through greed when they have everything at stake none more so than their reputation as being a law abiding citizen. He would have been the last person you would have suspected of being so dishonest.

Working in sometimes stressful situations when the opportunity arose to socialise with colleagues it was good to enjoy the freedom of a day out at the races. We worked hard but also played hard. I remember this one day we were off to the races having to travel some 100 miles by coach. After the main event was over we would stop off at a pre-arranged location to have a meal with drinks before the journey home. The rear of the coach had been converted into a bar with a couple of kegs of beer with several bottles of various brands of spirits.

We all acted responsibly as being police officers you were always aware you had to behave at all times even when not on duty, a rule some officers quickly failed to remember. However on most of the events I attended it was a mixture of CID, other beat officers and various sergeants who forgot about supervision switched off and mixed in well and it was just a good friendly day out. I recall I had a double scotch in one glass and a pint of beer in another coupled with a King Edward cigar and it was only 9.00am in the morning. What a way to start the day, still it was our time and some 12 hours later I still had possession of two drinks. I think I had drunk myself sober as I could still walk when I was dropped off home. Like most of our colleagues in the emergency services as a break from the stresses of work, there is nothing better than letting your hair down, enjoying your free time in any way you wish. After all we like everyone else are only human.

On one Bank holiday Monty and I were off duty and had received an invite to attend an Indian christening held in a local community centre where there was beer on tap and all the families attended with refreshments. It was nothing like what we expected, the families were highly respectable, clean and tidy and their generosity was evident with all of the guests. On every table they placed a large bottle of whiskey and a pint of beer was placed on the table for each of us. The food was remarkable, a homemade Indian beef curry which was cooked to perfection in which we both had our own three pint casserole dish with freshly cooked rice. Our taste buds were working overtime, together with the alcohol and pleasant company it was an experience I have never forgotten, with so many kind and thoughtful people. Call it race relations but we could not have met a nicer group of people. The compliment was later duly returned when the main organiser was invited to attend free one of our functions.

CHAPTER 13

DECEITFUL, CLEVER MOTORING OFFENCES

I recall stopping this vehicle one mid-evening and the driver seemed quite plausible. I checked him out for his details despite this from the information provided there was nothing held against him on the police national computer. He agreed to produce his driving documents at a nominated police station. I had a little intuition there might be something wrong so whilst the man was in my presence, I noted distinctive markings to his face I decided to draw a rough picture of him, he had scruffy hair and a moustache. He stated he was due to go on nights and was making his way to work. I asked for the details of his employer which he provided.

He failed to produce any of the documents, so I made enquiries with the owner of the vehicle. This person stated he did not know who was driving at the time and if anyone had been, the car must have been stolen. I gave him full description of the driver and of the place given where he worked to which he denied any knowledge. I asked him where he was at the relevant time and he provided me with the details of a friend where they had met for a drink. Enquiries were made with this person who confirmed the story. He stated he often travelled with his friend in the vehicle, but he denied all knowledge of knowing the person whom I had stopped. Something was seriously wrong and I was being taken for a fool. Not for long.

With dealing with so many things in the normal course of duty, this matter went on the back burner for a while. When the opportunity arose I managed to call round to the firm he had named and surprise, surprise, there was no record. This was a small engineering company, but nearby was a large steelworks which was open 24/7. I made enquiries with the Personnel department at this other large factory site and checked his name against all the work force, where a three shift system was operated. In confidence I spoke with the main Contract Manager and I was given the name of a person working there who fitted the description and that his next shift was mornings. The name was similar to that given but did not match exactly. Coincidently I was working that very same shift the following day. I advised my sergeant I could be committed at the end of my tour of duty and I waited round the corner where I had full view of the work staff leaving. All of a sudden I recognised him and took him to one side. I subsequently arrested him on suspicion of theft of the motor vehicle and took him into custody. He came clean and admitted he had given false information and that he was a disqualified driver. He stated that the owner and his friend had covered for him knowing his predicament. He was informed he would be prosecuted and the other two men further questioned and also reported for summons. The driver pleaded guilty and was sent to prison. The other two men were charged with aiding and abetting the offence, denied knowledge but were found guilty. During the time at the magistrates court they continually shouted abuse and made threats and I warned them if their action continued they would be arrested for even more serious offences. They were both fined and eventually changed their behaviour. All three men were disqualified from driving. The man sent to prison received an extension to his current period of disqualification.

This offence is always treated serious as apart from voiding any insurance, the courts view it as a form of contempt showing total disregard for the law. In addition the circumstances of this case were bordering criminal offences of conspiracy to pervert the course of justice all because of protecting someone driving whilst banned. So here we are again with people going to any lengths to escape justice over something fairly trivial, implicating others all against the risk of all involved possibly going to prison, rather than coming clean. Still in the end they were found to be the fools and paid the ultimate price in receiving a conviction.

It is amazing the attitude of some motorists who resent being stopped by the police. When a person claims he is being victimised and I suppose if he has been continually stopped for no reason fair enough that is annoying and can soon be addressed by the authorities. This of course providing he is not committing offences and has not done wrong previously. In fact this situation arose involving my own sons.

My elder son had passed his driving test and had bought a good second hand Austin Metro. He turned his pride and joy into the most smart and attractive vehicle in spraying the car red, with a chequered pattern on the roof which looked the business, very sporty and extremely unique. I explained drive carefully as you can easily be identified and it could cause you problems. Never a truer word said, as within 6 months he was stopped 20 times by the uniform police and continually produced his documents so in the end he carried them with him. After 12 months he sold the vehicle for a profit and the motoring issues became someone else's problem.

It was a time when jobs were difficult to find, so my son worked at a garage rubbing down cars and masking them for respray. Good experience and my son learned to spray cars, all for a measly £28.50 per week on YTS. The boss could see his potential and really using him as cheap labour. He paid him by cheque on a Friday which meant he could not cash it in and have it cleared until the following week. This one week it actually bounced and quite rightly I had strong words with his employer who apologised and from there on paid him in cash, with still no extra, but that's another story.

My other son also fell foul of the police and was also stopped several times and asked to produce his documents. In fairness he had a tendency to travel a little faster than he should and I warned him about this. He got stopped one day by uniform police from my station for travelling a little erratically, fair enough. I was in CID at the time and the officers told me, omitting to mention they had dragged him out of the vehicle and roughed him up in the back of the police car. Holding his hands behind his back which was painful and totally unnecessary, until realising who he was. I did not make an issue of it, as time had passed on. The one officer later did an attachment to CID. He was well into body building and had more braun than brains, in fact he could have learned to talk to people properly for a start, considering he had been in the job for around 5 years he had completely the wrong attitude in my book for being a decent police officer. Needless to say he did not qualify to be trained as a detective. His conversation was as boring as he was, what a pedigree for working with the public.

There was a male driver who had been banned from driving motor vehicles and I received information he had changed his name by deed poll through his solicitor which in itself is not unlawful. But when you are banned and take out a provisional driving licence in a different name you are just heading for trouble. Some officers having this information would just stop him, confront him and simply arrest him for driving whilst disqualified.

These challenges just need a little forward planning and I remember stopping the person in question driving on the road in his motor car. I asked him his name and if he had his licence and insurance. Very calmly having the documentation with him, he handed both items to me for examination. He confirmed his details, being a provisional licence holder and his insurance was in his name, ignoring the fact he was unaccompanied and without L plates which were less serious offences. I then challenged him over his true identity and that he had changed his name. He admitted this was the case and that he had been previously convicted in his old name and disqualified from driving. He was arrested taken into custody and charged with driving whilst disqualified, no insurance, making a false declaration to obtain both documents and producing the same with intent to deceive. Some of these offences could not have been dealt with if he had been arrested with no questions asked of him about any driving documents. He went off to prison for 18 months for a really stupid thing that he had done, as it was inevitable sooner or later he was bound to get caught.

One dishonest scam which was frequently committed back in the time before technology took over was the excise licence or road tax used on vehicles. Although it applied to most vehicles the worst offenders were owners of motor lorries and other goods vehicles. A vehicle tax disc would be obtained for the annual fee which was between £300 and £500, which was a proportionate charge then, compared to today which would be £3000 up to £5000. The disc would either be issued in person or sent through the post. Within a short time the owner would falsely report that the disc was lost or stolen and for a nominal sum of about £2 a duplicate disc would be issued.

The owner would then wait until the first month was due to expire and fill out a form stating the vehicle was off the road. He would return the duplicate licence and be refunded the remaining cost of the term not used, which in most cases would be just one month off the whole years contribution. The local taxation office records would then show that the vehicle was not taxed and they were unaware that the owner would simply place the original tax disc on the windscreen and continue to drive on the road. To any unsuspecting official it would appear the vehicle was lawfully using the road. I detected several of these offences during my time in uniform. They were always convicted of theft or deception. As stated due to increasing technology it has been difficult to commit these type of offences without getting caught, but most people intent on avoiding payment, just drive anyway without tax until they are stopped. In fact just having no tax means exactly that so any attempt to hide conceal or corrupt the system and you deserve what you get. These offences were the ultimate challenge to an investigating police officer and took the boring factor out of the word committing traffic offences to becoming criminal offences.

A very similar crime was like with a passport, using forged driving licences, Mot certificates and certificates of insurance. Some of these obviously were very hard to detect because even then with technology they would appear almost perfect. Officers would have to rely on information being circulated through various official sources, containing specific details relating to each forgery. This would include serial numbers and other information relating to the documents, which were being used widespread throughout the country.

I remember stopping a young man driving and he was from a background where I suspected forged driving documents were being used. I stopped him in his vehicle not far from his home address. Not waiting for him to produce his documents at a later date at the police station, he stated they were at his home. I requested we go to his address where he could show them to me. Looking at the driving licence it was of the bound small red book types issued at that time and was in completely perfect condition. I checked the issue number with the control room over the radio. Needless to say the number was consistent with a batch of forged items and he was arrested. All the other documents were correct, however he admitted buying the licence in area of London and I gave full details to C.I.D. short for Criminal Investigation Department for enquiries to be continued.

He was subsequently charged with, being in possession of a forged instrument, producing a driving licence with intent to deceive, no driving licence and no insurance. To have insurance you must be the holder of a valid driving licence so his insurance was voided. Today his vehicle would be seized sold or crushed. He was convicted of a criminal offence disqualified and heavily fined. Just because he could not stick to the rules.

Even with the vehicle recognition scheme now in place some motorists still carry false or forged documentation in the event it can be produced to an unsuspecting uniform foot patrol officer. No different to fraudulent use of an excise licence, known as swapping a tax disc out of date, for another current tax disc allocated to another vehicle, in some cases which may be stolen.

CHAPTER 14

ANOTHER COUPLE OF INTERESTING ARRESTS

An interesting case that I dealt with involved a man I had arrested for burglary of office premises and for using a stolen cheque book. He was cooperative and admitted being responsible for all the offences and was subsequently charged. Normal checks with Scotland Yard revealed he only had a couple of minor convictions. He was put before the magistrates and allowed bail. Needless to say he failed to attend and went on the run.

Back in those times if a person was using several aliases we would take his fingerprints and post them off to Scotland Yard for immediate comparison, as we had no fax facility or computer scanners. It would be done as quickly as possible but where the identity was dubious the courts would always remand the person in custody pending the result of the check. In this case we had no need to suspect anything untoward as the results initially showed only minor convictions. It was not until I received a phone call from Scotland Yard, where the past of the man absconding finally had caught up with him. His fingerprints had only recently been received from us and other forces and it was established in the previous month he had been arrested several times for various burglaries, each time using a new alias thus escaping justice.

His true identity was finally put together in one criminal record file. It established he had used up to five different surnames, each time when arrested, however it was noted he always stuck to a 1945 year of birth and the same Christian name. The pressure was on the catch this illusive criminal, but where did we start he could have travelled anywhere. So the gloves were off, we left no stone unturned. He had access to a Bedford motor van which I circulated as being in his possession on the police national computer, incorporating all the aliases he had previously used requesting sightings. Nothing materialised and it was over a fortnight the trail was becoming cold and it was a month since we had last dealings with him. Then one day I received a report the vehicle had been found abandoned in the suburb of one of the main cities within our force area.

With Monty we donned plain clothes and pursued our enquiries in that direction. It was possible this offender was living somewhere in the surrounding area where the vehicle was found, unless he had moved on and the chances then of finding him would have been extremely remote. Armed with a list of aliases he had used I decided to visit the local benefit offices under warrant, to continue our enquiries. There were three in question which covered all the general area. My particular concern obviously was my interest in new claimants, any one male with a 1945 date of birth using the same Christian name. If I had the correct surname used that would have simplified the problem but things are never that easy. It meant checking thoroughly with my information against that of every new claimant and it was more time consuming than I anticipated, even during the short period he had absconded from court. Still I persevered I was determined not to go back empty handed.

We covered two of the local offices and had drawn a blank. Finally we had to check the last office which could easily have been a miss, but it proved otherwise. It was a genuine hit, our instincts had paid off. Looking through all the records I found a claim with the same Christian name and year of birth he used. From this I asked for his application papers and upon examining all the forms, there I established it was his handwriting on most of the papers without question. Although the man on the run was something of a rogue in the past he must have been educated somewhat as he had the most beautiful neat handwriting and this was to be his downfall. When he made a written statement under caution, he wrote the caption as required in his own hand. I recognised the handwriting to be exactly the same as written on his application form as a new claimant. With an address also given the net was closing in.

It would be close to teatime and Monty and I visited the address given which was a bed sit on the first floor of this large house. Upon knocking the door a man answered, who shouted, "Who is it boss" I immediately recognised his voice. He opened the door and there he was totally flabbergasted and captured at last. This time he did not get bail and all his offences committed under different aliases were all linked together and he was committed to Crown court where he pleaded guilty and received 3 years imprisonment. At least we had the credit for bringing this man finally to justice.

I had then just over nine year's service and had various increments in my wages as Constable. This was good but after all I didn't join for the money just the job. So when I picked up my wages at the end of the financial year I could not believe my eyes. Apparently my wages were three times more than normal and that was the net amount after stoppages. I thought no way am I touching that it must have been a mistake. I checked with the pay office and was informed it was correct. For the previous seven years I had been underpaid and not the correct increment and this was all the back pay. What a lovely surprise. I treated the family.

However as a joke I could not resist showing my pay slip to one of the detective sergeants and stating that I could not see the point in being promoted, when I could earn overtime every month for the amount I had picked up. He just didn't believe it and walked off in disgust but it went round the department like wildfire. I just smiled with amusement. The seed had been sown, it nearly caused uproar. I stuck it out for a couple of weeks when I came clean with the truth of not having been correctly paid for such a long time. It was if you could sense the relief as jealousy over wages creates rivals and that was not my intention, or fair, after all some of them worked equally as hard as we did. It was all taken in good fun and we continued to maintain our good relations with the department. So after the excitement it was back to foot patrol to see what else we could discover.

We mixed with all kinds of people in our tour of duty from Managing Directors to Doctors, School teachers, Social workers and everyday hard working people to the extreme members of society, vagrant's, incorrigible rogues and of course our everyday criminals. It was a skill which I continually learned to improve as each person is an individual and basically you had to raise and lower the standards of conversation to communicate accordingly.

This was a task not everyone was capable of adapting to, especially some senior officers who often acted pompously towards some of these people. Why, we are all human beings just because you are in a privileged position does not mean you are better than that person. He or she may have unknown skills, had tragedy in their lives or not been able to have all the chances in life many of us take for granted. It is of tremendous importance in being a police officer of whatever rank that you are accepted in society by everyone where possible.

We had a report one day of a man seen acting suspiciously in possession of a handgun which he had some kind of ammunition for, which we had to treat seriously as he was a potential danger to the public. It was decided that Monty and I would just call round to his address and just arrest him for being in possession of a Section One firearm. This was a very serious firearm offence. Having made our way to a ground floor bed-sit kind of flat, we knocked the door and there was no immediate answer. Looking through most of the windows we could see the only activity in the premises was coming from the bedroom. All of a sudden there was a kind of scuffle and eventually this man came to the front door in his dressing gown and all flustered.

We explained the nature of our enquiry and the man immediately showed us the location of a handgun. It had the appearance of a blank starting pistol or firearm replica, where the barrel of the gun had been drilled. We subsequently arrested the man on suspicion of being in possession of a Section One firearm. We commenced a search of the premises including all areas, leaving his girlfriend still in bed to protect her dignity. Despite a thorough search no ammunition was found. He was later taken to the police station where he cooperated fully stating it was a replica gun that he had bought through a mail order magazine. He admitted to drilling out the barrel but denied ever having any ammunition for it. This man was just infatuated with firearms and had a fascination for handguns and ammunition. He was allowed his freedom on police bail pending further enquiries.

In the meantime the gun was sent off to Firearms department for thorough examination by Ballistics section. Within a few days we had a report back confirming that the handgun which was previously a replica which had been modified with the barrel being drilled out converting it to the definition of a Section One firearm. There was no evidence to support any ammunition had been fired from the gun, which was possibly a lifesaver for the offender as if used could have had devastating consequences. With any crude alteration to a weapon of this description it was most likely only the user would have been injured. Nevertheless the report strongly advised the offender be prosecuted for his actions, as a possible deterrent to others.

At the first opportunity Monty and I called round back to his address. It was late morning and the man was again engaged within the bedroom prior to answering the door. He was advised of the action that had been recommended and he was taken back into custody. He was a likeable sort of fellow but not the brightest sparkplug in the box. We charged him accordingly with the offence and wrote the report favourably covering his cooperation.

One amusing part of the enquiry we could not resist was when we did the documentation, which included photograph, fingerprints and antecedence. Monty had dressed in a white paper suit to take this man's fingerprints and looked like something from out of a science fiction movie. Our man never batted an eyelid gave his prints and had his photograph taken, whilst I completed the antecedence questionnaire as to his background. I went through name, date of birth and occupation pointing out the part on the form indicated as male/female. Showing him the relevant section of the form, I told him I needed an answer. I just said, "What about this question sex." He said, "I ain't answering that." So I just carried on completing the rest of the form including school and employment history when he said, "Can I go back to that question about sex." He then said. "Can you just write in occasionally?" He had no idea I was joking. I found that was just so comical if you could have seen his face trying to be so discreet. He only had two previous petty convictions and when finally dealt with he received probation with an order to have the weapon confiscated and destroyed in accordance with police procedure. We often saw him around the town after that case and he was always polite when he spoke to us.

CHAPTER 15

AMUSING SITUATIONS BUT WHERE CAN I HIDE

We must always never under estimate the qualities that a sense of humour provides, not only does it take the heat out of nasty situations, it can be stimulating for all the boring periods when the action is replaced by routine.

I was on duty one day in the police station when this one young man came into see me. I had locked him and his brothers up several times all for different cases of crime. All the family of brothers were troublesome but also amusing in certain ways and often at loggerheads with each other. Most of the time firm and friendly advice was all that was needed, keeping their problems to a minimum but always paying them attention as they would always come to me with information even if it meant shopping one of their own, which they often did. In addition they always had faith in you when they were arrested especially when you had a reputation for being fair. So it was no surprise when he came to see me after having had an altercation with another of his brothers. He had received cuts and bruising to his head but did not wish to prosecute and asked if we could warn the offending brother as to his future conduct.

As we were going out and in the direction of the general hospital, together with another colleague he was taken into the casualty department. I spoke with one of the senior nursing staff who I knew well and he was examined. In fairness this man needed a couple of stitches to his head. Having a similar sense of humour to myself the member of staff listened intently as I put forward my proposals of impending suggestions. I left the patient in the care of the extremely proficient medical team and carried on with my daily routine of enquiries. All the time I was thinking to myself what magical delights can you unfold for us today. As a result of this wild unusual collusion within the casualty area, later that afternoon I saw the same injured man walking towards the town centre. I couldn't believe my eyes he had a dressing to his head in the form of a surgical sponge which was secured by a bandage that was wrapped round his head under his chin. I pulled up in the car to enquire how he was, trying my utmost to stop laughing, when he thanked me for my help. I informed him his brother had been warned about the incident and his future behaviour.

He told me the hospital staff said he was to keep the dressing on for at least another 7 days, which made me almost hysterical. Looking at his shadow against a nearby wall he had the silhouette of a Gonk or Goon. I thought if he is stupid enough to commit crime during the coming few days he would be instantly recognisable as the Honey Monster. Today these are just memorable gems that are irreplaceable and would never play such a part in a political correct society, but I assure you this certainly did take place. As a good first class patient he was still wearing the dressing several days later. All I can say is that he loved playing the role of a victim and playing the sympathy card at every opportunity. He appreciated being the centre of attention in that everyone was talking about him in more ways than one.

Another perfect example of having a good sense of humour, although some may choose to disagree was when we reported for football duty. I recall was one Saturday, I was with Monty, when we all attended a main police station in city area of the force. Two first division football teams were playing later that afternoon and the canteen on the fifth floor was over filled with staff and the queue for service half way round the room. I said to him that we would be eating our lunch within a couple of minutes and he stared with apprehension. I just walked out into a corridor and to an unattended office. I dialed the operator and asked to be put through to the canteen.

A lady answered and I purported to be the Superintendent requesting all divisions to attend immediately at the parade square downstairs at the rear of the building. All of a sudden there was a mass exodus of some 150 police officers from the canteen, with all officers rushing down four flights of stairs to the outside of the building. Seeing all these officers running to a given location, just so I did not have to queue was like something associated with a scene from a slapstick comedy movie. I was hysterical and could hardly talk through laughing. I went directly up to the counter and asked for two bacon and egg sandwiches and was served immediately.

Halfway through our lunch the officers started to filter back into the canteen and I subtly asked and queried, 'What's going on'.

I was told the Superintendent wanted us on the parade square but it was cancelled. Again I nearly choked with laughter, but I dared not show it. It was just so funny. God knows what would have happened if they had found out. Funny thing was no one ever queried with any senior staff why they had been sent outside in the first place. Not a trick I could use too often.

Attending football matches in those days was no different than today with some matches displaying dreadful violence and poor fan behaviour. The main difference being today there is the privilege of close circuit television which may help corroborate your evidence in certain circumstances providing you had made a fair judgment or acted in good faith. In most cases today, persons committing offences are normally identified after the event by way of press releases via the television and national newspapers and subsequently arrested. However back then it was down to action at the time where sometimes you needed reinforcements to help when there was large scale fighting. It didn't stop the idiots throwing coins though which was an extremely foolish and dangerous practice, whereas today where possible they could be filmed as stated and they are arrested several weeks after the event.

In the early days whenever we attended major demonstrations, or serious unplanned incidents of rioting or disturbance, again there was no such luxury of close circuit cameras, or riot equipment. You had to grab whatever you could, such as dustbin lids for protection from missiles. At times when outnumbered it could become quite nerve racking and apart from upholding the law, self-preservation was always high on the agenda. Police horses were the ultimate deterrent in splitting up hostile crowds, as they still are today. When things had calmed down the appearance of the police dogs on the streets would help maintain order. High profile policing is then an absolute must, once control is gained. As a result of these basic practices, riot equipment was issued together with proper training being given, which included crowd control. However the training which involved some police acting as demonstrators became as realistic as possible using riot shields for protection, some missiles struck officers and it had to be toned down because some staff became victims of serious injury.

As time went on we had to face not only missiles but petrol bombs and that was an extremely frightening situation when involved with race riots and the National Front marches especially when under staffed. Sadly later in my service our Chief Constable disbanded the Horse Branch due to the expense, but I felt that was a big mistake but who am I to say someone has to be in charge and make those decisions for reasons unknown to us. Same as disbanding the Under Water Branch who played a vital role in helping to search and recover dead bodies, being victims of drowning or murder and the recovery of stolen property. We then had to rely on other forces supplying these facilities. Eventually we had telescopic truncheons instead of the wooden truncheon or peg, as it was more commonly known. I just couldn't get used to them. New style handcuffs were issued which you applied directly on both wrists together, again there must have been research to prove the new ones were better, but I found these cumbersome and not always practical.

The ratchet type were easier as I recall handcuffing a burglar as he half opened the door to his home, realising it was the police he tried to shut the door and his wrist became exposed. He was going nowhere as the other part of the cuff was applied to my wrist beforehand and I had the keys. He soon opened the door and was taken into custody.

In most cases today, as soon as a person is arrested and taken into custody handcuffs are automatically applied. Some people may feel this is unnecessary but apart from being a health and safety issue, you can never predict how a person will retaliate either by fighting or attempting to escape. All in all, I believe a good improvement in police practice, for the protection and safety of everyone. As for the issue of CS gas canisters as standard police equipment this was well after my time but again there are good and bad points involved in them being issued. When you see the vast increase in violence by some members of society it is easy to see why, but I am sure extreme caution and justification was an essential ingredient before use is considered. Sadly today with extreme use of illegal firearm and terrorists our police have no choice in certain areas to be armed. The trouble is one slight mistake, even if unintentional can cost an officer his career, possibly resulting in imprisonment. In the event of a death all has to be scrutinised and investigated thoroughly, but when you are facing the potential of someone pointed a loaded gun at you, or other dangerous weapon you only have a split second to make a decision, before it is their life or yours depending on the threat. Yet we still have 9.00 o'clock critics from every area of the media who would never be able to swap roles in the same situation. It is becoming a sad world with violence increasing in nearly every country on the planet.

Walking your own beat became the best days of my uniform service not only did me and Monty have excellent job satisfaction we also had the praise of the senior officers who were responsible for implementing our role. We were always encouraged when listening to stories told by more experienced officers some retired and all of different ranks and departments. It made intriguing conversation, often fascinating and despite being rude not to listen, as a policeman would be very naïve. After all no one learned anything from talking as by listening instead that is where you learn things. Sadly those experiences and times are now a far memory as far as real uniform police work is concerned.

I had a case that went to crown court where the offenders charged with burglary had put forward an alibi and had made complaints about another officer. Naturally I had assisted in the investigation so too I had to be implicated. I understood completely the investigation involved complaints and cooperated with the enquiry, but the investigating officer was not exactly the most practical of policemen. He was a little out of his depth or so I was told and could have resolved the matter more efficiently. Owing to the court case his presence was required and he may have had to give evidence against us. We were seated in the main corridors of the building waiting to give evidence, my colleague had already started and I was alone with the Superintendent. Whilst there I noticed this officer was wearing a toupee which was slightly blonde and did not match his remaining grey hairs and being slightly skew-whiff, this immediately drew my attention. Having a slightly receding hairline myself I thought he could not object to my level of inquisitiveness.

I politely said to him, "Excuse me Sir, but is that a wig you are wearing." Red faced he put his hand immediately to his head and said, "Why can you tell." I said, "It looks very smart. Do you think one would suit me? Are they very expensive?" He did not know what to say and I said," Do you think a blonde wig would suit me or should a chose a different colour." He said," I cannot really say." I had the impression he wished the floor would collapse and cave in, so I said, "I hope you did not mind me asking these questions because I am sure one day very near future I shall have to consider getting one." He just smiled reluctantly. Deep down inside I was hysterical. I would not be seen dead wearing anything like that. You are what God made you and if you have any character at all you certainly do not need a wig. I could not help feeling if he had been cross examined by a barrister in the court, like most serving police officers involving any aspect of the case, it could not have been as embarrassing as our private conversation. The case was finally dealt with and we were both completely exonerated of any wrong doing.

Where we were stationed we had a large Fun Theme Park which was popular with the local people as well as outside visitors. Most bank holidays with it being a tourist attraction it was necessary to police with extra officers due to large members of the public attending. I was with an officer who knew the complex well as it was within the area of his beat. This officer had well over 20 year's service and was close to retirement. On reflection his appearance was identical to Oliver Hardy of Laurel and Hardy fame, as he was plump and round with a moustache and in full uniform just looked the part. He even had a personality to match.

All of a sudden there was a report of a disturbance at an area some distance away and it was necessary to get there quickly. With no cycle or vehicle available the officer told me to follow him.

What happened next will remain with me forever as it was like being in a part of children's program and thank God video or mobile phone cameras were not invented. He only took me to the miniature railway where there was a train in station which he then commandeered. He got on a seat and of course I had no choice but to follow. There was just no place where you can hide when you are in full view of the general public and dressed in full police uniform complete with helmet. When people are looking at you and laughing and I did not blame them, I felt you were being considered the same as Noddy and Big ears, Wallace and Grommet or any other well-known comical children's characters. Whatever did the general public think of this? If it had been a lifesaving mission or an important emergency I could have held my head high but it was a little nonevent which was all over upon our arrival. Can you image the press being there or a television camera filming, it would have made us become celebrities all for the wrong reasons. With Facebook and Twitter it could have gone all around the world.

In police work you meet people from all walks of life and believe me I am not snobbish. I recall it was an enquiry on Monty's patch which I conducted whilst he was on leave. I visited this this large housing estate where the dwelling in question bordered onto fields. This was a house that was not for the squeamish and I am trying not to be unkind but they say cleanliness is close to godliness and this was a household where you wiped your feet on the way out instead of when entering. On the occasion of my visit I was alone at this time when the door was answered by the young tear away lad in his mid-teens. He knew me well as I had previous dealings with him and the family.

I explained the nature of my enquiry and was promptly invited inside. As I entered the hallway several un-skinned rabbits were hanging from the clothes rail alongside coats and other clothing. The inside of the property downstairs had not been cleaned since time immemorial and the stench was consistent with a pig farm. All over the floor there were half eaten take away food containers strewn everywhere from the freshest to the stalest, some containing mould with all kinds of lovely things growing inside. God knows how long they had been lying there. The lad invited me into the lounge where to my shock I saw the mother of the house aged in her mid-fifties, with un-washed untidy greasy hair, seated in an armchair with both her feet soaking in a bowl. Not only were her feet soaking but also in a glass on the nearby table were a set of false teeth. It was obvious they belonged to her as when she spoke she was without them, something reminiscent of guest visitor on one of today's most popular television shows.

One might think that the elder son of this house knowing his mother was in a state of undress, would have politely asked me to wait a moment, this was not so. In any case it was obvious her behaviour was an accepted practice in the household. Perhaps their definition of broadmindedness extended to all and sundry, but for visitors to witness was just shameful. That might have been acceptable as these things happen in some households, but apart from the woman wearing just a dirty white tee shirt, she was otherwise undressed. Thank God the tee shirt was oversized and protected most of her dignity. It was fair to say that when she spoke, every word was as uncouth as it could be, as she would just rant on uncontrollably using language utterly revolting.

Even the postman, social services and health visitors used to cringe when calling at this address, as they too were confronted with such unnecessary behaviour. If I am a little unkind I make no apologies in describing her mouth as big as her backside as far as volume is concerned. I politely stated that I would leave and come back later, or she could make herself more presentable. She made some crude un- repeatable comments and I went into the kitchen where I spoke to the lad in the presence of his father. She covered herself up and I spent about twenty minutes or so completing my enquiries with all of them. The father was preparing a meal and cooking sausages with a line of them all laid out along the window ledge. The state of the cooker was just indescribable, I don't think it had ever been cleaned and was riddled with stale grease. How they had never caught food poisoning was beyond me, but perhaps they were immune, who says a little dirt does not harm you.

I had to smile this woman was wearing a tee shirt with a motif showing the union jack flag with a note underneath stating Made in Great Britain. As I left the way I had entered I thanked them for their help, the lady was still sitting down reading the newspaper. All I can say is although her feet may have been clean, there definitely was room for improvement in the remainder of her and the families hygiene, as most parents, including my own would always say there is just no excuse for dirt and filth after all soap and water comes fairly cheap. I just thought to myself in a materialistic yet comical way that it is occasions like this that it just made you feel proud to be British.

You may perhaps wonder whilst reading this book why include such paragraphs, but apart from the majority of front line working staff from all professions, I bet some senior management from all these occupations have possibly never experienced people who live like this in the modern world. This I suppose naively applies to many people throughout the country who have never seen anything, or visited such properties to see first-hand for themselves how people can live like this. Can you imagine the television or media visiting or royalty, the mayor, or dignitaries of a town hall, it would never happen. In their own way I suppose there is a little amount of ignorance and they find their way of life to them normal and acceptable, not that they are all bad people but living in such squalor it is their choice and so despite any education they will never change. Thank God there are not too many properties like this, but I am sure every town has similar families like this.

Another example of friendly banter was one day I found a photograph in a newspaper of a young boy, who had the appearance of a delinquent, and showing a childish cheeky grin, wearing a school uniform. I cut it out and typed - Do Not interrogate C.I.D. informant. Photocopied it and stuck it on the notice board in the C.I.D. office. This was together with a similar notice showing a photograph of an old man in the late 1920's putting his hands up in front of a push bike. This time I cut it out and typed - C.I.D.

latest arrest theft of pushbike. It was all good fun, especially when I was interviewed for theft of two sheets of photostat paper, by the practical detective Inspector. Naturally I denied all knowledge but complimented the unknown offender stating whoever had done them had showed extreme and accurate professionalism. I cannot begin to repeat what he shouted back at me. But he took it in good spirit and it was just friendly banter, knowing we both had respect for each other.

This brings to mind, the time I set Monty up with this amorous young lady in her late forties. She had a crush on my mate and was fairly large in weight for her height. She had no teeth and her dress code was something else, not the most attractive female on the planet. She lived on the beat and the general word was she put herself about for 50p a time and that was too much. I never had any evidence supporting this alleged offence, thank God. I just told her my mate wanted to see her and gave her the time that he finished work.

We both left the station later that day around 6.00pm and there she was standing by the main entrance to the police station. As we parted I said to Monty, "I'll leave you with it then." The next day I learned it took him well over half an hour to get rid of her, as she did not take kindly at all to being rejected. I suppose it was a cruel thing to do at time because it is not normally my nature, but the opportunity was too good to miss. In any case he did get me back but I cannot talk about that it has been censored as being unprintable.

Another intriguing story Monty told me about was when out on traffic patrol with another colleague, when he had enquiries to make via landline at a sub-station on our division which was close to the border of adjoining police forces. Although a smaller section station it housed facilities for some C.I.D. staff and local resident beat officers. At that time it was manned over a 24 hour period with a station police constable who was present at all times to offer services to the public. As both officers entered the building he was spoken to by the station PC, who was an old fashioned type of officer, very likeable but also a little eccentric. He drew attention to the fact that it was St George's day and he felt it was his duty to ensure the relevant flag was flying correct above the station on the main mast. He stated it had taken a while to find the flag which had been crumpled up inside an old cupboard and that he had put it on display regardless of its condition as it was the only flag available but it was better than none. This was despite the fact that even though it was utterly filthy, torn and ragged and looked like an old bed sheet that had been ripped apart in a washing machine. Monty listened intensively believing the PC was again exaggerating the issue, which he immediately dismissed as it was often the case with most conversations with this person. He made his necessary enquiries and bid him farewell to carry on his duties.

Upon leaving the station Monty with his colleague walked to the police vehicle, their eyes immediately were drawn to the flag which he saw had been adequately described by the PC on this occasion. It actually looked worse than portrayed which was bad enough and in actual fact would have been better to have been thrown into the dustbin in the first place, rather than being out on display in full view of the public. They both thought about the whole issue and then became engaged in fits of intolerable laughter. As Monty and his colleague travelled to the next town centre area continuing his patrol duties he just could not stop thinking and smiling to himself of the whole charade over the displaying of such a worthless flag, when suddenly an extreme sense of wickedness overcame him and he was again drawn to the telephone. On this occasion he disguised his voice to that of a person of mature seniority and rang the telephone number of the police station where the flag was displayed.

His call was politely answered by the station PC who enquired as to the nature of the conversation. Monty stated, "I am Major General KIDDING from the Ministry of Defence in London. I live locally in your police area and I have to tell you I am absolutely appalled with the disgraceful condition of St Georges Flag that you have displayed upon your premises. Who is responsible for displaying such an atrocious piece of ragged material, representing a patron saint on one of the most important dates of the calendar year, "I demand your full name rank and column number." This information was politely given by the officer who was completely dumbfounded by the whole affair. The call was ended by Monty still purporting to be a Major General in the army, who insisted the flag be taken down immediately and that a full report was on its way to the Chief Constable.

Flummoxed by such an embarrassing issue the station PC thought it was time to put pen to paper to cover himself and admitting his mistake in flying the flag in such a state of deterioration and the comments made by Major General KIDDING. In addition he also reported the full facts to the duty Inspector who in turn contacted the senior police officer on duty, who was an acting Chief Superintendent. As a result of this contact the senior officer on duty made a personal visit to the section station where he saw the station PC and listened intently to the officers concerns, where between them they were pondering how to deal with the issue with the minimum of fuss to avoid any bad publicity. The officer was told to scrap the report originally prepared and submit a new one requesting a replacement St Georges Day Flag, denying that it had ever been on public display. Strangely enough nothing was ever heard of the problem again, panic over, but I know who had the last laugh over the complete scenario resembling a Dad's Army comedy sketch, which we still laugh about today.

I remember one Christmas Eve I was on patrol and with another officer who was young in service. It was close to midnight and at the address which we attended we had dealt with the complaint to the occupier's satisfaction. He was a middle aged Jamaican fellow living with his wife and he offered us a small Christmas drink. Albeit drinking on duty was not allowed but it would hardly affect my ability or driving and being the festive season I gratefully thanked him for such a lovely gesture. After all what a better way than showing we are all human, race relations never came into my mind as are all equal and he was a good human being. I accepted a small whiskey and the kind man offered my colleague a drink. He went through every drink he had in his cabinet which was very impressive, then he went on to state he had orange juice, fizzy pop, cordial, tea, coffee, cocoa, milk or water. He asked for a drink of milk. The man just laughed out hysterically. It was a wonder he did not offer him the beano or dandy comic book to read. Never mind we enjoyed our short break and wished the couple season's greetings bidding them goodnight. Sometimes common sense overtakes all the rules and sowing good seeds can never be a bad thing. It was not as if we stayed there on a binge drinking session, just being friendly.

In my next chapter I explain how at times walking the beat I had the assistance of the public to get from one destination to another. One interesting situation occurred one night when I was out of uniform and walking home. On route I went into a Chinese takeaway restaurant that I had not used previously. Looking at the menus on the wall I saw a sign advertising Order your Takeaway – Free Home Delivery. I just could not resist the temptation, I ordered the usual two chicken curries with egg fried rice and can you take me home please. The gentleman behind the counter a middle aged Chinese chef looked amazed and asked me, "What did I mean". I repeated the order and stated can you take me home, pointing to the message portrayed in the sign – Free Home delivery. I couldn't resist laughing and he too became amused seeing the funny side. He offered to give a lift, but I was not too far from home and politely turned down his kind offer.

Just shows a sense of humour is always welcome. Now this is food for thought, every time you call into your local takeaway these signs are still on open display today that clearly have a double meaning. This issue is something definitely to ponder over especially when you have a long walk home ahead, or on a wet or cold evening, a most tempting idea to put into practice.

CHAPTER 16

CLEARING SERIOUS CRIME

Majority of the time when I walked the beat and towards the end of a shift, if I had over run my time and was late finishing, I would flag a male motorist down and have a quick ride back to my base. Upon stopping him I would ask in which direction he was travelling. Explaining I had to attend the police station urgently, I had no amount of willing drivers prepared to give me lift and found this a very useful facility even if a little tongue in cheek. It was also a good way during the day of getting quickly from one place to another especially where time was of the essence, where reliable information was forthcoming and the opportunity was there to catch a person in the act of committing crime. Of course these people were always given full appreciation for their kind assistance, it was so helpful to have such public spiritedness. Some drivers or occupants of the vehicles asked if they could help and they were given brief descriptions of offenders and vehicles in the event they saw them in the vicinity after dropping you off. This sometimes worked out very well in your favour, but at that time there were no mobile telephones which would have been so beneficial back then.

It was just as important to note certain activities when you were off duty, as with various events happening with people acting suspiciously, or known criminals in different vehicles or with new contacts at unusual locations. It was always good practice to make a mental or written note, recording all important facts at the first available opportunity into your police note book. In committing such sighting to memory, there would be no doubt instincts would remind you that such sightings may feature in either your current or future investigations, or could be invaluable to any other officer's enquiry as you will see in later chapters of this book. Sadly a minority of some officers could not show enough interest when they were at work yet alone off duty and this practice never entered their heads.

One saying popular amongst serial criminals is the comment, 'I wish I could steal enough to become an honest person'. Sadly this is the philosophy of many of all nationalities, involving corrupt people who are drug dealers, corrupt businessmen, dishonest entrepreneurs, politicians, or just utter career criminals. Many of these dishonest people may eventually become millionaires by any corrupt means possible, then purport to be a respectable person in society dressed smartly in Saville row suits, or smart dress who never get detected.

I have always ensured when travelling from one job to another it is when you always may see things are happening elsewhere, so it is important not to be distracted and look for the unusual which can result in identifying the wanted criminal or catching other criminals in the act of committing crime. This is especially true when being sent to the scene of any crime where the offenders had been disturbed or made their getaway on foot or by vehicle. It was imperative you kept your eyes peeled for any such activity.

In addition, sometimes I travelled to work on the bus and would normally be in either plain clothes or half uniform. I recall one day seeing a man who was wanted on warrant for failing to appear at court and I discreetly informed the bus driver who stopped directly nearby the police station. Having quietly informed the man my identity and the reason he was being arrested, we both got off together. The remaining passengers were all unaware of what was going on keeping the man's private business confidential.

There were times when we had to use a marked police vehicle to continue enquiries which spilled outside our area. Always on the lookout for the next episode to take place, I saw this car being driven by a dodgy person to say the least. He was not a man with many convictions but lived on an estate which had a history of villains and a reputation in crime to match. What he did possess was a mine of information as to what was happening on the current crime scene.

I stopped the vehicle and saw that the tax on the vehicle related to another car. This is termed as fraudulent use of an excise licence and can be punished by imprisonment. Whether it fell from the corner part of the dashboard or was removed by the driver after he stopped I didn't notice, but I did see it on display when I first saw the vehicle. He admitted having no insurance and Mot for the vehicle, which of course was not taxed. I explained he could be done for fraudulent use of the excise licence for which if convicted may receive a prison sentence. I had no intention anyway of prosecuting him for that offence as he would simply say the disc was not displayed and it would have been my word against his. He was duly reported for all the other offences and later summoned to court.

What I did do was to use the situation to my best advantage. I told him I would state he had been cooperative in my report especially, if he could come back to me with any information of a criminal nature. I gave him my details so he could leave a message for me. You had to try at every opportunity to get the best out of these people who had a wealth of knowledge of the criminal fraternity, but I never raised my hopes just another seed planted.

However to my surprise it worked, within a couple of days he got back in touch and I met him at a given location. He mentioned two names of well-established villains who were planning a robbery over the coming weekend. He had no more information than that, but stated he would get back to me if he learned anything else. The weekend passed and he came to see me at the police station. He told me it had happened but did not know anything until it was all over. He stated £2000 in cash was taken, which was a lot of money at that time, equivalent to the sum of £20,000 at present day, so it was classed as a very serious robbery. Apparently the steward of local social club situated on a neighbouring sub- division was on his way home after securing the premises. He was travelling with his wife, and 10 year old daughter.

As the vehicle pulled up at a road junction a short distance from the social club premises, two men approached the front of the vehicle. The windscreen was completely shattered by one of the offenders using the handle of a garden fork. This was followed by the same man ramming the prongs of the fork directly into the driver's throat. Both his wife and daughter were hysterical, as this was very nasty experience for them to have witnessed. The husband was told to handover the money or else, with further threats of violence made. A briefcase in the back of the vehicle was taken by the other man and both men ran off into fields nearby. There must have been some inside knowledge as to the actions of the club steward, as it was just asking for trouble in having such a large amount of money to be in his possession. According to other club members he was renowned for keeping all the weeks takings and going to the bank only once a week.

Monty and I spoke with our Superintendent and it was decided in the interests of protocol, we had no choice but to pass this information over to the C.I.D. covering the area. This I did giving names and full details of everything we had established to be passed to the senior officer in charge. After all, even though we were not to deal with the matter in any way, it was still a feather in our cap.

In the meantime our sub-division was experiencing the worst spate of burglaries ever involving public houses. During the early hours of the morning these types of premises were being broken into nearly every night and sometimes involving more than one location. Large amounts of cigarettes and bottles of spirits were stolen along with large amounts of cash in the form of coins from gaming machines and in some cases takings left in the tills were also removed. It got to the point that it was becoming embarrassing and so much of a problem the C.I.D. created an Incident Room solely to coordinate enquiries with a view to catching the offenders responsible.

My friend Monty at the same time had cultivated an informant who was close to giving us some good information, but would not confirm any details at that stage. It had been two weeks since I had spoken to the C.I.D. on the adjoining sub-division about the social club robbery and no arrest or action had taken place to arrest the named offenders. I just could not understand it, when all of a sudden the penny dropped, detective GLOVER had been moved to work there under a cloud from our station. I am sure he put poison down on our information that was given, which I later positively established was the reason why no action had been taken that was so infuriating. A short while later, one evening close to midnight, I was on duty together with Monty when his informant finally came across with the goods, or in other words the information we were waiting for. He mentioned a couple of names of the ring leaders, one being our suspect responsible for the robbery we had told the C.I.D. about. In addition he was told they were responsible for a couple of public house burglaries.

We knew of a multi-storey flat, on the 11th floor where they would all be later that following morning. We both decided to finish duty and start again at 6.30am the next day. So there we were right on time, both in plain clothes and able to stake out the target premises from another flat which was vacant and insecure just across the landing. The control room had been informed of our activities and the location where we were situated. We saw absolutely no movement whatsoever and being there for well over four hours we thought nothing was going to materialise, but our patience proved dividends. Then shortly before 11.00am that morning after this long period we suddenly heard the door to the flat under observation being unlocked. It was time to make a move. Two girls aged in their twenties, came out each carrying two heavy duty carrier bags, which we found later contained plastic bank bags of silver coins removed from gaming machines. Four men were with them, two being adults and two juveniles in their late teens. They also each had carrier bags in their possession. All had spent the whole morning counting the coins into banking bags for later exchange, being proceeds to several individual break-ins. We entered the flat showing identification and contained them all in the one room preventing their escape. The control room staff were immediately alerted and sent assistance, as officers had been briefed and were ready to act. They were all arrested with other officers arriving giving assistance which came within moments. All were searched and taken into custody. In addition the flat was also fully searched. Hundreds of pounds in cash and notes were recovered together with a large amount of cigarettes and bottles of spirits. A large motor van was needed to complete the removal. We had caught them, the pub burglars but did not anticipate all their total involvement.

On arrival at the police station news had spread like wildfire and Monty and I were both summoned to the detective Superintendent's office, where we adequately explained how we came upon the gang and the events leading up to it. We were allocated a detective sergeant who was reluctant to assist and quite frankly just didn't want to get involved. It was fair to say they did have egg on their faces but it was not really intentional. In fairness they did not have a clue to the description and identity of any of any persons responsible, who had been arrested by us. At the end of the day we had achieved a result and Monty and I were both complimented by the more efficient of the detectives, for which we had great respect. Sadly the other small minded minority members of C.I.D. did bear a grudge against us again through plain jealousy.

Back to the interview Room and the detective sergeant allocated, sat in the corner of the room whilst we interviewed the prisoners in turn. The named suspect for the robbery with the garden fork was amongst the person's arrested. This one man suspected of committing the robbery also admitted full responsibility for his involvement in the burglaries. While he was in full flow and coughing his heart out, the robbery was also put to him and bearing in mind all the charges facing him, he decided to clear his slate and admitted this as well. When someone admitted coughing it, it has nothing whatsoever to do with smoking or having a cold, this was merely a slang word for admitting the offence. A term which I believe is still used in present day. So much so the detective sergeant couldn't believe his ears and nearly fell out of his chair in disbelief of what we had uncovered.

Due to the amount of property retrieved the gang, admitted being responsible for all public house burglaries committed during the period in question. Altogether a total well over eighty offences of burglary were cleared, and of course a very serious armed robbery. Our Superintendent and sergeant referred to us as policemen with extraordinariness which was the biggest and nicest compliment we had ever received. This followed with many internal politics which we were not privy to, but I did know our uniform Superintendent was flaunting our success directly at them and it was a wonder me and Monty ever made it to C.I.D. but we eventually did. After all we were only doing our job acting on information and working hard to achieve the results that we achieved.

None of the monies from the robbery were recovered and the main offender received a substantial prison sentence for this and his involvement in the burglaries for which he received a total of 4 years. In addition all the remaining offenders were also prosecuted, with all men involved receiving custodial sentences.

We made further enquiries into the robbery arresting other persons but they denied all knowledge. The one man implicated his co-accused and another man who assisted in disposal of the monies from the robbery. In the absence of any other evidence we were not able to charge them. Perhaps if more help had been offered from those initially receiving the complaint and help from C.I.D. we may have got further, but it wasn't to be.

You can imagine the protocol I retained, when I later telephoned and spoke to the C.I.D. at the adjoining sub-division to advise them to cancel their current enquiries, if any were actually made, from the information I had given two weeks earlier. We advised them the main offender was in custody and had admitted responsibility. Most importantly the matter was being dealt with us both. What an embarrassment for them and no more so than detective GLOVER.

When the original officer dealing with the case, realised good information had been decimated, through the criticism laid down the negative action taken was something he bitterly regretted. Dc GLOVER's future in C.I.D. was hanging on a thread, but from what I had learned it was always in the balance anyway, as his sponsors were getting less and less as they moved towards retirement. It was common knowledge for whatever reason no one would work with him. Dc GLOVER had been posted to his current station from our sub-division several months previous. I heard that in front of all the staff he was in the CID Office and had a vote of no confidence in that no one was willing to work with him. I was informed from a reliable source that in front of all the staff he was just crying his eyes up, for a man of 45 years I found that simply pathetic.

Why he remained in the role was beyond apprehension as he was certainly pulling someone's strings to keep him in the department. It was hard to belief that when I eventually became a detective constable I got posted to the very same sub-division where he worked and some of the hostility I later experienced came as no surprise, as I even ended up having to work with him. As you can imagine, yes of course there were many explosive episodes which feature in future stories.

Ironically the main adult burglars and robber were remanded into custody to committal to crown court, but due to industrial action by the prison service, they were remanded into the police cells for long periods of 7 days. In addition there were 8-10 other prisoners also in custody at the police station, all this additional expense was met by the Home Office, These prisoners were segregated from the everyday prisoners and police staff on overtime manned this facility. The station was able to house these additional prisoners but the building itself was not designed with prison security in mind and this was realised by those in custody, natural instincts had worked overtime in their minds as they we continually planning and scheming their next move with escape on their minds.

Perhaps in fairness in mitigation if they had a brave solicitor or barrister defending the escapees, they could have blamed the Home Office arrangement for meals as being an element of torture. Our station in the town was close to a popular Chinese restaurant and they supplied a good substantial meal in the form of freshly cooked chips, peas and gravy with a fried egg laid to rest on the top, all neatly put together in a foil wrapped container with plastic utensils. Not bad you might think, but this was three times a day, 7 days a week for as long as they remained in the cells, with no alternative choice. I think if I had been in custody I too would have tried to escape. Today the Human Rights lawyers would have had a field day suing the establishment for cruelty and you for once would have to agree with them.

Two officers were on duty in the block on the evenings and nights and this was when they made their move. They found a point in the exercise yard which they could climb which was accessible to the roof and out into the courtyard of the police station and eventual escape. What on earth were these two lazy officers doing, other than taking absolutely no notice or sleeping on duty. How embarrassing a total of eight prisoners escaped and this became a major news event hitting main stream television radio and national newspapers. Away from the eyes and ears of the media, the officers put forward all kinds of answers, but the more they spoke the more stupid they appeared, proving exactly that excuses are the words of the incompetent which summed them up exactly. Both officers were reprimanded for their actions due to the unsuitability of the police premises acting as a prison building, but that made the matter no easier to forget. Within a few days all escapees were re-arrested and faced further charges being remanded to a proper prison on this return visit.

Like with the carpeting from the other burglary arrest, up to information gained from out of a traffic offence, just proves some of the petty parts of the job can give fantastic results and should never be under-estimated for the usefulness in solving crime. I believe a lot of crimes are screened today and filed immediately on the basis they would be undetectable. If these were looked at and investigated, sometimes it would give leads to more serious offences. For example a person who commits robbery also commits minor offences such as theft from a vehicle, or take and drive away of a motor vehicle, known commonly as TADA for which evidence can be connected. This is where looking deeply and scrutinising minor offences it can lead to clearing more serious crime. I previously referred to this as a cold case review.

At Christmas we had social events at the police station. Sadly I believe through the country various forces have closed police clubs on police station premises and there are not many left with hardly any alternatives in place. In my service it was a good way of mixing with your colleagues and friends especially for formal occasions and it was a meeting place for leaving and promotion events. It was a place where retired staff would visit and reminisce the good old days and children could attend parties and discos.

In my view there was nothing wrong with that as most people behaved and being sociable was a very important morale issue. This was proved year by year at our station where the club was well away from the public area. The Superintendent each Christmas would authorise an all-day buffet of very high standard where every officer could invite one guest normally from friends and acquaintances met during our everyday work. This was always appreciated and fondly remembered. Sadly those days are no more.

CHAPTER 17

MINOR, SILLY, DANGEROUS MOTORING OFFENCES

I could never see the point of booking someone who is in the process of putting his seat belt on even though he had only just moved off, yes technically an offence but a verbal warning is sufficient. No different to a driver who attempts to enter the road but on seeing the police decides not to for any reason even if he just crosses the pavement. He will come again and get stopped when driving completely on a road and will pay the price for any offences committed. Anything short of this he will deny and be given the benefit of doubt. So all these partial attempts can be treated as warnings as if they intend to carry on driving and committing the offences they will always come again and discretion saves a lot of wasted court time.

Just like some people in positions of authority who resent being stopped driving vehicles. I had many incidents like this in my earlier service when these people complained, why after all no different to me no one is above the law. If they had to produce documents, or take a breath test on suspicion of having driven when under the influence of alcohol so be it. Just because for example, they may have been a police officer of whatever rank, licensee, managing director, solicitor or on the police committee, magistrate or doctor, so what is wrong with them being stopped when driving vehicles in the execution of my duties. They are members of the public subject to the same laws as everyone else, but it was amazing how some would show resentment as if it was wrong for them to be stopped and complain. The higher in society the worse they would behave. My philosophy would be to treat everyone equally and fairly and not listen to unjust criticism.

No different to people from all walks of life purporting to be a friend of the Superintendent, or the Inspector or play golf with the Assistant Chief Constable and believe me there were many of them who thought in this respect they were privileged. I used to ignore this where possible as when I came into office I swore to uphold the law without fear or favour an ingredient some police officers of all ranks easily forget. None so much as in present day when we appear to have politically correct police forces, dealing with stupid incidents and in some cases ignoring serious ones. If I had a friend in the police or in any other walk of life, that would be it he would be a friend and nothing else and I would never use any person's position to give me an advantage. Like your relatives or friends who never speak to you, they are always the first to say my uncle, mate or cousin was in the police, or is in the police, as if it raises their role in society. These people are just hypocrites in every sense of the word.

Apart from looking for all kinds of crime whist on patrol, I always took it upon myself to learn the identity of vehicles owned by disqualified drivers and where they were located. Not all disqualified drivers committed crime, but majority I had dealings with always did. During the early hours of the morning with about an hour to go before the end of the night shift was ideal, things were quiet and it was amazing what you could find. This is what made the job interesting and a challenge except for those officers who thought they could park up and get an hours sleep and sadly there were too many of those in the job. At the rear of some garages there was a space where a vehicle was discreetly hidden and checking the details it belonged to a person who was disqualified. When I visited the same location during different times the vehicle was missing so obviously being used.

When I was out on patrol the next time on nights around 1.00am in the morning, I discovered the vehicle missing. I decided to park in the very same place and just waited. It was not long before I saw headlights and as the vehicle travelled from along the road to the waste land. I pulled out and stopped alongside the vehicle which was being driver by the man I suspected. You can image the shock on his face seeing a marked police vehicle with flashing blue lights, at the point of his final destination. He was arrested and charged. He did not learn by this because by accident I saw him again driving just two days later so he was stopped and taken into custody. He was not treated with any sympathy by the magistrates and went straight off to prison. As always in these cases his period of being banned was extended. Today his vehicle would have been impounded and crushed as previously explained.

Every town sadly has its fair share of idiots or people without common sense and although some can be likeable characters, they too do the most dangerous things without hesitation or any conscience. Later in my career I was at the hospital when five casualties came into Accident and Emergency department. There were two men and three women who were all occupants of a large estate vehicle, which had travelled along country road at high speed in excess of 80 mph and had lost control. The vehicle subsequently had overturned three times, not on its side, but from front to back which must have been totally horrific for all especially passengers, during which all three women seated at the rear where all thrown out through the rear window. Fortunately no other vehicle was involved. All occupants who were in their late twenties had extensive injuries apart from the one girl who sadly was paralysed from below the waste. I recall the seatbelt law was not in force at the time this accident occurred, but it is debatable whether or not this would have made matters worse as staying in the vehicle instead of being throw out, could also have resulted in fatalities. This is especially true if they had been trapped and a fire occurred.

All were known to me and when the police officer arrived, I helped him with his enquiries ensuring all were properly identified, as he was from another adjoining police force. I informed him to check the identity of the driver as to my knowledge he had never passed a driving test. In addition enquiries to look into the background of the vehicle and establish if the same driver had hired the vehicle with production of a valid driving licence. I was aware the driver, who looked older than his years, had the same full name of his father who was deceased.

With this information in mind the officer made the right enquiries and established exactly what we suspected, that he had purported to be his father and the holder of a licence in order to hire the vehicle. This of course was classed as criminal deception. He pleaded guilty was given a substantial prison sentence, but the girl who was paralysed came off worse, as with no sign of any recovery or improvement to her health, she was sentenced to being in a wheel chair for the rest of her life.

I cannot forget while they were all lying on stretchers in casualty awaiting treatment, both the driver and his mate were shouting out across to each other about what vehicle they were going to drive next. Their behaviour was just totally unbelievable they had no remorse for the chaos that resulted, or that they had come within an inch of possibly losing their lives or being seriously injured. The fact that they had caused a young person to be severely handicapped and all they could think of was what was going to be their next vehicle to drive, shows their total lack of respect for the law and their irresponsibility. Words just escape you in these situations.

Still on the subject of idiots or people without common sense I recall the time I saw an old Jaguar motor car being driven erratically along a country road. There was also a front seat passenger and despite indicating the driver to pull over he ignored my requests completely. Eventually when the opportunity arose I managed to pull in front of the vehicle which veered along the wide grass verge where he came to a halt with a tree causing severe damage. Fortunately both occupants were uninjured who were a young married couple. I established that the woman was even expecting her first child. The husband the driver was becoming awkward and failed to answer my questions and was close to being arrested. His wife finally came clean and told the truth he had bought the car for £20 and that he was without any documents whatsoever.

I arranged for a vehicle examination, as at the time of first seeing the Jaguar motor car, it was found to be travelling well over 30 miles per hour. It was later established the vehicle had no braking mechanism and was a virtual death trap thus explaining how the vehicle was not able to pull to a halt correctly. What if there had been a pedestrian, cyclist or a horse being ridden on the country road as often is the case it all could have ended in a complete disaster. As for the occupants of the vehicle they too could have faced severe injuries or worse. Whilst the traffic Officer took over the issues in having the vehicle removed, I took both persons back to their home address. It was obvious the young married couple were of low intelligence and that the wife was the better person. I established their identity and the husband was reported for a host of serious traffic offences as he had never passed a driving test and was without insurance. Although the husband was prosecuted, I just hadn't got the heart to involve his wife. This again provides another example of where today another vehicle would have been automatically crushed.

Looking at the fireplace I saw a picture of their wedding photograph outside the registry Office. I couldn't help but smile when I saw two women standing at the back in the picture who had curlers in their hair. I recall asking what are they doing dressed like that and the couple told me that's how they came as they were attending the reception on the night. They clearly were just starting out in life together and their flat was in need of basic furniture and fittings. I tried to give positive advice as to priorities in life and that there were more important issues than just having a motor car. In the end I later got in touch with social services covering the area they lived to see if they could offer them some help, but I had a feeling it was all clearly out of their hands and fate was down to both individuals.

I recall one incident way back where an arrogant middle aged man I stopped was driving a motor car in the town centre. He was approached and I asked the driver his name to which the man said," Fuck off" This was followed with the question again, "Give me your name and address." Again the man replied, "Fuck off." He was immediately arrested on suspicion of theft of the vehicle and taken to the police station. The vehicle was duly seized and despite further questioning the driver he would not give any details. I made enquiries to locate the owner of the vehicle and left a note at the address recorded for the owner to contact the police. At different intervals the man in the cells still gave the same reply of "Fuck off" to every question that was asked. Time went on and I had the last laugh, something you would not get away with today. I walked down to the cells some two hours later and the man shouted out to me finally giving me his correct details in the form of his name and address. Payback time I then said to him, "Fuck off" and walked away to investigate. Wrongly or rightly let him experience his own type of behaviour.

It transpired the man lived some distance away and was disqualified from driving. After keeping the prisoner in suspense with the same answer to all his questions by telling him "Fuck off", the owner eventually attended the station. He stated he had no idea the person driving was without documents and had allowed him to borrow the vehicle. The driver was later charged after admitting his responsibility and given bail. The car was returned but I am sure that man always gave his full name and address when requested in the future. The morale of the story was in those days if you acted like an idiot you were treated like one.

Another amusing incident was one day on a busy Saturday morning, a local but shady Car Sales Manager at a town centre garage had left his vehicles unattended in the street. Altogether some 20 cars for sale were parked in restricted areas causing chaos and obstruction. I walked into the premises and some jack the lad with a dickey bow said, "Can I help you Gov." I firmly explained I was not going to tolerate all these vehicles being parked in the street.

He said, "I don't know where the Boss is Gov." and he told me that he was out of the area and that his boss would not be back for around for a couple of hours. I just said, "Fine I will get them all towed away, I will issue tickets for them all and you can pay storage until they are collected." In his presence I pushed the mutt button on the radio and spoke as if my call was going direct to control. I wasn't actually speaking to anyone, just purporting to. I stated that I required the presence of the vehicle removal squad to come immediately and to start ceasing the vehicles. The man went into a frenzy or state of panic and within less than five minutes the owner conveniently returned. He immediately apologised and stated he would remove the vehicles from off the road, which he did into a compound the back of this garage. There is no way you cannot minimize the power of the police uniform combined with the use of common sense. Calling a person's bluff you nearly always achieved positive results. I later established that the finance company involved within the business had seized the vehicles pending repayment of owed monies and had returned them that day leaving them all in the road.

The owner of the garage always failed to pay parking fines from all over various parts of the division and it was necessary for us to interview him several times a week over a long period in connection with various vehicles, as being the owner at the material time. This was very time consuming especially when having to deal with other more serious matters in the normal course of events. This procedure was always a nuisance part of our duties and the owner of the garage used to thrive on such behaviour. Today this is dealt with effectively by the local council. One achievement was all his past came to haunt him and we had a special afternoon court hearing solely for this proprietor and I gave evidence fifty times in relation to his possession of the offending vehicles. He was fined £2,000 in his absence as he failed to appear, the equivalent of £20,000 today, for his failure to conform to the law. Within a month he had totally repaid all the fines. What a way to run a business.

Walking the beat in full police uniform in a busy town centre having achieved several year's experience I would pride myself on using discretion and patience when dealing with members of the public, especially motorists. Despite this you would always come across a person who would not accept a firm but kind warning and just had to cross the line in being offensive or abusive.

I recall this one afternoon traffic was busy and this inconsiderate motorist had parked and left his vehicle unattended in the approach side of a pelican crossing. This caused pedestrians and traffic having to be extra vigilant because of the obstruction. It was my intention to give the driver a stern warning in the politest way possible; however that was not to be. He had no respect for the role I portrayed having cleared numerous offences of crime and dealt with so many tragedies; nevertheless he was never ever going to get away such an abusive behaviour. The driver eventually appeared and before I could utter a word he sarcastically shouted go on then give me a ticket if it makes you feel better. He was a sales person who in his job role, regularly treated parking tickets as an occupational hazard. I pointed out the offence he had committed and all he could do was smirk as if he did not care less. I changed my mind and thought how arrogant, this kind of person does not even deserve a warning and without hesitation I requested his details and in full view of everyone passing I recorded all into my official notebook. He was duly reported for parking within the restraints of a pedestrian crossing. During the whole time he just could not stop sounding off and prior to me issuing a form for him to produce his documents he stated he would just add this other summons to his collection remarking that it did not matter anyway showing a completed attitude of conceitedness, as his firm would just simply foot the bill to be included all in his expenses.

I commenced to walk away after telling him the full facts would be reported. I just had to add that the firm may well absorb the full costs, but they would not have points on their driving licence, as that only applied to him and him alone. For the offence he had committed did not warrant just a fine but an endorsement of points on his licence following conviction and remaining there for 3 years. These days it is now 4 years. That took the smile off his face realising possibly he had used up his nine lives under the totting up system and that he had the prospect of being removed off the road for driving. Whilst I appreciated sales representatives have a difficult occupation, all this action on that occasion was due to his own stupidity and bigoted behaviour, which he had bought on himself. There are some people in society who do just not deserve your help. Thankfully the majority of people accepted advice and warnings given rather than face court action.

I recall one afternoon shift had ended and I popped into the police club so I could have a couple of drinks before making my way home. I was travelling along a main road and decided to stop for a take away. I had pulled up and switched the engine off, when all of a sudden a car travelling towards me in the opposite direction suddenly swerved and veered right in front of me crashing into the front of my vehicle. He then reversed back driving off and failing to stop. Fortunately no-one was injured but I was a little shaken up. The damage was severe but the car still driveable. A lady on the other side of the road came across to me and stated she was able to get the registration number and gave me the slip of paper with it written down together with her details. How lucky was I. I thanked her so much and advised her I was calling the police to attend.

A sergeant and a policewoman arrived from another station whom I knew and they asked if I had been drinking which I admitted. He advised I was to be breath tested which I knew was routine for all road accidents and I cooperated fully. I could see the test was negative and all he could do was check it against the glow of my headlights and then with the police woman's torch to see the result more clearly. Eventually after scrutinising the result for about a minute he finally confirmed it was a negative result. No problem I knew I was not over the limit as knowing I had to drive, you just had to be sensible. I made a statement later at the police station and produced my documents and thanked him for his help. The other driver was traced and prosecuted. I admire his principals he did his job correctly, but he was not a person of integrity as discussed in a later chapter, when he fell from grace. For being a supervising officer he became the subject of a serious case of gross misconduct involving himself with another policewoman.

This was the same police station where the retired uniform Superintendent abused his position in having his own chosen chairs in the police club, which I bought to an abrupt end and embarrassed him as being of a bigoted nature. I think this must have been a breeding ground for recruits into the masons as many constables also joined the elite club to enhance or protect themselves.

The reason also to justify this, was that anyone appearing before the Chief Constable at that time on a discipline charge for being convicted of driving over the prescribed alcohol limit it was automatic dismissal. We had at this station, an Inspector who was driving when involved in a road accident. He was breath tested positive where he pleaded guilty at court and was disqualified. He appeared before the Chief Constable on discipline charges and was allowed to keep his job and pension. What double standards, a rule for one and a rule for another. He clearly was in the masons but no one ever admitted it.

CHAPTER 18

PUBLIC NUISANCES AND OTHER STRANGE BEHAVIOUR

During the course of my uniform duties, I have dealt with several different kinds of incidents, majority of shoplifters, and cases involving drunkenness, domestics and sudden deaths. It was busy and at all times I had help from more senior colleagues, it was refreshing to have firsthand advice from officers who had seen it, done it, and had got the ticket. To me they had gained my respect and those worthy of promotion had earned it in every sense of the word. Driving around the town centre alone at night was always a challenge. Attending licensed premises due to trouble in those days was frequent, in majority of cases just removing the potential trouble maker outside and being spoken to firmly, they would see sense and calm down and move on and failing that arrest would follow. In those days it was rare for further action as the uniform carried a good amount of authority and respect, only in the most serious of incidents of drunkenness and assaults, was arrest necessary.

At those times public toilets were open all night unlike today, but even then in those days men and women were all caught urinating in public places too lazy to go to the correct place, even when a short distance away. We always summonsed people in these circumstances committing offences. Another offence that was not tolerated was deliberately throwing down litter especially uneaten taken away food which not only was unsightly, was also a serious health issue with the community with the increased population of vermin including rats and foxes.

In fairness with most of the public being extremely tidy people letting off such offenders in my book was an affront against all the law abiding people. There was always a low tolerance policy with these kinds of nuisance matters that was just a small problem then compared with today. In some areas of the UK these offences seem to be completely overlooked and dismissed, no wonder we are getting branded untidy and dirty and the graffiti capital of Europe.

Yet in present times despite Police Community Support officers regularly out on patrol, I never hear of anyone being prosecuted for such types of litter offences which are in abundance, perhaps their powers do not extend to such activity. This is so much of a nuisance crime which sadly is only enforced by some council areas and rarely by the police. There was nothing better than a habitual criminal having to go before the court on a charge of litter, it was if that person was humiliated more than anyone else as he or she was not performing up to their usual pedigree involving other offences of crime. Anyone caught swearing in public could be prosecuted under the byelaws. Can you image that today, it would be totally unworkable but without all the swearing the world would be a much better place.

People today all over the country do not understand why after early evening public conveniences are closed up until the following daytime. It may be simply just down to costs or other genuine reasons which remain unknown. This could also be connected to a small percentage of criminal damage or graffiti merchants who spoil life for the rest of society. Putting it simply, in addition it does not stop just there as from police experience public toilets were deliberately targeted by men who frequent such locations for the purpose of cottaging, or meeting new acquaintances to indulge in sexual activities involving gross indecency, which could also be another reason. Even twenty years ago we could not say that any such establishment was free from such activity in most places throughout the United Kingdom.

I remember at various locations throughout the division we had set up plain clothes observations at or near such places and regularly people from all walks of life were arrested for committing acts of gross indecency in a public place. Sadly this type of offence was not restricted to lower class people but many prominent people, Judges, senior Police officers, Barristers, Solicitors, Accountants and lower ranking Police officers, to Doctors, Dentists, male Nurses and married men and so on. One might find this disgusting as I certainly did as really there is no justifiable reason for such revolting behaviour in public locations. These types of offences also included many prominent politicians over the years, some in high office. All these offences being grounds for many blackmail offences involving all sorts of victims to avoid embarrassing publicity in being found out or exposed to the public or families. All were prosecuted with many being found guilty after a trial had taken place which usually ended up with a fine. I suppose in present times meetings are arranged between internet websites and take place more often in private which is no menace to society.

However behaviour at these locations always put innocent decent men and boys at risk to being subjected to these types of activities when attending public toilets when making a call of nature. It only ever in my experience ever involved men at these locations, as women even in gay relationships would never visit such places. Sadly in present day we still get nasty incidents where young children visit toilets alone in major supermarkets and other fast food outlets who are prey for pedophiles who have attacked and molested such victims, whilst parents wait nearby for their return. Every decent person in society is revolted and appalled with such disgusting behaviour. Clearly these kind of individuals are a menace to society and potentially extremely dangerous where in such cases it has sadly resulted in murder.

In the main, majority of gay couples of either gender who are living with each other in honest, loving and now legal relationships keep their intimate relations private. They are never any problem to anyone and would never dream of visiting public toilets to commit sexual acts with strangers. So in my view there should be more private public toilets available where entry is subject to a small reasonable payment. This is sadly long overdue where a parent with child or just single adults can use facilities, especially at night, in areas close to public scrutiny. These facilities should be plentiful in every town, city or village locations, as it would save the embarrassment of people having to discreetly urinate elsewhere due to every toilet block at present being closed.

In present times with facilities of the internet being available to everyone, it is quite depressing to see so many individuals convicted of downloading child pornography, or making indecent photographs of children to upload onto the internet. All children are precious being God's gift to mankind, how awful they should be abused or subjected to such degrading situations.

Whenever you were out on patrol in a vehicle, there was never any better experience than stopping and taking time to walk around for a short while, always in close proximity of the police vehicle in case you were called out urgently. It was on these rare occasions when looking for crime you came across sometimes embarrassing moments for all young couples. Either by walking round a corner or driving past parked vehicles you would sometimes unexpectedly find couples in compromising situations. If it was a case of walking past on foot patrol and couples were engaged in obvious sexual relations I would just walk by so I could be seen. Possibly asking if they were okay ensuring everything was above board and no force involved was the only thing necessary for me to do. Ensuring their dignity was intact so long that they were well out of the public eye and well behaved, I would turn a blind eye. Finding a police officer had disturbed their amorous intimate advances was deterrent enough for them not to return again or for any repeat performance, but we have to realise after all, we have all been young once. A similar case when driving by parked vehicles when looking for crime occasionally you would see couples together inside doing what comes naturally, but also in reality if things were underhanded or sinister at least some attention could be raised by the unwilling partner. It was never done intentionally but when you are thorough in your patrolling duties it is inevitable these things take place and that is where it is time to use common sense and discretion in closing your eyes to the tender age of discovering love.

Naturally if this happened anywhere in close proximity of the public or at places it was obviously they could be easily seen you would have no choice but to take other action. In less serious instances just telling them to move on, or if you had a formal complaint by anyone a different approach may be needed. Either way in my book fairness and dignity greatly outweighed any minor breach of silly behaviour. It wasn't as if it happened every time you were out on patrol.

This makes me think of my courting days when I was with my girlfriend and we parked up to have a talk. We were only embracing and kissing when all of a sudden a bright light shone into the car and we were disturbed. All of a sudden the driver's door was opened and I could see a uniform police officer. He stated, 'What are you up to then?' I replied, 'Just talking and cuddling. Is that against the law?' He was abusive and I saw he was not a regular officer but a Special constable. He had special constabulary on his uniform, a part time police officer walking alone unsupervised. He slammed the door after saying, 'Just behave yourselves.' I thought all was unnecessary as we were doing no wrong and then it clicked. He possibly was a pervert just like a peeping tom, deliberately looking for something more sordid, all the ingredients that should never be associated with enforcing the law in such a way. What would be wrong in just passing by or even saying, 'Are both alright?' If this action was in fact needed. If things were not and if it was another scenario, the female passenger could have shouted for help. That's all that he needed to do in my view, not a nice person.

During majority of my working time the police force was responsible for clear passage of the highway and such things as road works left unattended would not be tolerated. Today some roads have contractors setting up road works at numerous locations where they have won contracts possibly through greed do not wish for any other contractor to take over. This would have been stopped in my day in the police and if they started one job it would have to be finished. These days we have a small hole in the road coned off completely taking over half the carriageway, with traffic lights in either direction. As we all know left unattended for days on end but causing really serious traffic build ups for no reason all under the umbrella of health and safety, when the hole could have been filled in just one day, or a day allocated to sort the problem out. Sometimes causing chaos in towns or villages when all really unnecessary. On the other hand we also have to compliment the good local authorities and contractors that do not allow such activities and regularly monitor contractors who are deliberately causing inconvenience.

One area of nuisance which is now undertaken by local authorities who in most cases do an absolutely wonderful job is that of noise abatement, whereas the police who had limited resources had to attend noisy parities in households. Where thoughtless people played televisions, radios or stereos extremely loud just to infuriate neighbours causing them quite naturally to complain. Quite simply the police would warn these people only for them to turn the noise down and when the police left the scene to restore it back to the same level. In these cases we could only use a breach of the peace for arrest or summons for minor public order offences which nearly always would be contested.

Today most offenders who repeat their performances are given anti-social behaviour orders known more commonly as ASBO's, which have resulted in eviction of some tenants whose behaviour would otherwise be uncontrollable. This is definitely a positive step forward providing positive action is maintained by the magistrates in combating the problem. Councils with ongoing complaints now have the correct equipment in measuring decibels and do very excellent work in this field, so warnings can be served, or prosecution can follow with serious offenders facing court action or justified eviction.

In present times however there seems to be extraordinary policies between different forces in the country, where sadly some police officers and police community support officers alike and council enforcement officers report individuals for summary or non-indictable offences where discretion at the very least should be used instead of prosecution. Members of the public mostly of previous good character are reported for all kinds of ludicrous issues which should either be ignored completely in the interests of common sense, or not proceeded with at all.

To give obvious examples, there was a case when a person took a pet dog for a walk in the park. Sitting on a bench started to comb the dog where hairs were falling onto the ground and was given a fixed penalty by a PCSO for dropping litter. Really is this justifiable, when there are some other blatant cases. A council enforcement officer reports a person who walking from his home having had the mail handed to him by his postman continues walking to work. On route discovering the contents relate to unwanted junk mail he decides to discard them in the street litter bin. Other irresponsible people may have thrown them to the ground. This person was reported for depositing household waste into bins specifically designed for street litter. It was a one off, not as if this person had taken his black bin liner half full from home to throw in the bin which would have been totally different. The whole of this book could be filled with ridiculous stories that have taken place so frequently throughout the country and quite rightly reported in the media. The problem is these incidents are still regularly happening and some guidance on policies in some cases, in my view should be looked at again.

With so many more serious other offences being committed where the offence can easily be detected goes unchecked, where efforts should be made to prosecute the offender. No different to my theory when being on patrol if you look for serious offences they take a little longer to detect but you only find what you are looking for. Such as throwing food from motor vehicles which is a regular occurrence, or where lazy people abandoning shopping trolleys well away from their place of use, which is theft being too lazy to carry the goods inside. Cases of graffiti or criminal damage all too often overlooked. Yet some police forces and councils have the complete opposite in having low tolerance policies, but just have to use discretion and common sense in applying the law. Some councils with close circuit television in their town centres have operators monitoring activities warning offenders to pick up rubbish which is costly but effective.

So much damage is caused when people are fined by fixed penalty for really frivolous offences and despite appealing and apologising are ordered to pay. Nothing is more irritating and one police force in 2018, their Chief Constable announced anyone speeding just one mile over the limit would be prosecuted. What an utter idiot. No allowance for any technical fault with equipment, or common sense decisions where a warning would suffice. This senior officer was in my view a disgrace to the community he served. What damage to the justice system as it is hard enough to encourage members of the public to come forward if they witness any crime. Does he not know the public are utterly fed up with poor detections of crime, that's if many reported crimes are even investigated due to police cuts all over the UK in the recent years. This when other criminals get off lightly with police cautions sometimes for more than one offence of dishonesty including robbery and house burglary. In my view it is the difference of avoiding court appearances for the really guilty and making those in society made to pay fixed penalties for petty offences knowing the legal alternative would be extremely expensive. During my time of policing many of these kinds of offences were dealt with by way of either no action or a police letter of caution. In that way fairness was more controlled and the public as always were more forthcoming to assist the police.

Today decent members of society, who fall under this umbrella together with victims of crime, are least likely to ever assist the police in the future as they are aggrieved and annoyed in their view of being treated badly. They are not happy with the cautioning of some habitual criminals, when they for the pettiness of their offences are made to feel like criminals themselves. Where a person suffers the indignity of being burgled and in restraining the offender who is subsequently arrested makes a frivolous counter claim of assault and they themselves are arrested appears completely wrong. I know it is a fine line where sometimes justifiable force is used but still the innocent person is arrested and has to prove their innocence. Not that the householder has a right to assault anyone but common sense should always be considered in the rules of arresting anyone. It is through being treated badly that these decent people are now sometimes the witnesses who see crimes and do not come forward. This is all this because of what happened to them, not that this is the correct course of action which I cannot condone but it generates a hatred of authority for being so unfair.

Some decent people inexcusably have also turned to crime especially when hounded for offences of pettiness. It is about time the law now was changed to protect the innocent person and new rules of guidance for what is a proper nuisance offence is and what is not, but again that is only my view. In addition perhaps there should be better training for the individuals responsible for issuing fines for ridiculous offences. This is where they could be taught to use discretion and common sense, which should always be a priority before such action to prosecute is taken. In addition it could be pointed out the negative effect it has against decent members of society who are the real victims in these blunders.

CHAPTER 19

WORKING RED LIGHT AREAS - OFFENCES INVOLVING PROSTITUTION

We had growing intelligence that certain licensed premises within the boundary of the town centre were allowing their premises to be used for the purposes of prostitution. There were two female prostitutes who were plying their trade, encouraging sexual activities with acts of lewdness and indecency. All being performed in public places and at other bed sit premises nearby.

Monty and I were both requested to investigate even though it meant moving away from our own areas for a while, faced with the challenge of achieving a positive result. We planned our task ahead it was a completely different side to police work never experienced before. Its location was alien to our everyday policing and the fact we were not known by any of local drinkers or other cliental, assisted us greatly. We had a Technical Support Unit, who loaned us for that time, state of the art high quality zoom lens and fast action cameras capable of taking professional pictures of high clarity. Sounds good, but they were cumbersome and easily attractable and we had to be very careful, bearing in mind our role would be incognito and we did not want to blow our cover. Due to this, we were aware the camera could not be used in gaining all our evidence but it supported the identity and behaviour of the persons involved. When I think now of changes in electronics with micro size high definition cameras, video recording and picture taking facilities, evidence gathering today would have been much easier, but that's progress. The use of a camera proved to be an asset but with other evidence we had to keep logs of everything we considered relevant and these were made up at the time, or as soon after an event as possible depending where we were situated.

We commenced our enquiries over several days during a four week period, mostly early evenings at the location targeted and parked at secluded vantage points. We used an old car we had borrowed from a garage proprietor we both knew and the job fully reimburses our costs for petrol and taking out appropriate insurance cover. Our dress was appropriate to the area and we soon fitted in the environment remaining unnoticed. It was not before long, within a couple of weeks we had built up good evidence of two prostitutes who were openly soliciting inside the main bar of the licensed premises. In addition we saw growing evidence supporting a man who regularly accompanied the women who on occasions picked them up in his vehicle driving them to various locations. He was later identified and it became clear he was their Pimp, being the man responsible for controlling them both.

Majority of occasions they would take male clients out to the rear car park, which was quiet and unused except for their activities. We were able to keep watch from other outside places concealing the camera inside our anoraks. At every opportunity we were able to take pictures with a view to identifying those involved. We also frequented the public house and for a short time mingled with the locals. The purpose of the exercise was to identify criminal offences, as prostitutes working alone from a private home is not an offence in itself, except where there are two working at the same establishment and the premises then are classed as a brothel where they would all commit offences.

We noticed a pattern emerging amongst the girls and their pimp, sometimes up to three times each week he would collect them early evening from outside the public house and drive them in his vehicle towards the main city within our force area. Bearing in mind this man was unemployed he was certainly living above his lifestyle driving around in a flashy two tone convertible which was virtually brand new. In the decoy vehicle we followed them and this soon became easy. They were all heading to the infamous red light area which was well known to the authorities. If we lost them at any time in heavy traffic, we always drove back to the same area where we soon located both girls soliciting openly in the streets. Both girls engaged with several clients. The one girl was short with auburn hair and in her early thirties. She was possibly attractive at a distance, but the closer you saw her it was clear she was not in the high class category and this obviously reflected on the prices charged. The second woman was of similar age with black hair and despite being pretty she was well overweight again reflecting the income she too could expect to earn. What a dangerous occupation with continual risks of violence and the risk of infection through unprotected sex. This at a time when Aids and HIV infections were at their greatest they certainly were dicing with death. At least when the matter was finally dealt with we could refer them to the correct authorities to ensure they were offered counselling or appropriate advice.

If not present on our arrival, they soon returned being dropped off by punters using their own cars. The main business was conducted by kerb crawlers which later became an offence in itself. Today this restricts the practice to a certain degree, but some men still run the risk of being caught and having their names published in the local newspapers following conviction of offences committed by them. We soon had plenty of evidence including photographs, showing the pimp associating with both girls regularly transported them to these locations. In some cases both women would stay at the pimp's home overnight, other times the girls went to their respective addresses. Not being discriminatory but the girls in question were not the cleanest by nature and to some degree were quite scruffy in appearance. Whether it is in the town, or in the city or just round the corner, it is the local people who suffer from this undignified behaviour where children can be vulnerable and other women young and old can be propositioned when just going about their own private life, totally unconnected. It is basically a social menace, not only having girls parade for prostitution on the streets, but the ever increasing volume of traffic associated with kerb crawlers in any location.

In addition to this, back on our area there were times when the girls used one of their home addresses to continue their business. One Saturday afternoon we were parked in the street and fairly inconspicuous to the activities surrounding us. We couldn't believe how blatantly this queue of men were all waiting in turn to enter this house where the girls were conducting their trade. With the pimp also being at this location, they were all involved in running a Brothel. We were able to take pictures even from a short distance away, as we had our camera well positioned slightly protruding from a newspaper we were purporting to be reading. One thing we learned from our experiences of these kinds of observations, you always think that you have been clocked, when in actual fact you have gone on unnoticed. The worst part is to panic and this proved to be a valuable learning curve as discussed in the next case.

All in all between them they were each earning a fair amount of money, plus the added luxury of having rent, council tax paid together with employment benefit. When we had sufficient evidence we took out warrants and all were arrested. They all admitted responsibility when confronted with what we had seen and recorded. Both prostitutes cooperated with our enquiries and rather than them being prosecuted, they were both used as witnesses. As for the man running them he was charged with the offence of living off immoral earnings of prostitution. He pleaded guilty and although this main offence against the man was serious, there was no evidence to suggest violence had been used towards either of the women who both willingly participated in their activities. He was sent to prison for 9 months.

An interesting point was this was the first time in the history of our local town that the Magistrates had ever had a conviction for these kinds of offences, something Monty and I were solely responsible for. Today all his earnings or his vehicle would have been confiscated and sold. Although the area where these offences had taken place was policed by a colleague from the same sub-division we could not believe the comments he had made prior to us starting enquiries. The resident beat officer had covered this area for well over three years and blatantly told us he had never seen any signs of prostitution as discussed in the last chapter. It just shows the difference between some efficient experienced officers meticulously clocking everything that moves whilst walking the beat and those others with completely no interest in what is going on around them. Eventually he moved back to working shifts and guess what he later got promoted. He was sent to another division and as soon as he had completed his probation he was transferred back as a sergeant and spent the majority of his career in the custody block. This was a role which he enjoyed, but definitely not our cup of tea and not for us.

The following year, I was again asked to look into reliable information where five men were running prostitutes as a wide scale enterprise and each conspiring together to live off the immoral earnings of prostitution. At this time Monty was completing an attachment to the CID and was working elsewhere. I was with another colleague Pc WATSON who later got promoted into CID. He was also very industrious officer and took pride in his work and like Monty was a very good thief taker. We both later worked together for several years when I later transferred into the same department.

This time the running of the prostitutes was far more organised and we had two teams of officers, conducting separate surveillance where before long four known prostitutes were identified. They were of a higher class and dressed to kill. The girls this time were reasonably attractive, all initially coming from fairly good backgrounds. The one girl in particular was of extremely high standing as her father was a senior military officer, totally unaware of his daughter's associates and her new found pedigree. Eventually when he discovered her role he was utterly devasted and very deeply hurt. All the men were unemployed and the common denominator which drew us to their attention was the fact that they were regularly hiring motor vehicles to take the girls to various vice areas in three different cities. One city was located within an adjoining force area, the other two within our police area. All the men lived within the town area where I was stationed and again we soon recognised a pattern of travel to assist us in culminating the evidence required. We again had access to decoy vehicles and professional camera equipment. They would initially travel in the direction of the one city then divert all of a sudden in the opposite way to confuse any police presence and travel to this other location. If they used the motorway we knew they were travelling out of the force area to the other city. We liaised with the Vice Squad of this city and on our behalf having photos of the men and girls involved assisted in obtaining evidence supporting our case.

With all men using hire vehicles, every time they were stop checked by uniform officers, they would simply return that vehicle the following day in exchange for a replacement. There was one occasion where we were keeping observations from a vehicle and one of the men we were watching who was heavily involved came up to us.

Unknowing to him, we actually had him on photograph a short moment before in possession of one of the hire vehicles. He had come to a block of flats to pick up one of the girls and he directly approached us. He said, "What are you watching me for?" He recognised me and I immediately replied, a little tongue in cheek, but convincingly, "We are watching a stolen car over there can you go away now you are blowing our cover." He said, "Okay, sorry mate." He then walked off satisfied we had nothing to do with him, but I had to keep a low profile after that as I could not be seen twice. We also adopted their style and changed our motor vehicle. I had to smile later in the case when I introduced this into the evidence and combined with the photograph taken, he knew he had fallen for the third card trick.

As soon as this was realised we built up good relations with senior staff of all the major car rental companies and were alerted in advance of which vehicles they would be using. All girls would solicit for the purposes of prostitution in each of the three city centre red light districts. With their fairly attractive looks as stated, each had no problem plying their trade at every opportunity and raking in monies which gave them and their pimps the lifestyle they could not otherwise afford. Not only were they putting themselves at risk to infection but also when not under the protection of the pimps were vulnerable targets for the weird and depraved. You may wonder why on earth did they subjected themselves to such a degrading enterprise. Surely nothing is worse than selling yourself to complete strangers, or running the risk of their families finding out about their secret pastime which is exactly what did eventually happen. I just hoped they found a new and more honest pathway to enjoying their lives than being exploited in such a degrading way.

When we had sufficient evidence, arrest warrants were obtained for each of the men and like in the last case all were arrested. Sadly out of the five men involved one was not present in the arrests and he remained wanted for some considerable period of time before finally being arrested. When the men were confronted with the evidence they admitted their involvement, but each one minimising their role. All the girls cooperated and made witness statements, but denied they had been threatened in any way to pursue their activities.

As for the outstanding fifth man it was imperative he was found and arrested as quickly as possible, as this complicated the prosecution file. The offender was a convicted criminal for various offences and well known by most of the efficient police officers at our station. Naturally having four in custody all to be interviewed, statements from the girls and enquiries to make, we were completely absorbed in our work. The fantastic thief taker whom I gave the information to about the dishonest nurse stealing purses in the hospital was in our briefing room. He stated he was uncommitted and this came as no surprise to ourselves. This officer stated he knew the outstanding man extremely well as he had previous dealings. I produced the offender's record with an update photograph and in front of several officers he confirmed it was the same person he had previous dealings with. Although dubious of this officer's professionalism I explained how imperative it was that he was arrested and bought to this police station. We knew where he was to be at a certain time later that afternoon for a job interview and this was again confirmed by the source. The sergeant told him to take assistance and keep observations in plain clothes.

Later that day we received a message that the offender had indeed made his visit and had stayed at the premises for several minutes but left without having been arrested. It transpired this officer we had involved, who had several years' experience, decided to go alone for the possible glory of bringing the offender to justice. We later established this officer had his facts completely wrong, it had been someone else he had dealt with and not ever dealing with man in question. During his observations he had failed to recognise him at all and allowed him to go. What an idiot I know he had a justifiable telling off from our Superintendent. Just one weak link in a chain, just what we did not need. These type of people really frustrate intense dedicated workings of any active police team. So we had no choice but to circulate this outstanding offender as wanted and on the run, causing duplicate the work in separating the case into two files.

It was suggested some of the girls had been confronted initially with threats of being burned with electric irons but this was venomously denied by all implicated. I felt deep down I could not help believing sadly there was an element of truth about all these allegations, as some of the men had reputations for violence, but without any evidence to support the matter the subject could not be raised. The four prostitutes were all previously found guilty of offences of soliciting for prostitution in public places, some having several convictions. The daughter of the military officer was a person of good character at the start of our operation, but twice she was arrested and cautioned for this offence and the third time went to court and was convicted of the offence. This is normal police procedure and necessary to prove our offence as for living off immoral earnings all had to be convicted prostitutes.

In addition to our evidence we also had evidence from another city outside our force area when the same prostitutes had been see soliciting in red light areas, having been dropped off in their cars by their pimps. All this evidence was incorporated into our file.

There was considerable evidence of high spending amongst them all, on vehicles, taxis and fast living. I checked production of driving documents registers at two main police stations in our area covering the whole period of surveillance. This was hard painstaking work as in a month or so you can just imagine how many drivers had elected to produce documents. Today these forms are rarely issued if at all, due to the vehicle number plate recognition system where any offences committed are mainly taken by street camera, or police vehicle camera and followed up by police visits to the driver's home addresses. All documents are today all available online with insurance, MOT and DVLA for excise licence and driving licence, providing full up to date details. After searching the registers against all those drivers named I found positive results. My dedicated efforts had paid off. I had three occasions when one of the same defendants using his own vehicle had been stopped by the police and had given in his documents for recording. All were in order, no wonder from the money he had been earning but upon scrutinising each entry I came up with amazing information. Today this kind of manual search would not be possible. It recorded the garage location of where the car had undergone an MOT test and the date was directly in the middle of our surveillance period. I made enquiries with the garage proprietor and established apart from the test he had paid for a full vehicle service and extensive mechanical repairs amounting to several hundreds of pounds. The owner had documentation bearing the car owners signature that the work was successfully carried out and he was given a receipt also signed by the defendant that he had settled the bill paid in full by him in cash. In addition the owner informed me the defendant paid a similar sum of cash at the adjacent premises, where he had his vehicle completely resprayed and re-upholstered. Excellent corroboration of living well beyond his means and full detailed statements of evidence were obtained.

In addition I made enquiries with many taxi drivers and established all those charged had often used their facilities hiring taxis for small journeys. Many whilst the drivers were paid for waiting for them to visit licensed premises and supermarkets to complete vast amounts of shopping. A luxury for anyone yet alone the unemployed pimps. Again written evidence was obtained from all witnesses. All this evidence along with the full cost of hiring brand new vehicles at 2 or 3 days at a time and sometimes two vehicles hired together, which also amounted to a very high figure of money paid out.

Eventually all those arrested remained in custody and were committed to Crown court to stand trial. At the trial all pleaded not guilty and the evidence commenced. All prostitutes involved turned up and gave evidence along with several of the car hire staff. Midway through proceedings all barristers advised the judge their clients had decided to change their plea to that of guilty. I went into the witness box to give evidence of antecedence history and of previous convictions and to my surprise whilst there the judge made a compliment, something I will never forget. He commended myself and other officers in respect of outstanding police work bringing the offenders to justice. It is not very often in the police service that you receive a Judges Commendation and so I considered myself very fortunate. In addition he thanked the business staff for assisting the police and those turning up to give evidence. All those convicted received prison sentences.

I recall back at the station I was asked if I wanted a Chief Constables commendation for my part in the investigation, but I politely declined stating it was a team effort by all the officers involved and felt it was unfair to take full credit. I could see why because one of the officers who received the judges commendation, unknown to the judge he only played a minor part. He was off sick after his first day, again not very experienced in this kind of police work, although he had several year's service. We were watching at one location for the offenders to arrive. He purported to walk around drunk to see if he could get a better view all to my annoyance as he was clumsy and drew attention to himself. He might as well had of been drunk because he fell over and twisted his ankle and was off duty for the rest of the enquiry recovering from his injury. What an embarrassment so a well-deserved judge's commendation awarded to him just for falling over and placed onto his personal file. As for the outstanding offender he remained at large for several months living in an unknown area believed one of the major cities in the UK. He later was arrested and was interviewed by myself and another colleague as I was then working in CID which I discuss in a later chapter.

Yet today in 2018, prostitution certainly has not gone away, in fact it is now a lucrative sordid business as many woman from abroad, mainly third world and Eastern European countries are sneaked into the UK or have entered legally believing they were entering work contracts. These poor women all to be run by mobsters and people traffickers. Many of these women having been tricked then possibly drugged and kidnapped or subject to threats and intimidation. They are mainly forced to participate in sexual activities in make-shift brothels, where those that control them receive reward in regular high earnings. Those that are wanted by police and border control agencies avoid escape by moving around various premises and different areas.

So on the subject of prostitution this is the worst possible example and as a nation we appear to have gone backwards. Many people in this country go about their lives quietly, who have absolutely no idea this is going on, or how these criminals work and are totally unaware of how commonplace this all is. The fact is, this sick, disgusting, evil criminal behaviour is in most of our towns and cities and sadly involves also many decent people British citizens of all races and ages. On this issue alone the police today certainly have their hands full in dealing with this escalating problem.

CHAPTER 20

VIOLENT ACTIVITIES REQUIRING POSITIVE POLICE ACTION

Today Great Britain is still a fantastic country for allowing freedom of speech with strong support for people from all walks of life. With the Human Rights Act and other controversial laws passed for separate detection of offences, some organisations and local authorities were virtually in some isolated cases perhaps close to playing the role of big brother. They had been given powers to prosecute many of the byelaw offences and other nuisance matters independently of the police. However, discretion and fairness must always be a priority in dealing with such cases which thankfully most organisations and local authorities adhered to.

Whatever happens we should all try and pull together and although Scotland voted to stay in the UK, we still have politicians above the border still trying to go independent, who knows what the future will hold, especially if Wales and Northern Ireland follow suit. Let's hope common sense prevails. The consequences for the police will however remain the same under English law. We just need those in society who offend and continue to commit acts of crime to be dealt with more positively. The issue of law and order to be correctly restored so there is a deterrent to committing crime reclaiming real credibility for the future. In present day there is so much information claiming crime is down, but being realistic is it a play on words. Are crime figures being played down, or people not reporting them or are they being classified as less serious crime than what they really are.

Either way crimes of violence and murders with firearms and knives tragically seem an everyday event.

Over the years of policing, violence against officers has continually increased with any severe deterrent getting less effective due in my view only to soft sentencing. Then you get the situations where arrest is inevitable as the offender refuses to come quietly or tries to escape, knowing he has committed an offence which has clearly been explained to him. In many cases they just accept it but then at times some offenders just lose it and become violent and enraged and commence fighting. The amount of force used in restraining such persons can fluctuate considerably, as each incident is different. This is where the nine o'clock critic often feels justified in making comments. The fact that he or she was not present at such time is immaterial to this person as all they can do is criticise police action taken. An easy thing to do giving negative views when not confronted with any danger, where the police officer dealing often has to make a decision on the spur of the moment.

Sometimes when attending a violent incident action needs to be taken without delay, to prevent serious injury to the officer or any other person, especially when it is impossible to speak common sense to get through to such person who refuses to calm down. In incidents that happen in current times police in certain cases have no alternative but to protect themselves and members of the public. Of course there can be occasions when an overzealous police officer has acted unreasonably and just gone too far and self defence has become an act of hostility and classed as assault. This not acceptable under any circumstances and should never be tolerated, but all circumstances must be thoroughly investigated and judged by their merits. Yet whenever an officer defends himself either with pepper spray, taser type stun guns or use of a truncheon or the worst scenario the use of a firearm there is always an enquiry. When the officer has himself been threatened with a loaded gun or has been fired at or indeed injured there is a public outcry in some cases even more so when the offender was the victim. Did he contribute to the dangerous incident giving the police officer no choice but to protect himself from injury or the public. Was the officer under threat and alone when facing violence from more than one person, or was it the opposite situation with the offender outnumbered by police. All important factors to consider.

When you go back to earlier days of policing things were so much different and I recall several examples where such arrests were made, which possibly would be frowned upon today where some people would imply perhaps excessive force was used.

I recall a dog handler telling me of an incident he was called to attend at a fish and chip shop where the proprietor was having trouble with a known violent drunkard, who refused to leave his premises. Upon arrival the man was shouting and swearing and when confronted by the officer took a swing towards him with his clenched fist. The officer without hesitation struck back in self defence with his fist striking him to the jaw where the man fell to the floor. This man was a regular trouble maker and had a serious reputation for being violent through drink where normally two officers would be needed to apprehend him. Although six inches shorter the officer stood no messing the last thing he was going to do was end up rolling all over the floor perhaps allowing this man to gain the advantage in being able to overpower him. He then placed the offender into the recovery position and held there whilst awaiting assistance. The man was then handcuffed by other officers and taken to the police station. The shop owner immediately showed his disapproval of the action taken. Can you believe it? The officer had attended and dealt with the incident positively, without any assistance from the proprietor who otherwise may have been a victim of a nasty assault. When people are violent and assaulting you the time for talking is over, but perhaps not in this politically correct world as some people would have you believe. You cannot have it both ways where violence is imminent and the issue is self-preservation and safety after all, the officer in these circumstances is entitled to reasonably defend himself. This was put forward into his evidence and accepted by the court.

Another similar story was in the main town where I was stationed. We had a very tall uniform police Inspector who was some 6ft 6inches in height. He was a typical gentle giant and a Geordie, well-mannered and extremely approachable. Despite his politeness, make no mistake he was no fool and he certainly did not suffer foolish idiots at any price. This officer had obtained a law degree and later became a clerk to the magistrates after retiring from the police force. He was in the main shopping precinct in the town when two well-built youths in their late teens were misbehaving and becoming abusive and threatening. He warned them firmly about their conduct but their behaviour continued resulting in him arresting them both for public order offences. It was quite amusing when he restrained them both on arrest and held them firmly with each arm in a headlock and quietly walked them both in his grasp, the short distance to the police station. How embarrassing for these two louts who thought they were above the law. I think their future behaviour was a little more respectful as a result of that encounter. Following a later visit to the magistrate's court they made their apologies and were duly fined.

It was no different when a violent escapee from prison had committed a very nasty robbery whilst still out on the run from prison. Information came into the control room that he was seen drinking in the main bar of his local public house. This man had been at large for over 6 months. Officers were directed to the scene and this one officer, a former rugby player of stocky build well capable of handling himself entered the premises on arrival to confront him. Immediately the criminal at large without hesitation smashed a pint glass and lunged towards the uniform officer with intent to imbed the glass into the officer's face. As a result in self defence the officer struck the man immediately to his chin, with one blow from his right hand putting him down onto the bar floor where he was restrained dis-armed and placed into custody.

This horrible creature even had the audacity to make a complaint of assault before the station sergeant on arrival at the station, which was later investigated and found that the officer's actions were fully justified. This offender's picture and profile was earlier that year shown on a crime television series and the public informed he was wanted and requested sightings, with a warning for members of the public that the man was extremely dangerous and not to approach him. This was clearly good advice and could not have been more true seen by his behaviour on arrest. The man was charged and returned immediately to prison. He later got convicted for escape from prison and committing armed robbery, where the sentence reflected the behaviour of this criminal.

It was just so good to see positive policing where a dangerous man was taken off the streets, to be held in a more secure prison for several more years which he clearly deserved. Yet again some justified do-gooder would probably criticise this kind of police action taken, pity they were not the victim at the receiving end of his most serious crimes, they certainly would take a different refection on things or perhaps not.

Back in 2013 on the television news and other media, a man in possession of two large knives was behaving strangely in front of members of the public outside Buckingham Palace in London. Police officers were called with some uniform officers carrying firearms. Although several officers were present this man clearly was a danger to everyone including himself. No direct threats had been directed at the public due to the fast arrival of the police, where the man started becoming aggressive. One police officer immediately used a stun gun to incapacitate him and he was taken into custody which definitely saved him from causing injury to himself and possibly others.

Whist this news clip was being shown during a television discussion program a female presenter criticised the use of a stun gun. This again is an ideal example of the nine o'clock critic, making comments from the comfort of her armchair away from any threats or danger. She suggested a stun gun was unnecessary and that a pepper spray would have been more effective. This is easy to point out and was possibly stated in good faith, but when confronted with a man with razor sharp knives time is the essence, as he could have used the knives slashing his own throat or elsewhere and lashed out in all directions attacking police officers. Would the same person then have stated it could have been dealt with some other way or have been avoided. In the eyes of some people it was seen to be justified and others not. In this politically correct world you just cannot win, but I am sure common sense must always be applied. The officer only had a split second or two to make his decision and then act. With the eyes of the world's cameras trained upon him, in my view it was well done to him and his brave action. I had to smile when this positive police action was supported by a second television presenter on the same show who stated the complete opposite to that of his colleague. He pointed out that the police officer was also carrying a firearm and that almost certainly if this had happened in other parts of the world the offender would have been shot. In this case he clearly was not. Enough said.

Then you have the situation where today there are marches where political groups quite rightly are allowed to protest their views to protest their views and thoughts over various issues. This is fine providing it is a peaceful demonstration and there are no threats or intimidation made against any individual or member of the public or police officer. What I believe is no one should be allowed to cover their faces to hide their identity, nurses, doctor's firemen, railway staff and many other workers always demonstrate peacefully, apart from sometimes the odd individual acting alone and breaking the law. Those hiding their identity often turn a peaceful demonstration into a full blown riot, where petrol bombs are thrown and vehicles over-turned and set alight. In many cases this is a premeditated course of action and those hiding their faces should be arrested as a deterrent for such trouble. In fact covering your face in public is a serious threat to security and in my view should be a serious offence in itself.

Naturally the police for intelligence purposes video such events as a public safeguard. It is interesting also to note that whilst demonstrations are in progress members of such groups are also involved in videoing police activity also. It is only fair if a police officer found abusing his position with excess force, should be rooted out and prosecuted and for this reason video filming is good, but unfair where those covering their faces are allowed to get away with it. How things have changed over the years, modern technology at its most intriguing or is it society gone mad.

With most individuals in possession of modern mobile telephones having camera, video and audio recording facilities the policeman today is very much in the eye of the public. All the more reason for police having body cameras at all times when on duty, but where will it all end. The term the public seeing your good points as a police officer, but also your bad points has never been more appropriate. It is a sad indictment but today in some isolated cases someone would rather video a police officer dealing with a difficult incident, than going to his assistance when clearly he or she is in need of urgent help. No different with the same people standing around and doing nothing when others are attacked. Thankfully there appears to be more cases when the brave citizen steps in to tackle the lout committing such offences. Indeed we have had examples of ladies of pension age stopping robberies and other crimes, not that we encourage this, but they must be commended. No one can blame anyone for not getting involved as every case has to be assessed on its merits, but when the offender is surrounded by numerous people capable of stopping his violent actions, it is sad and disgraceful no one gets involved to stop any further attacks on innocent people.

This is where the punishment should fit the crime as without a proper deterrent to punish offenders, members of the public feel they are not protected enough, so you cannot blame them completely. Those that do assist the police should be paid substantial payments from public funds and the offender made to repay even if from his benefits. With all this technology in use at any time, any police officer who crosses the line whilst on duty today can expect what he or she deserves, after all if the police cannot behave and show restraint no one can.

Whenever members of the public, video or photograph someone badly injured or close to death, or person sadly been killed, leaving these people or the deceased without any dignity is just unbelievable and totally unacceptable. This is especially disturbing when downloaded onto various websites and sent around the world and should amount to a criminal offence in itself, especially causing alarm or distress to friends or relatives. All the offenders should be named shamed and prosecuted.

CHAPTER 21

GETTING PRIORITIES RIGHT –
HOW NOT TO POLICE

M ajority of beat officers who worked at our police station were selected for their many qualities in being able to communicate well with the public, in giving high profile policing in the neighbourhood combined with close contact with communities in liaising with schools and other organisations. Giving talks where necessary on everyday policing and crime prevention, together with visits by school pupils and other groups to our main sub-divisional police stations. This would involve showing them police equipment, with a visit to the police cells providing no one was in custody at that time. In addition the radio control room the nerve centre of ongoing normal police operations. Later they would all be shown traffic fast response vehicles and motor cycles and police dogs. All this created a fascinating experience for our younger generation where professionalism was of extreme importance.

In addition officer's walking the beat were chosen for various skills necessary to get the best out of the job in that they developed good intelligence skills in monitoring criminal activities leading to the detection and prevention of crime. This was of particularly importance in assisting in serious criminal offences involving rape, robbery and murder, as the knowledge gained by a meticulous uniformed beat officer's in knowing their patch was invaluable in such investigations in identifying suspects and witnesses in various parts of the community. The regular movements of tradesmen or people visiting the area of their beat with whom knowledge could be obtained and who the investigating team could contact who was approachable, reliable, or trustworthy. Also most important was the activities of certain known criminals and who they were associating with. All issues which make it easier to build up patterns of behaviour in detecting crime. In my view anyone falling short of this criteria should not be a uniform policeman and certainly not solely responsible for their own police area. It is all about getting priorities right in everyday policing which I am happy to say during my whole service detecting crime at all levels was a priority.

Of course in all organisations not everyone is the same, some beat officers amazingly have different priorities. One would think that the ultimate goal of every walking policeman would be the detection of crime and other offences. Not the case. We had one policeman on the beat that had a red light area on his patch and didn't even know it or believe it. He used to walk through it every day and night without realising it was happening all around him. Later this was proved in a positive way when Monty and I both dealt with a case of living off the immoral earnings of prostitution, within that same location. It was to our amazement the person covering that beat actually told us to our faces there were no prostitutes active or any red light area within his policing territory. What was he blind he later learned to regret those words as he was proved totally wrong more than once.

On another busy beat consumed with crime, we had another officer who spent most of his time chasing offenders who allowed their dogs to foul the pavement or lawns and reported many who committed these offences. Fine I agree very commendable providing there is at least a mixture of cases especially some who are involved in crime, after all locking up criminals should be the number one priority for any policeman especially those walking the beat. That's why they were selected in the first place but for some it was more difficult than what they had thought. The problem was this particular officer, he became obsessed with dog fouling offences and at one time was the talk of the station. If he wanted to pursue a career in that direction I was sure at the time there were plenty of vacancies in the parks department of the local council.

We had this other policeman who had joined the force. He was an excellent runner and extremely fit and although coincidental his character, is closely mirrored by the role of PC Penhale stationed in the fictional television comedy series Doc Martin featuring the seaside village of Port Wenn real name being Port Isaac in Cornwall. He entered all major police sporting events, all paid for in the firms time while we carried on doing the job paid to do being police work. I will never forget they gave him his own beat, in one of the other crime ridden housing estates on our sub-division. However he was a unique individual and very friendly. This officer was gifted in teaching chess and at a local youth centre on his beat he regularly tried to learn teenagers which was admirable. Fantastic for community relations, if we had wanted a social worker we could have employed one. However the main purpose on the beat at that time was dealing with the high volume of crime and building up local criminal knowledge, but I believe that area of police work like so many then and today, was not his priority.

I remember he had this man in custody that was well known for being an easy target and had admitted several burglaries. Certainly this officer had improved in my estimation and clearly had the potential after all to be a good thief taker. The prisoner had given all items of property to other associates and there were a further six people to arrest and bring into custody. He asked for my help but I only had one day, as I was soon due to go on leave. However I was able to assist in one of the interviews where one person eventually came clean with the truth and admitted responsibility. He was charged with handling stolen goods. The remainder of people to be seen were all down to him, he would have to spend the next few days fetching them in and dealing with them accordingly after all I had done my best and was looking forward to valuable time with my family and a good rest. I told him to seek help and advice if needed from any other experienced colleague, which I later found he had chosen to ignore.

When his file of evidence was submitted for prosecution, only two people out of all of them finally arrested were dealt with at court. The burglar and the one man I assisted with in interview for handling stolen property. The main investigation went downhill thereafter, obviously no proper interviewing skills were applied and no action was taken against all remaining offenders. I decided to look through the prosecution file, which immediately saw was heavily criticised by senior officers, in bold green ink, with advice – insufficient evidence to prosecute. No wonder when I read witness statements, I saw that this officer had taken several independent witness statements from the man charged with burglary. His correct details were shown and I could not believe he had given his occupation which was accepted and taken down as a criminal. The first paragraph being he was a criminal and earned his living by breaking into houses and other buildings, as a trespasser and stealing property. Is it lawful to be a professional criminal, would this affect his benefits or should he be charged income tax. Just how on earth did these reports even get past his supervisor sergeant who like most of us was normally very thorough, but perhaps he thought it was all correct and just signed it off. I am sure he did not read the file fully, as from the comments made it also sadly would reflect against him. Obviously he believed the file was up to the normal high standard and should have checked it meticulously, I know I would have done. However we can all make mistakes. For a man who had three year's service and had passed his exams to sergeant, he had absolutely no idea as to putting into place the practical elements of police work.

Guess what happened he was promoted to sergeant and transferred division, how on earth could he supervise other officers. It is no good being able to run and catch a criminal, better to know his identity in the first place, especially when you did not know how to deal with him when caught. This is just one example I relate to when criticising bad choices for promotion and was an insult to the more suitable candidates.

In fairness it was not always the younger officer I came across, but also many senior uniform constables who just had not got a clue when dealing with even the lesser criminal offences and that is a sad indictment. What had they done in their service in their role as constable in clearing crime, hardly nothing. Not even enough detail that you could write and fill on the back of a postage stamp. You could not state they were unenthusiastic as they would sort out all the offences involving bad behaviour involving youths and obviously had many other qualities. When they came to you asking for advice on extremely basic issues concerning just theft it was amazing. They just did not have a clue I would have been completely embarrassed and ashamed. Surely those in supervision must have known what the real levels of experience were. Thank god there were many other uniform colleagues who were the complete opposite and were actually excellent thief takers in their own right.

Sadly you also had the other kind of officer who like many for no reason would be completely obnoxious when dealing with members of the public. It was when I had transferred from a rural force to an urban area and with this one officer who had several year's service but clearly lacked experience and should have behaved better. He approached this middle aged lady who had parked her car incorrectly and in breach of parking regulations. To say he had given her a telling off was an understatement, far worse than anyone who has received a caution of crime. His behaviour just resembled a typical Hitler character and all so unnecessary. He made her feel lost for words, upset and completely demoralised. I remember thinking even a traffic warden would not behave like that. I walked away in disgust and later told him if he ever spoke to anyone again like that in my presence I would report him, regardless of his length of service.

Small world a few years later and he too came to me for advice of a petty nature involving a theft. I thought all your service and you don't even know the basics. How would he have dealt with that same poor motorist if she had been involved in a serious crime he wouldn't have had a clue. Some officers just had no shame and no sense of priority of offences. He to me was an embarrassment to the whole police force.

We had another officer at the station who worked a separate beat area. He was also very popular and friendly, but also extremely limited in his abilities. He was described as being thorough or meticulous in his work was an over statement, but all for the wrong reasons. Yes there are times when this quality is essential and important, but occasions warrant where dignity of a person should take precedence. The officer who also had several year's service received a complaint from a victim being bitten by a dangerous dog. A common type of incident you would believe, not when this officer had finishing taking the witness statement from the lady, who was in her late forties.

The story starts seeing a pack of dogs at the other side of the public park, while she is some distance away reading a book seated at a bench. The dogs get closer and the one dog in question goes immediately up to her. He wraps his front legs around the ladies one leg, where he allows the poor witness to describe in graphic detail the dog having sexual gratification at her expense, resulting in her smacking the dog which eventually bit her. The officer just could not understand what all the fuss was about but unknown to the poor lady a copy of her statement circulated like wildfire throughout the organisation of a prime example of what is relevant or not in a witness statement.

All we see patrolling on foot and around the areas I have lived and worked are PCSO [police community support officers] who appear to have replaced uniform constables, whether this is true or not I do not know, or if the same takes place in other parts of the country. In fairness we have to ask the question is, 'Where is the old fashioned bobby who used to patrol our streets?' Is he now fully committed all of each working day, or are resources just unable to provide this type of policing anymore. It just feels sad as having as having a local policeman on duty, it was always the public that would trust you and they would confide in giving useful pieces of information concerning offenders in all avenues of police work.

I think it is appropriate to mention this style of policing is sorely missed in today's society and how PCSO's are in no way comparable to having a bobby on the beat. So nothing really can substitute the police officer in this role, as PCSO's are not qualified or trained up to this standard and have no direct powers of arrest. So if someone confided in giving information, the PCSO can only really pass it on through proper police channels. Even a special constable working voluntary and part time has more power than a PCSO. It is not their fault they are restricted in their duties as some do show initiative and work hard. As for these good officers who show potential they should be encouraged to re-train, qualify and apply for the position of constable. Should a vacancy arise they should be appointed, but like all things in life it is down to costs and restraints on the police service in today's financial climate.

CHAPTER 22

ANNOYING DANGEROUS DRIVING HABITS

In my first chapter I related the facts of a car chase revealing some of the most dangerous aspects of motoring involving serious traffic offences. It was just fortunate that no person was fatally injured. In that car chase the driver was disqualified which means automatically having no insurance.

What people do not realise is that it is a privilege to be able to drive or ride on a road and not an automatic right, a privilege that can be removed as quickly as it is given if you decide not to conform to the rules. Whatever the excuse in majority of cases if everyone drove or rode defensively there would never be any accidents and anticipating the actions of other motorists and riders including your own driving manner is a main ingredient in performing this exercise.

This was especially true when policing rural areas of the countryside. Going back to those times and even today the amount of drivers of all ages, whether men or women who just drive without thinking. Travelling round bends even at 30 mph they fail to anticipate exactly just what could be presented in front of them. A tree could have fallen across the road, or a pedestrian walking immediately in the direction of your vehicle. A horse and rider or several of them, a tractor, sheep or cows all where undoubtedly they possibly could not stop or take action to avoid a tragic accident. Those travelling even faster many racing and travelling blind round these bends are a dangerous menace on the roads. The ultimately kill someone else or themselves or passengers. It is a common fact there are more fatal road accidents on country lanes than all other roads apart from motorways. Sadly many could be prevented by driving safer and defensively.

This brings back a sad story my father told me when back in the 1930's. He was in the countryside walking down a steep hill leading to a small village. With him was his girlfriend, both were in their early twenties. It was a narrow lane and they were walking on the side facing the oncoming traffic. They had just cleared a sharp bend and out of nowhere a man on a bicycle just whistled past at 30 to 35 mph and in second was down the road and out of sight. When my father looked back his girlfriend was on the ground after being knocked over, hitting her head violently on the hard road surface where she had died instantly. There were no other witnesses, or any other traffic or people about. It was an early summer evening and he had the awful task of carrying her dead body over his shoulders down to the village where he stopped at the first cottage he came to. Despite police and ambulance attending nothing could be done. There was an inquest and it was ruled accidental death. The cyclist failed to report the incident and was never found. Even back then all totally unavoidable as this was preventable by slowing speed and anticipating other road users. This tragedy stayed with my father for the remainder of his life.

No different to reckless motor vehicle racing by younger people of all races on roads and motorways in fast cars. Sadly today this is on the increase, especially when several cars all race together at isolated areas and organised on the internet. Local byelaws have banned such practices in many areas, but it is still very much a major problem. These are labelled in many areas as 'boy racers'. They are a danger not only to themselves but any other motorists in the vicinity where that drive erratically.

When I was in the police we did not have the instant vehicle recognition number plate facility. This is an extremely valid tool for identifying vehicles that are not covered with road fund licence, Mot or a certificate of insurance. With powers to seize and impound vehicles breaching the law and failing to pay penalties, results in the vehicle being crushed are a giant step forward. Everyone now should know exactly where they stand so if they drive and are not insured they know the consequences, so if you are unsure check before you drive in the first place. One new change in the law which I find hard to swallow now being a retired police officer, is the removal of having to physically purchase and display an excise licence. Some people will find it hard to understand this and sadly some police officers of all ranks. I believe this is a huge mistake and many, many dishonest motorists are getting away driving vehicles without tax. Possibly denied by the authorities. It is good for the honest motorists of all classes of vehicles, but definitely not for police detecting serious criminal offences, in fact another bonus for the criminals. Apart from detecting a vehicle not being taxed, which comes under the umbrella of instant vehicle recognition number plate facility, it leaves a big loop-hole for the dishonest who can regularly drive their vehicles on different false and dirty registration plates. This is one way of avoiding detection for all offences and choosing locations where there are rare police patrols, no cameras and traveling at remote times of the day or night.

At least when the excise licence was displayed, vehicles stood out from each other. Altered stolen false discs would be detected either when the vehicle driven was stopped, or when seen unattended on the road or waste land and known that it was being regularly used. This would lead to many other criminal offences and detection of stolen cars all disguised into a ringed motor vehicle, sometimes all due to the display of an excise licence. The obtaining of discs however was made much easier with the introduction of the internet, which is why I cannot understand the licence being scrapped. In addition the procedure in obtaining the discs, in my view also kept people in jobs which was a bonus for all local post offices for those people who preferred this method of purchase. Retaining the discs in circulation, had more benefits for police and everyone else.

Back in my time without all the technology it was down to skillful questioning of all occupants stopped in vehicles to detect the most serious of offences. The most important issue when you stopped a driver was to establish a positive identity, in case he was purporting to be someone else or using that person's or any other person's documentation. The importance of questioning all passengers was that they may be involved with the driver in covering for him and this would lead to aiding or abetting counselling or procuring the offence. The most obvious for hiding true identity is that the driver may be a wanted criminal, or a person wanted on warrant. The next in line that he is disqualified, which when I was a serving officer always meant the sentence would be custodial with no exceptions.

We had the perfect answer for people driving vehicles with tinted screens thinking they were above the law. Most people I must say when stopped by the police would always give respect and cooperate fully. But hardened villains found this kind of vehicle the perfect excuse to deliberately behave awkwardly and refuse to open doors and windows. In these cases you would need assistance to block their escape. Informing them threatening behaviour and obstructing the police in the execution of their duty, could lead to their arrest was enough to ensure revealed their identity and cooperated. As for today again this is another former problem that is now addressed. Anyone driving with tinted screens today is subjected to a screen visibility test, which if fails is an offence in its own right and if not rectified, possibly renders the insurance for the vehicle invalid.

As far as traffic offences are concerned there is no doubt speeding is an important ingredient when it comes to serious injury road accidents. The traffic department during my period of service were extremely professional in catching persistent motorists who regularly drove recklessly and dangerously and invariably on conviction would lose their licence, some for very lengthy periods. Members of the public would report incidents of seriously bad driving and where justified, possibly with more than one person complaining, these dangerous drivers would be targeted with traffic officers using plain un-marked police vehicles in the normal course of their duties. This was a positive step in taking such people off the roads for the general safety of the public.

With the introduction of speed cameras, this was seen to be controversial with many people, as although it was a deterrent for many an offender, it was also seen as a money making machine for most. In some cases it sometimes created more hazards but there is no doubting without them completely there would be more accidents. I think the main criticism present day is that the main offender responsible for inconsiderate and careless driving or the reckless dangerous driver goes un-detected, as the demand for traffic officers to be used for other general police duties restricts such policies.

I recall being told by a traffic officer back in my earlier days of policing, that discretion in reporting of offenders for speeding offences would always have to be considered and that in some cases it would not be in the spirit of the act to prosecute. This basically related to any minor infringements and would include just being a couple of miles over the speed limit, especially where the offence was found to be committed during the early hours on the morning when there was no danger involved and no other traffic on the road. Whether or not there has been any change in policy today I do not know, but offenders who go through speed cameras are not afforded this air of grace which justifies criticism for these types of equipment being used as a money making scams.

As soon as the Government of the day direct police to weed out the bad drivers who often commit offences away from speed cameras will we see some improvement in driving standards. This is especially true with some foreign motorists and heavy goods vehicle users and other motorists who clearly cannot drive safely on our nation's roads. If these offenders were routinely banned from driving this would tackle the problems with bad motoring and the increase involving sadly deaths of all road users. Where reckless driving causes the death of any other person, the penalties are to be increased substantially in very long periods of imprisonment. At the moment only a Manslaughter charge would allow this. This is very welcome news, especially when the person committing the offence shows no signs of remorse or sympathy for the families of victims.

In addition another major problem is the amount of abuse involved all those people found using mobile phones whilst driving, who not only make telephone calls, but also send text messages and access the internet with iphones and ipads. The offenders would think twice if there was an instant ban tied into a first conviction if only for 3 months, which would act as a real deterrent and would virtually stop offending overnight. Recently the points on the licence has been increased and the fines, but will never sort the problem out, only instant disqualification from driving will.

Another area for concern is the amount of elderly drivers, and those with defective eyesight, who clearly cannot see properly yet continue to drive. I regularly tested these motorists especially following a complaint of bad driving or involvement in a road accident and sadly a significant number failed the eyesight test. All those I dealt with surrendered their driving licences confirming also that their eyesight was below standard and could not be corrected. I appreciate it is sad when a person comes to the end of their driving life, but not at the expense of causing injury or death to other people or indeed themselves.

Another annoying issue is the people who deliberately fail to keep clean their number plates. Some may just forget, but to some drivers it is an excuse not to get traced, especially if they commit crime with a vehicle, fail to stop at road accidents or drive a high speeds through areas with traffic speed cameras. It is hard to distinguish whatever reason may apply to drivers, but for me I would always report them. Having an unreadable number plate is no different to having false plates displayed, as it achieves the same purpose. To some this may seem petty but I always took the serious view for the reasons clearly mentioned.

CHAPTER 23

REAL COURT EXPERIENCES IN THE OLD POLICING DAYS

Magistrates or JP's, known as justices of the peace were first introduced in England and Wales many centuries ago, possibly as far back as the 13th century. Since that time many changes have taken place over the years within the legal system but offenders when charged with criminal offences they first have to appear at the Magistrates court. The less serious offences such as litter, public decency, begging, minor traffic offences, minor theft and common assault plus many other matters are known as summary offences and can only be dealt with by magistrates. Naturally serious criminal offences like in older times have to be dealt with at higher courts known previously as the Assize courts and Quarter Sessions. Today these venues are known as Crown courts.

In the Magistrates and some Assize and Quarter Sessions courts all defendants and witnesses sat together in the same area waiting for their particular case to be called and this was also the case in many Magistrates courts. Back in 1970 each case would follow on, firstly all the guilty cases would be dealt with and then those contested trials would follow on all being in the same large open court area. All witnesses to each individual case had to wait in a room outside the main court until called by the usher.

Majority of the buildings used for such purposes were of extremely historical character and architecture and were indeed places of where justice was or not delivered. In particular the Assize courts in that many were old and established and had that eerie feeling of punishment being duly served out. This would be either in harsh prison sentences or indeed where Judges donned the black caps in giving out the death sentence mainly for crimes of murder, but in older days for many crimes less serious. With certain parts of the court such as the Judges seat facing the dock and the witness box, all at a much higher level than the remainder of the court which of course was at ground level. How intimidating for both witnesses and offenders alike. In some towns or cities some of these old buildings are now used as Magistrates courts. Imagine standing in the dock where condemned prisoners once stood only difference being your offence is speeding instead of murder.

There were funny times, perhaps embarrassing, but all under the umbrella of the law which must be adhered to at all times. We had a police officer give evidence of a man offending who had been charged with drunk and disorderly. As the officer told the court the full facts, he repeatedly referred to the bad swearing used by the defendant which mainly involved the f word. As he gave evidence this word was used in nearly every sentence. Upon cross examination the officer was asked, 'Well what did you do then?' I recall him saying without realising, "I just fucking arrested him." No problem mentioning what the defendant said, but no reason for him to use the same language. The court was in uproar momentarily, until the noise was quelled by the chief Magistrate sitting. Nevertheless the man was found guilty and fined.

I remember a police Inspector telling me the story of when he was a young police constable in Yorkshire and present in a small magistrates court in a quiet country town. The man appeared on a charge of theft, to which after a short trial, was found guilty. In summing up the magistrate told him, 'If I thought you had done it, I would have sent you to prison, so that's why on this occasion I am going to fine you." The police Inspector was close to the end of his service, so the incident was during the 1940's, whatever happened after that I don't know. In any case I could have imagined it having taken place back in those days. If that happened at my time or in present day, it would have been on the evening news and travelled all around the globe. Barristers and solicitors would have had a field day, especially with the Human Rights Act, how times change.

In one other case, I remember a traffic policeman went into the witness box, to give his evidence in full view of a packed court. He took the oath and gave his name rank and number. Then a sudden unusual silence occurred, which seemed to last for ages resulting in the officer, who was to have given his evidence verbatim, admitted he was sorry. He stated that his mind had gone blank and that he could not remember any of the evidence he should have given. Case dismissed and I am sure the officer had some explaining to do with his superiors.

In those days most people pleaded guilty to offences unless they thought they had a chance of getting off and this was especially so with persons summonsed for keeping a dangerous dog. There was always the threat the animal could be put down so in majority of cases it was not guilty. Just a dog bite if not to serious was normally a fine. I never experienced any offence life threatening, or any animal being put down, unlike today when cruelly some dogs are unlawfully breed for just for fighting and personal protection. Sadly it is all too often these types of dangerous dogs often maul or mutilate people, especially young children when the animal is not muzzled or left unsupervised often resulting in death or serious injury.

There was one straightforward case where this ladies dog bit the postman and in my presence he was able to identify her dog as responsible. She would not accept it and went to court pleading not guilty. I remember giving evidence and during cross examination her solicitor showing me a selection of photos of similar breed dogs for me to pick out the dog in question. This was a little unfair as the postman had identified the dog anyway in my presence and that of the owner which was all that required of us to prove the offence. The police Inspector prosecuting winced and looked towards me, where in fact he should have objected to such cross examination. I calmly looked through the large selection of photographs and pointed out to him one of the photographs. "That's the one." I said to him. The solicitor said "No further questions." and I left the witness box. She changed her plea to guilty and was fined and an order made to keep the dog under proper control. No one ever knew that apart from identifying the dog on the photo, I recognised the back garden at the home of the offender.

In a similar story which sadly came much later in my service, a young experienced detective who had full potential to a promising career, suffered similar problems in giving evidence. Without any real explanation half way through cross examination he had lost his memory and was later deemed unfit for purpose as a detective. He was taken off C.I.D. duties and returned to uniform working inside the police station. He was extremely well liked and I would say now sadly long forgotten. It transpired the initial cause of his problems was the onset of multiple sclerosis which sadly caused him to lose his life before the age of forty. This just goes to show we are only human which should never be dismissed from our minds.

It's a pity the same does not apply today when solicitors hound our troops on shady or flimsy evidence from the enemy in wartime conditions resulting in the trauma for them and their families after so many years to be found not guilty where many cases if in civil life would never even reach court. Human rights going overboard. No one can condone murder of course, but there has to be real and strong evidence so such actions can be justified. It is always suspicious in my book when these people do not voluntarily come forward and their cases only are allegedly detected through possible incentives by some solicitors, decent law abiding solicitors of course presenting good evidence must always be complimented.

I remember frequently having to go to the city magistrates to obtain urgent search warrants, where no entry would be allowed into premises, or buildings that were secure and we suspected the occupants had hidden stolen goods and were not answering the door. Leaving another officer outside such addresses to ensure nothing was removed. Just walking into such an old atmospheric Victorian building was itself fascinating. It was so nostalgic steeped in history of famous criminal cases. With well over forty separate courts all housed in one building the main clerk would arrange one for you to attend without delay. The Ushers would clear the court so evidence could be given in private. Based on the evidence given, a warrant would be issued, for premises to be lawfully entered and by force if necessary. From start to finish the whole procedure took less than 10 minutes. That was the justice system at its best.

In my earlier days of being a police officer we were in most cases always able to get back items of property from the crime, valuable or sentimental goods which sometimes could not be readily or easily replaced. What job satisfaction nothing could replace the happiness given to the owner, especially when belonging to the family of bereaved relative's items so precious they were irreplaceable.

I recall a story told to me by one former police Superintendent relating back to when he was a detective Sergeant. He had a colleague of the same rank who was well known throughout the criminal fraternity as being a hard- nosed gritty detective who was dedicated and extremely hard-working, honest, yet ruthless in bringing those to justice who well deserved it. He had a case at the city Assizes where some 10 defendants were each charged with affray with varying offences including grievous bodily harm and offensive weapons. They were all due to appear before a red robed Judge for establishing plea. Either that of guilty where they would be sentenced or not guilty where a trial would go ahead, that day or in the future. They were all in the foyer of this major city venue when they saw the officer in the case, this detective sergeant walk alone to the main downstairs toilet area.

Altogether they followed and confronted him alone where they made threats and suddenly attacked him. Ten nasty men against one policeman they certainly were brave individuals. To his credit he was more than able to defend himself and one by one he pushed them off and at every opportunity defended himself with an appropriate exchange of fisticuffs. In turn his retaliation resulted with all men suffering bruising to the face and upper body where they had fallen into a heap on the floor. He was certainly more a match than they ever could have anticipated. This officer was eventually joined by other police colleagues both uniform a plain clothes officers, who assisted in rounding up the offenders and taking them into custody to later appear before the judge who was made aware of their conduct. No further charges were bought against any of the accused but the judge certainly bore this in mind when it came to sentencing upon receiving their guilty peas or findings of guilty. As it turned out all pleaded guilty and they all went to prison. Today security together with CCTV would either prevent these incidents taking place or provide sufficient evidence to convict them of offences.

As time went on it has become acceptable practice when the accused has been questioned over the whereabouts of stolen property for them to give a ridiculous answer, such as "I sold it to a bloke I met in the Pub" or just simply "No Comment". Defence staff knew the accused was lying, as so did we, but that bought no comfort to the victims. In many cases victims lost out, with having no insurance to cover them, or had to accept poor reduced settlements from inadequate insurance claims.

With society changing in many directions, with sometimes the wrong people winning huge amounts of money from winning by the pools, lottery, bingo or gambling, no account has ever been taken for covering compensation. When criminals have been convicted and through criminal activity have banked large sums of money it is good under the Proceeds of Crime Act that losses can be recuperated. This can only be excellent news. There should be procedures in place for winners of competitions who have not paid compensation for earlier crimes and any cutoff date for such claims, should be abolished and judged on merit. Anyone who has never worked and has been a prolific criminal should in my view be made to pay back from winnings, any reasonable claims against property stolen. The same could apply to legal aid where there has possibly been some abuse.

In the recent cases of some criminals becoming millionaires there shouldn't be need for any lawful prompting. As a matter of conscience they should make up and pay out themselves as a form of voluntarily retribution, which would complement any proper way of going straight and giving up crime. As with legal aid in my view it should not be seen as an automatic right just because you are not working or earning very much money. We can argue human rights but when a burglar is repeatedly charged with offences, he should only get limited representation for his first or second offence. Anything more than that and the offender is using the system to fund his own criminal career. I know a good lawyer would argue there could be a miscarriage of justice, but if the rules were in place he would have to behave properly or tolerate the consequences. All these issues are of course debatable of course in a free democracy, but do make sense to prevent abuse.

Today we have the Human Rights Act and the European Court of Appeal, both controversial areas of law. In many cases some victims can benefit, but the wrong people seem to attract high profile cases such as uncomfortable prison beds and not being allowed soft pillows or radios or televisions, when they are pampered instead of serving simply their sentence of punishment. Possibly living in better facilities inside than being free.

In addition legal aid used for the wrong cases and not for other cases deemed more genuine, when it is in fact for all people in society to use provided honestly and fairly. Sadly today we seem to get people committing crimes from all spectrums of the legal profession, on the defence and prosecution sides where the genuine dedicated honest professional in all areas should be quite rightly fully respected.

CHAPTER 24

EVERYDAY EXPERIENCES AND ACTIVITIES WITHIN THE CORONERS DEPARTMENT

The Coroner is a very professional person a former doctor or lawyer with a least five years previous experience. They have some of the most important powers in the country and can and do change the law in many respects for the better.

It was only a small Coroner's department made up of two police constables, an ex-sergeant and civilian typist. Needless to say they were all characters in their own right. Although the female typist was a lovely person, her typing was just absolutely terrible. If anyone blamed their tools she did, it was always the typewriters fault yet other people using the same machine never experienced problems. She would use so much tipex, which in those days, was a white fluid used for covering printing mistakes and my god did she use it. It would have been cheaper to buy a tin of quick drying emulsion paint. When you held the pages of the completed typing against the light it was if it had caught the tail end of a shotgun being discharged, but she got away with it how I will never know. I think it was a question of personality came before experience as even I could type better and I was just a novice.

When in the Coroner's department one of the saddest experiences whilst working with this team came as we were about to leave one of the major hospitals. We had finished attending a series of autopsies and a call came over the radio, that there was a D.O.A known as dead on arrival certified within the casualty area. Sadly the deceased was the victim of a road accident, a very pretty young girl, one of three all aged 8 years who all ran out into the path of a vehicle, in attempt to cross the road. The other two girls were being treated in casualty who had sustained serious injuries. It transpired that all three girls were related, with two being twin sisters. The other girl was their cousin. All parents had been summoned to attend. It was a very sensitive issue, no parent had been informed of the death and with all girls very similar in description and wearing identical clothes it was of the utmost importance we had our facts completely correct. So one by one we went through the process of elimination, first speaking with the parents of both survivors and established the deceased was actually one of the twins. This information was given to the nursing staff and the doctor in charge broke the sad news to the parents.

The worst part was yet to materialise. I had the task of arranging identification of their daughter such a young body in a private chapel. So how do you console a young father who has to view the dead body of his very own daughter this is such a difficult task. It is what every parent dreads, an experience that never goes away. Like any other loving person you can only hug them and offer condolences be sincere In every respect and be there for them, regardless of their background.

The post mortem of any child is the worst experience I can ever describe and I admire the pathologist and his assistant immensely, showing total respect and professionalism at all times. As they will tell you, it is something that you just do not get used to we were all extremely sad and finding it hard to control our emotions. Every young person, especially a child is very special and everyone is affected with total sadness. Having children myself this kind of tragedy never leaves you and makes you appreciate each other all the more. So with a death of this nature it affects everyone especially, family and friends of the deceased and the driver of the vehicle who was absolved of any blame whatsoever.

I also recall another tragic case, when I had to arrange the identification with the parents of deceased girl who was just 12 years old. The father completed the difficult task no different to the previous case. This time I knew the girl, who had gone missing from home a couple of times in the previous twelve months. She was found on both occasions, the one time by myself and returned home. I spent some time talking with the family during these difficult times, so it was even sadder for them and me when I had to deal with her death, also as a result of a road accident.

Working in the role of a policeman having a sense of humour is an important quality never more so than dealing with death, but it must always be discreet and with respect and dignity. Like the time two electricians walking along the hospital corridor asked directions to the power room. The porter having a wicked or warped sense of humour back in those days sent them both in the direction of the mortuary entrance. Unsuspecting they walked straight in and to their horror interrupted an autopsy

265

taking place. In shock I recall one them shouting out, "Is he dead?" referring to the deceased, before himself collapsing on the floor with his colleague just running outside in terror. To some people this may appear to be funny but could also have again resulted in devastating consequences. No one owned up to the misdemeanor but from there on the doors always remained locked. Not that I am a kill joy, but in my view another example of a joke portrayed in extremely bad taste.

A few years after my role as Coroner's officer the one police constable that I worked with in that department suddenly died from a heart attack. He was still in service at the time of his death which was unexpected. Despite being very sad his good friend a serving colleague the ex-sergeant, attended the autopsy. I was told that apart from watching his friend now deceased and lying on the slab which was bad enough he indulged himself eating cold liver sandwiches during the examination, not that his friend would have minded.

This same ex-sergeant was the same man who told me when he was younger he met his girlfriend inside the cinema, not outside meaning she had to pay the entrance fee herself and he took along his cold liver sandwiches. How romantic. He was also the same man as desk sergeant when someone selling boxed Christmas cards entered the station. They all laughed when he responded, "The only box I want for my missus is six by two." I am sure he was only joking.

Today not many officers attend post mortems or are attached to the Coroners department which is now a mainly civilian post, whereas it can be an extremely helpful experience, rewarding and ultimately very interesting. Not only to bring out the sensitive side of your personality but also prepare you for the sight any serious injury or scene of death you may encounter as part of your duties. The same applies to our other colleagues and friends who work in the emergency services such as fire, nursing and paramedics, not forgetting mountain rescue and lifeboat service crew.

A couple of years later walking the beat I was directed to a 14 storey block of flats where on the landing of the 10th floor there was a report of a suspicious death. It involved sadly a young black youth in his late teens who had hung himself from a stair rail. He was found hanging between floors and some residents had actually discovered the body of the deceased whilst walking downstairs to exit the building. A young couple raised the alarm, but the female witness was naturally traumatised, fortunately her male friend was consoling her. Assistance arrived and we cleared the area, the deceased being covered with a sheet which was kindly provided by one of the neighbours. Scenes of crime officers attended together with the police surgeon and someone from the Coroner's department who dealt with the case.

Enquiries later revealed tragically the young person had a history of depression and had attempted to take his own life some weeks previous. That same day I recalled speaking to his parents who lived a short distance away when they visited their son's address. They were such good people, religious and law abiding, who had to live on with the consequences of their son's actions. With such a sad loss one would hope the pain would ease with time, as everyone who experiences a tragedy of this kind will know life is never the same but at some time we have to carry on our lives and remember all the happy memories of the person passed. Although no note was found from the deceased, it was established the cause of death was due to hanging with no suspicious circumstances and at a later inquest from the evidence provided it recorded a verdict of suicide.

Families who go through life without these awful experiences are indeed very fortunate, but sadly many do not, with some having more than one sad experience. Despite my father losing his girlfriend in a road accident as detailed previously, some 10 years later, tragedy struck again. My parents were both attending my uncle's sons christening, when again sadly the incident took place. There was a family disagreement and words were exchanged. His brother who was a little hot headed jumped on his motorcycle and rode off erratically away from his home into the countryside. He was gone for ages and eventually police called at the home where the christening party was being held bringing the sad news that his brother had crashed into a tree and had been killed instantly. Naturally everyone was devastated and this stayed with my father for the remainder of his life. With both horrible experiences as stated previously, time was a great healer, but sadly for my father this was not the case and he often during his life was extremely distraught and this affected his mental health for many years as he blamed himself, even though he was not at fault.

That is why I will never forget some few years after I had retired from the police force. My old neighbour who was also a police officer came home one morning after working nights and suddenly collapsed with a fatal heart attack. He had less than twelve months service to complete and his death was a shock to everyone. A duty uniform Inspector who worked at the very same station as the deceased, visited shortly after to offer condolences to his widow. When referring to her deceased husband he got his name completely wrong. How hurtful and insensitive for his family especially his widow, just as if it did not matter. This deceased officer had served nearly 30 years at the same station and the police Inspector who also had worked there several years, could not even get his name right. How insulting is that, not just with the deceased being a police officer but with any person. Surely of whatever rank you are this is one role where there is no excuse for not being professional. You get your facts right especially in such tragic circumstances, as you only get one shot at it and you must always give your best. So I make no apology if I offend anyone, as in my book there is just no justification for such a poor performance in offering condolences, at such a sad occasion, by an officer representing the senior management of the police service.

This Inspector showed complete lack of empathy and failed one of the basic requirement at such a sad sensitive time, getting your facts correct. Would he have liked the same treatment had it been a member of his family whose name they would have expected to know and had got it completely wrong. He possibly regretted saying it but it is disrespectful and you cannot remove the hurt and insincerity shown, in not being fully aware of the facts. Clearly if this had been an officer of lower rank he would have been criticised, whereas no action was taken against this Inspector. Thank god for the good officers who are always on the ball and get their facts right no matter what the rank. What better reason for staff having attachments to the Coroner's department and learning to be respectful and sincere where the lesson of avoiding such mistakes would be a requirement for all.

CHAPTER 25

THE GOOD AND NOT SO GOOD SENIOR UNIFORM OFFICERS

Throughout the whole of my service I have always shown respect for the ranks from Sergeant to the top of the tree to the Chief Constable. I have to accept that exams had been passed and some experienced staff were very good leaders, after all they were fulfilling very necessary roles as managers having skills in administrative issues and organisation. This was even better if they were fully experienced officers in performing all kinds of practical and operational duties. Sadly like in any organisation that does not mean everyone was perfect for the role, far from it. This is something I would have loathed to have done, I was not into any kind of supervision that involved checking other officer's paperwork or procedures, not that I did not help other officers, but I really joined just to be an all-round operational police officer.

The annoying thing was midway through my service some staff did not get promoted on their own merit. Whether this is accepted or not, there was a genuine thread of promoting officers just because they fitted a criteria, had degrees with University background, or such as because they were black or a different nationality, female, or gay in whatever gender, which had nothing to do with diversity for everyone.

I cannot prove it and it is only my view and that of limited older officers of all ranks who had common sense, who regularly between ourselves discussed the issues. We would not have been at all surprised around that time, if some exam results had been doctored to ensure passes for certain officers. After all anything was possible, as promotion exams were marked by police personnel and un-scrutinised. With information possibly from a much higher level those marking papers may have been given carte blanche instructions. This being French for 'blank card', meaning one that can be filled in as a person wishes. With exactly the same principal being applied to marking papers to ensure one passes, even if the person taking the exam did not have sufficient knowledge to pass correctly or qualify in the subject matter. It was all about getting figures right to achieve political goals, whereas other more suitable candidates of the same description fell by the wayside. It would have been done cleverly if it happened and most certainly denied and very difficult to prove. It was so obvious as when these people who got promoted as a result, many just did not have sufficient knowledge or experience to fulfil the role especially that of Sergeant. Their knowledge of the law was extremely limited and strong evidence very likely they would never ever pass the strict police promotion papers. So in my view and only my view, people of these descriptions may have become supervisory officers just solely for political reasons. However majority of staff of all races and backgrounds did not wish to get promoted for these reasons, they wanted to be in the next rank because professionally they were suitable candidates having qualities in leadership, experience, integrity and being above average in character.

A few years later this was addressed with more stringent rules and practical tests with various scenarios of police work marked on merit, experience in how expertly the incidents were handled. This ensured the right person suitable for promotion hopefully was sufficiently qualified. Even so although having good knowledge in a background knowledge of theory, it is far different to genuine general police duties involving real life incidents, where practical experience combined with common sense is the ultimate testing point.

I can recall one time in this Metropolitan police force shortly after amalgamation, if you had passed your exams promotion was in most cases automatic as there were too many vacancies. Sadly too many staff became Sergeants who were not even decent Constables and it took a while to correct this through wastage and retirement, but not all were bad. We also had some good sound police officers who went on to climb the ranks. Thankfully today officers have to be well qualified for the role before any kind of promotion, but sometimes I cannot help feeling the desire to reach the top is not always matched equally with the level of real practical experience. The philosophy of learning on the job from various experiences whilst in the newly promoted rank may seem fine for the powers that be, but unfortunately in some cases is it unfair to that officer as he may not be ready and of course then the job suffers either through poor morale, bad results and cavalier policies which could be avoided when the ideal candidate is otherwise fully cable of performing his duties in the first place.

A few years on and I am sure the powers that be realised their mistakes especially where some had reached high ranks involving all races and all they could do was end up suing the police force who after all had treated them far better than most others. If the police force had been more ruthless and positive in demoting some of the supervision who did not make the grade it would have been all the better for it. Mainly for obvious reasons such as political views, areas of bad judgment or just plain inefficiency, I am positive a lot of the problems today could have been prevented.

In my earlier days senior officers did not live in the politically correct world, but they knew their profession and many were fully experienced with some sadly who were not. Decision making was forthright in most cases, unlike today where everything is damage limitation. Whether we like it or not, we now all live in a world where every mistake is magnified and scrutinised. Not my kind of politics sometimes I feel the world really could be a better place.

One set of circumstances I refer to, certainly would not fit into today's politically correct world. No different to the saying that you cannot have a police officer appointed in the job as if he was a Benny Hill look alike, same applying if it was a similar female comedienne. In my first police force we had an Assistant Chief Constable, who later became Chief Constable. He was a respected police officer who was known for his common sense, strict discipline and decision making. Whilst serving under him you knew exactly where you stood and providing you had done your job sensibly and efficiently he would in light of this evidence give his total support and backing. If you were at fault and had failed to do your job properly you knew you had to face the consequences of your actions. So if you crossed the line and were found out, depending on the severity of your actions you had to pay the price, resulting in discipline with a host of possible punishments from dismissal to demotion, fine, reprimand, or being required to move stations, or resign. You knew the rules and if you had any sense you learned by your mistake and where possible improved performance.

There was a very true story circulating through the ranks as told by several colleagues. This senior officer was in charge of promotion Boards when a sergeant appeared before him who was qualified and recommended for promotion to Inspector. After the usual formalities this officer on the Promotion Board, stated to the candidate. 'I have had feedback Sergeant from the division where you are stationed, that on the ground you are known as being a bit of a Pratt. Well I have looked into your background, so I have the decision that in this case I will promote you to Inspector and you will be posted to Newtown Wedge police station. [false] So we will just have to wait and see just how much of a c--t you really are, or turn out to be.' Believe me I am no prude but one swear word sadly used more frequently than ever is the C word. This is the worst of any bad language that I loathe completely. I am sad to say also that more and more this word is creeping into movies. Just what are the movie sensors doing about it? Completely nothing in my view but they have so much to answer for, in influencing younger people completely in the wrong way. I just hope in society it never becomes commonplace like the F word which is just used as a form of habit which so many people of all ages adapt to, but also is so unnecessary.

This senior officer was renowned for being blunt and a no nonsense individual who never used to mince his words. Can you imagine this today it would just not be politically correct and could even constitute abusive behaviour or misconduct. I do not know what the final outcome was of this newly promoted officer, but at the time several well- established police officers of all ranks all agreed with the comments made by this Assistant Chief Constable who was well regarded for speaking his mind even if not always kind in nature. In other words he was portraying the old saying, if the cap fits wear it. To me that seemed all un-professional, either he was suitable for promotion or not and any decision made to promote him should have been based on that alone, not with personal insults. To me it showed a lack of real character for the role he was performing, but that was how it was back then. Today sadly there are in my view, some Chief Constables in the UK who are far too politically correct in their roles and behave like social workers and can be compared to Boy Scout or Girl Guide leaders, who have no real experience in running Law Enforcement Organisations.

One perfect example I can give of un-professionalism involved a police sergeant who continued criticising the activities of another officer he was supervising to a Chief Superintendent. In other words, he was just talking about the officer behind his back. It was just at the same moment that the officer under discussion, was walking down the corridor towards them. The senior officer stopped the officer in question and in front of the sergeant, repeated exactly what the sergeant had said about him. The sergeant was all flustered and red faced when this senior officer reiterated what had been spoken and told them both he would leave them to sort it out with each other. The Chief Superintendent then walked off. This is exactly what the sergeant should have done in the first place. Rather than talk about someone who has no redress behind their back, just supervise and talk to the person concerned to correct the issue, with positive action or discussion to remedy the problem. This was just pure excellence, brilliance in showing how to manage staff as portrayed by the Chief Superintendent. If only everyone would follow in his footsteps, not only in the police force but all other professions government and private institutions the country would be in a much better place.

In most cases unnecessary criticism made by some senior staff would be against other hard working policemen, or officer's with skills that they indeed could not match themselves. These problems often occur when someone is over promoted and not ready to deal with the challenges involved. However in complete contrast, we had a uniform Superintendent, who fitted all the ingredients completely as an Inspector Clouseau character. You may think I am joking, sadly I am not. He came across as just absolutely barmy and I felt it was ludicrous to keep such a person in a senior position of authority. Rumours and an abundance of jokes had it circulated that he had had a brain tumour and the surgeons had removed the brain and left in the tumour. I did not know if this man had undertaken medical surgery or not and if he had, the comments of other senior officers and alike were deplorable. As sad as the situation was, either way his position was unacceptable. If he was incapable for any medical reason he should have received help, or if just unfit for purpose be dealt with accordingly.

There was an occasion he was completing staff appraisals with most of the station staff and had been in charge of the sub-division for several years. This one officer had also been under his supervision for the same period.

After conducting an interview for over half an hour, the senior officer stated," Well thank you for a good years work PC Richards." The officer replied, "That's fine Sir, but I am PC Grainger." Words fail me as most people could not believe it but let me assure you this most definitely took place. This Superintendent deserved better than to remain in such a demanding role but so did all the staff under his command, who at times needed strong support and backing in performing a very difficult job. This area of policing needed expertise which this officer was not fully capable of providing.

Okay anyone can make a mistake, but there was another occasion where this same senior officer had been to headquarters on a briefing where there was to be a staged mock terrorist operation. This was to involve expert crack military forces at a pre-planned location. All was set in place to happen in the area of a disused factory and the senior officer had been to all the meetings and knew the plan of action. Nearby modern offices had been set up as a command centre, we all knew the date but not the time and this was all being monitored as a national objective. All of a sudden on this very date, the make believe incident had commenced and nominated officers were directed to the given command centre. We had to drag a large wooden Incident room box, which was cumbersome and heavy, which would normally be taken out to the site of any real major incident.

Just to explain these major incident boxes were in use, well before the widespread use of computers without operational programs which in present day are designed specifically for murders and other major enquiries. Back in our day the incident room box contained all kinds of stationery, with witness statements and descriptive forms and all necessary documentation and equipment to be used for this same purpose. We were directed by this senior officer to the most filthy and unused area of old offices, which were void and without electricity. He supervised us in cleaning the place as a make shift command centre, which was quite frankly utter chaos. We all sensed something was completely wrong about the whole set up and this proved to be another example which questioned his ability and authority. We had been there for about 30 minutes and the Assistant Chief Constable for crime attended and gave the senior officer the biggest bollocking of his life and in my view unprofessionally, as it was in front of all officers present regardless of rank. Apparently at all the briefings attended by this senior officer, he had been advised all had been set up in place in the command centre, with telephones, fax machines and computers, all ready for operational use. This especially showed that there was absolutely no need for any wooden incident room box.

Surely his behaviour must have aroused suspicion with the Assistant Chief Constable as to this man's state of mind and credibility, but surprisingly this Superintendent still remained in post. After this dad's army charade, the nominated officers regrouped and commenced to play their roles in the incident which eventually resulted in a complete success.

I remember the same Superintendent, some several months later calling me into his office, as he was dealing with a serious complaint against police. He was asking me questions over identification of suspects. I could see he completely had his wires crossed. He stated as he questioned various police officers, was he allowed to ask the officers if they could identify the complainant. Come on get real we all would know the answer to that. It should have been the other way round, can the complainant identify the officers involved. What an annoying farce, another issue when his judgment was in question, after all he was earning well over twice as much as our rank and we deserved better. Eventually he was moved to another station at a separate division. It's hard to believe but he regularly turned up at our station several mornings, by mistake when he was actually employed elsewhere. This was within some nine months after transferring, all these warning signals with such a catalogue of disasters just being the ones we knew about and he still did not receive any help or guidance. If an officer of any other rank had behaved in a similar way this would not have be tolerated, but this officer remained in this rank for some five years with this unhealthy behaviour until his retirement. If the powers that be, knew his real predicament then someone should have authorised him to go into a less prominent post which he could have coped with, away from operational police duties. Otherwise this Superintendent should have been considered for medical discharge. This in my view was a clear and utter example of a person being over promoted, where the establishment should have acted appropriately in a reduction in rank or medical pension, again where the establishment clearly looked after their elite as anyone of lower rank would have been sacked or pensioned off immediately.

It didn't finish after he had retired. I met him with his wife in another local town and he had pulled onto the pay and display car park. He came over to speak to me asking if I had any change for the machines, as he only had notes. Who goes into town to park on a pay and display car park without any change in his possession. I explained he could have my ticket as it had over half an hour left, but really was not transferable, but he could be clamped or fined without one. I told him I had to go and left him with it. He probably stuck it onto the outside of his windscreen. Whatever he did I did not know, other than he hadn't changed much. Whatever his problems were, to me they still had not been addressed.

Over a year or so later I was also retired and out with my friend for a drink, when this same ex-senior officer with his wife came into a local country public house where we were situated. I introduced him to this business colleague a figurehead in the borough where we worked, whom he did not even know, despite being chief of police in the area for well over five years. We had an amusing lunchtime and both were getting slightly inebriated and the man's wife, in her late sixties starting writing down my friends details on her tights at her upper leg, with a ballpoint. It was obvious they would not be able to drive, so we arranged to drop them off on the way home ourselves in our chauffeured vehicle. They had left their car on the car park and off we went. As we left them outside their house, he had fallen over the privet into the front garden and she had leaned with her back against the wall of the house and had slid down onto her buttocks. We did not anticipate this behaviour and it was a complete surprise even though it was extremely hilarious and just plainly unforgettable. If only I had had my video camera it would have been a worldwide hit on You Tube. I bet there was no Sunday dinner cooked in their home on that day, but it was all down to them and their own self-inflicted behaviour.

We had a uniform sergeant who had 15 year's service and he had done a stint on traffic, the remainder of the time he was a chief officer's chauffer. What a luxury for an operational police officer, now quite rightly undertaken by a civilian role. This sergeant had been dealing with a fatal road accident on the shifts and requested my advice as I had been a coroner's officer and he wished to use the benefit of my experience. I naturally helped as I would anyone and gave him ideas on file preparation and policy, which he at the time was extremely grateful for.

What I could not understand was if he had been a traffic officer for so many years how come he had never dealt with a fatal road accident which should have been bread and butter stuff for anyone in that kind of role. After all the help I had given a few months passed and he soon forgot the occasion he had asked for my assistance. He had changed and had become rude, abusive and obnoxious and clearly frightened of his own shadow perhaps due to some other lack of experience. Another clear example of a person being over promoted. It was true to say I don't think he ever had a friend. Not that he deserved one from the experience that I had with him. He clearly was a very vindictive and misguided man who had failed to appreciate how good things had been for him.

It was while he was also sergeant that he arrested a fireman for stealing half a bucket of coal during their strike, where green goddesses were used instead of fire engines.

The fireman had taken the coal in the belief he would have had consent of the owner as at that time the temperature was well below freezing. With them on the picket line at such a controversial time, to arrest such a person at a time of conflict was insensitive and like showing red rag to a bull. This was immediately a refused charge authorised by an officer of higher rank, but the damage was done. What a way to insensitively treat our colleagues in the emergency services over such a petty issue.

Guess what this sergeant later got promoted, but again I am sure not for his experience, I believe it was to get well shut of him. He moved division after that and even made it to the next rank above Inspector. He must have had some good qualities somewhere, but in fairness if he did I never saw them. Just imagine a person of this charming character getting to grips in investigating any kind of serious criminal matter with such an attitude. I don't think he had ever solved any real important crime in his police career and certainly not during all the time I had known him. The alleged theft of coal gives you a positive flavour of his expertise in dealing with criminal behaviour. He was just the sort of person some anti-C.I.D senior officers would love to put in charge of detectives. If transferred as a senior detective officer they would believe in that role he would be good for motivation, when in actual fact he was one officer who portrayed the opposite and would have killed morale. To me and many others he was clearly over promoted. No different to a future Chief Constable who later was in charge of our force and did exactly that, which is explained in much more detail in a later chapter.

On the same note I was present a few years later at an address, home to a petty criminal family. You only had to listen in their conversations during your stay with them to pick up on local criminal activity in who was up to what and who with. They clearly had no loyalty to anyone whatever the consequences of their loose and informative speech which you just laughed at pretending to ignore and take no notice of. Whereas the complete opposite applied, but you were able to detect valuable information relating to other persons who were involved in some of the more serious offences. In this family there were a total four brothers living together who were all active in crime in one way or another, some petty others serious.

I remember this one late afternoon I was in the house when the elder brother returned not realising I was present in the main lounge and he had in his possession a couple of large savoy cabbages. It was clear in my mind knowing his pedigree that possibly they had come off the back of a lorry, or had been cut from a farmer's field without permission, either way I found it amusing what he was going to say or do. Unsurprisingly he stated he had found them on the side of the road when coming back from his mate's house who lived along this country lane. He was a typical character identical in many ways with the character of 'Greengrass' in the television series 'Heartbeat'

He told me to have one to take for the wife, I naturally refused in any case it was not my kind of vegetable. He insisted and not to be snobbish or show any unfriendliness towards him I politely agreed and he handed one of the cabbages to me as I left the address. I had to smile because I bet there were even more lying in the back of his estate, but I cannot say I saw them if he had taken others. I could see the cabbage was riddled with caterpillars and only fit for one purpose. However in accepting it he falsely believed that the trust was safe between us and in any case it got him off the hook, not that you could prove any act of dishonesty against him. To them I was approachable and trustworthy, but if I ever uncovered any evidence of serious criminal offences this would certainly not save any of them from arrest.

In any case on reflection you could easily imagine this sergeant if he had been in my shoes not hesitating for a moment to arrest this criminal on suspicion of theft of the cabbages, where he would take him to the police station. He would then question him for at least a couple of hours, engage fully the services of a solicitor, only for the final result with the brother being released with no evidence and charge refused. What a waste of time. In my view the practical issue being, use him for information and only lock him up when there was more positive evidence of a more serious criminal offence. After all police procedure has always been, can you prove the offence and are the grounds for arrest reasonable or necessary. This in my view was the only way to operate and achieve respect. Something this sergeant was utterly incapable of and could not detect where a valid defence was given or possibly could not be disputed and was not worth the amount of time for something so trivial. No different to someone having a shovel of coal. In any case the cabbage was properly disposed of at the first opportunity into its rightful place, adequately called the dustbin.

When he finally retired he ended up working for a solicitor not that there is anything wrong with that as some ex-colleagues with their expertise can be an asset in an honest and loyal way to both defence and prosecution. The annoying issue here was a former policeman who had never gained any experience in locking up criminals and without practical knowledge in many areas of police work undertook such a role. With him having some 25 years of service, he was working for an organisation that quite rightly help criminals in their defence get off charges, the kind of people which he couldn't lock up in the first place.

If you were the officer in charge of a case as detective or uniform constable or sergeant and identification was an issue, the law would state an identification parade would have to be completed by an Officer not less than the rank of Inspector. This was an often well used procedure and when you later appeared at court you were the subject sometimes of very unnecessary criticism or severe cross examination, when they knew anyway you could not comment as you would not have been involved under any circumstances. Just to explain for anyone who may not understand, when an identification parade is necessary the officer in charge of the case dealing with the burglary theft or other criminal offence is not allowed to take part whatsoever in any part of the identification parade.

This is to ensure complete fairness to the accused and prevent any collusion with witnesses. Just a way the defence could try to paint a false picture of your credibility, knowing you were not able to answer the questions in the first place. Then they would realise at the very last moment they would have to call the Inspector to give evidence, that's if they could find him or he was not on leave, because he was not initially notified to attend. This was often overlooked in some cases I dealt with, when preparing the order of which witnesses to call to give evidence.

When I knew a parade was to be undertaken I used to complete a full report covering all the ingredients of the offence, detailed description of the offender, all witness particulars and ask for the matter to be allocated for a uniform Inspector to deal. Then there was no come back on me and any professionalism issue was well away from me. In addition to this report I always insisted on a statement of evidence from the officer to include in the file.

I regularly had comments from that rank saying it was not necessary and it was not liked but just one example where you covered yourself and remained free from this element of unnecessary questions in the witness box. Later in my service it became general practice to call those in charge of an identification parade automatically along with other witnesses to give evidence.

What used to aggravate me were the principals of certain people. When I was walking the beat and doing what I was paid for locking up criminals, we had a uniform Inspector who stated we had the best job in the police force. This from an officer who was in charge of licensing and ran the police club, hardly ever working shifts. I told him, "You ought to look in the mirror Sir. You have the best job in the police force." He had done that job for over five years and still had another similar term to serve undoubtedly in the same position. No hassle with no arrests, no violence and no court appearances and no shifts. One might say was he a serving policeman yet alone an Inspector of police.

So many policemen in various ranks had posts where savings could have been made using constables or employing other suitable civilian staff. These were just time wasting areas such as crime prevention, road safety, summons and warrants, firearms renewal and applications. There were just too many in these roles where they remained in a cushy number regular daytime shifts, never facing any serous police work or putting their neck on the line. These officers in my view had hung up their boots forgetting the role of policeman that they had in fact joined to be and police the community. I cannot help but feel the powers to be were to blame for this after it was at their jurisdiction it was sanctioned.

Over the years thankfully many changes in this direction were finally made, but all was far from perfect. It would make you sick that when cuts were needed to be made in the service, from all levels but the poor low paid cleaners or odd job men who all did a very excellent job would be at the top of the list to be exterminated. It was never from top heavy management or those where their roles were completely unjustified. No different from back then to present day, with the same policies being implemented with schools, hospitals and many other government establishments especially councils. It is always the low paid who work extremely hard in valuable roles that lose their jobs, with others with higher positions with five times higher wages who remain in unnecessary posts, some cutback on savings.

A major issue with all operational officers affecting us all throughout majority of our service was associated with poor working conditions. Nearly all cell block areas had hardly any room for taking fingerprints or photographs and with several prisoners needing to be processed on many occasions we either had to wait until some officers had finished their individual documentation which was very time consuming. All because facilities only catered for one prisoner at a time this with some twenty cells sometimes housing two prisoners at a time. This coupled with the fact that the police station never had enough interview rooms and in emergencies it was necessary to find anywhere to perform this task. When later audio and videotaping was introduced we only had two or three rooms available and it became inevitable we had to wait. As for normal witnesses just a room for interview in many cases was hard to find, you could not go into the police station areas where the environment showed official documentation, under privacy and confidential issues. In a lot of cases we just over spilled into the doctor's room or anywhere we could, not exactly comfortable for making witnesses relax and feel at ease.

However in nearly every major station it was the complete opposite. There were large offices for senior officers of most ranks, Chief Superintendent, his deputy Superintendent, sub-divisional and detective Superintendent, uniform and detective Chief Inspectors yet alone uniform and detective Inspectors. All who in the main had the luxury of thick carpeting, posh furniture which in most cases was four times the size of any interview room, with additional rooms specially adapted for some of their secretaries. Somewhere the priorities were all out of place compared to the working conditions of many operational officers of the lower ranks. No different to parking arrangements all had their own spaces whereas operational staff of all ranks had to arrive at work well before duty time to even find a car parking space. Nurses and police all experience very similar problems today having to pay for park spaces whilst bosses get it all free.

The one force where I was serving with all six divisions had chauffer driven cars for use by Chief Superintendents and their deputies being Superintendents grade 11, with the drivers role normally fulfilled by uniform police officers. Upon amalgamation this luxury for divisional staff ceased, after all they were treated like royalty with such a lavish expense for the period which really could never be justified today, yet alone back then.

The senior role of Chief Superintendent was a very much respected rank and you could not just walk into his office without a formal appointment and being escorted and introduced by a uniform Constable. It was known as the Divisional office and a smaller type set up of the Chief Constables office. Divisional cars have since long gone and are only now reserved for staff at the Chief Constables office with the chauffeurs role performed by civilian drivers. As for the Chief Constable, with his deputy and assistants they are based at police headquarters where major policy making decisions are made with various functions carried out in the everyday running of the force.

No different to the Police Federation PC who was always taking time off to go to meetings and conventions all expenses paid and visit officers on sick leave. In some cases all did very good work away from the front line and operational police duties until I realised, when they retired they received a Chief Inspector pension and more than double that of a Constable. They never openly disclosed this issue and or from my memory clearly advertised these jobs, no wonder there was never any Federation vacancies for many ranks.

I recall one uniform shift Inspector was with his men enjoying a Christmas function at a local public house. We all were invited and off duty and I decided to visit for a short time. All was bustling in seasonal party swing when at different periods the inspector was challenging this young probationer to see who could drink a pint of beer the quickest whilst standing back to back. What the young officer did not realise was the Inspector had only picked up a third of a pint and this officer's own drink had been laced with 30% vodka and the glass was full to the top. This happened twice during my presence and I could see the officer becoming the worst for ware and could hardly stand and kept going to the toilets to throw up. How many he had drunk before my arrival I did not know but he was suffering badly from the results of drinking large volumes of alcohol and possibly alcohol poisoning. He was unable to stand up in the end, he had certainly reached well beyond his limit.

I thought if this continues this person was going to be seriously ill or worse and I went up to the Inspector and asked to have a quiet word. He was told in no uncertain terms that if anything happened to this officer, I would report him and that all this stupidity had to stop immediately. I am all for a game of fun, providing all is equal and fair, but plying his drink with large amounts of vodka if resulted in death, at the very least would be manslaughter. He was told that he should have known better and left. They didn't give you any brownie points for criticising senior officers, but I would have done it again anytime willingly. He was a disgrace to his rank. Today he possibly would have been sacked under health and safety issues and quite rightly too.

So here we are in 2017 and you have senior officers such as a woman Assistant Chief Constable and a woman police Superintendent before a discipline panel for alleged arguing at a senior police function where one woman I cannot describe a lady, pulled out her one breast on open display comparing hers to the opposite rank stating she had a gorgeous figure despite being a mother of children. How on earth can they maintain credibility in such senior positions and despite this both kept their jobs. This in front of some members of the public. You are always on duty as a police officer, whether actually on duty or not. Wishing not to be cynical, but I would bet they both jointly had never seen active police work in their careers, carried out by myself and many other colleagues of low rank. What a disgrace to a truly wonderful profession and bringing their colleagues to shame when many had so many better standards than those in power. A perfect example where they both should have been demoted, as a constable or sergeant would have been sacked.

Yet on the opposite end of the scale we had a sergeant turn up for work and he was in a state of drunkenness. Clearly he was experiencing enormous stress related problems, with alcoholism playing an additional factor. His wife had left him and he had no access to his children, clearly he was ill and needed help. He was put before a senior officer who demanded this resignation, albeit I think under duress. He left the service when in fact in my view he needed medical help, counselling and support. If he was not liked you could appreciate what had happened, but sometimes there are two sides to a story and he had gone through a very bad divorce and clearly had several problems. As a result he lost his job and pension. Needless to say he did not bother to appeal which he should have done and may have been reinstated after all he was suffering illness and the job took advantage of his situation. I remember in his earlier days he was a good thief taker, well liked supervisor and all round solid performer. When he needed help all he received in my view was a closed door which in some way was very sad. Just like the Inspector plying vodka without hesitation should have been shown the door, but in that case it did not happen. It just proves in life there is always a rule for one and a rule for another.

There were many instances of double standards involving senior officers. One such officer who was initially a Constable at our station, returned several years later as Inspector. He was as scruffy then as he was before and even more uncouth. He was not liked and many that did not even know him soon found him to be of poor standing. He was making life difficult I learned with abuse of authority against many officers, some who were long in service and just would not stand for it. As a result whilst he was on night duty, an unknown set of officers went to where his vehicle was parked. Together they raised it onto sets of bricks and when he finished duty returning to the vehicle he was at the mercy of other officers to try and help. Not that this is my style, it was so funny and went all round the lower ranks, as undoubtedly the senior staff. No action was taken and with assistance he was able to free his vehicle. From various sources this Inspector had an overnight personality change and was much the better supervisor for it.

Whenever someone was promoted back in those days, I can never recall a senior police officer being reduced in rank having completing a 12 month period of probation, on grounds of being an inefficient supervisory officer, except under discipline for unconnected matters. It was if it would have reflected on the promotion board, but in other dedicated traditional posts such as scenes of crime, CID, traffic, dog section we had no such protection. As a constable or sergeant especially if you made any serious mistake or were considered inefficient or your face did not fit anymore, regardless how good you were, you could be moved back to a uniform posting without any real redress. To me that was an abuse of power as you were dealt solely with a senior officer. His decision which may have been affected with bias or just plain dislike of the officer affected, who was not entitled to any kind of appeal or proper representation. Some may think it cynical but some senior officers upon achieving promotion thought they were superior to those of lower ranks, whose dedicated hard work was mainly reflecting their own performance. Some had the mistaken belief that being just constables we had limited views or outlook, where the truth in reality was completely the opposite, as some had far more practical experience and common sense than many senior officers.

A good thorough efficient and experienced senior officer well-liked and respected always received respect and would never act in such a pompous or unprofessional way and in fairness there were more of these officers than the other kind referred to. There have been occasions a murder or other serious crime has been cleared through dedication and ground work undertaken solely by an officer of the rank of constable. Where the more than one senior officer has accepted the glory for all the hard work done and overlooked completely the constables involvement. Fortunately these instances were only rare but they did happen.

This view is fortunately shared with some senior officers who were wise enough to have realised the full circumstances. When you are in the public eye it is the one and only time when you are expected to give your complete best in the true tradition of the police service.

CHAPTER 26

ATTACHMENT TO CID ATTACHMENT ESTABLISHING A NEW CAREER

Having achieved some nine years' service I applied for an attachment to C.I.D and put aside any previous small grievances. In any case I had the full support of senior officers based on my previous experiences and my enemy Dc GLOVER was stationed elsewhere. It was my friend Monty who put forward the suggestion of stepping across borders in venturing into this new area of police work, but insisted I go first then he would follow. You do not get many friends like that. So a new station and brand new team another challenge I just had to succeed after all it was my secret ultimate goal to reach the rank of operational Detective Constable.

One of my first cases involved circumstances surrounding a very weird person who had a dust phobia, perhaps I am being cynical but the person suffering the illness was also engaged in criminal activities. I had never experienced anything like this before in my life and with circumstances being extremely unusual I just had to incorporate the story into this chapter. Normally if a person is ill with a phobia the last thing on their mind is committing crime but who was I to say. It wasn't exactly crime of the century more of a nuisance crime.

It all started with several complaints being made from different retailers throughout the town who had complaints of joints of meat and chickens having been purchased and alleged to have been contaminated where full refunds and compensation were paid out. It may not sound very serious but it didn't stop there. From our enquiries with customer services the same man had made allegations to other similar branches and other local towns and involved locations at two other cities. In some cases he had receipts, others not, but in nearly every case he had received refunds and compensation was totaling in excess of £500. In those days the technology was not around like today and when I made my enquiries majority of the businesses were unaware of all the complaints being made to separate branches by the same individual.

So with a detective colleague we went to the home address of the alleged offender, a middle aged bachelor who lived alone with his mother. The door was answered by the man and we explained the nature of our enquiries having shown him our identification. We asked if we could enter and immediately he went into a state of panic. Eventually speaking sympathetically he calmed down. He explained he had a dust phobia and that we could come in provided he put paper on the carpet for us to walk on. This he did all the way into the lounge and kitchen and finally we entered the house. To say it was creepy was an understatement. He had suffered this illness from his late teens and was now in his mid-forties. He could not stand dust under any circumstances and you may think the only way to combat this was to clean, clean, clean and clean but no it was the opposite. He had not allowed his mother to dust or vacuum for well over 20 years and all you could see everywhere in the hallway and lounge was a deep film of dust. It just had to settle he could not stand it to all be disturbed or spread into the atmosphere and that was how he lived. His mother was kind and caring and had little knowledge of her son's activities.

It was established he had a downstairs room and slowly with his permission we made a search. Out on the table were numerous letters, all correspondence relating to complaints of bad meat and chicken products and cheques for various sums as a form of compensation and refunds were everywhere from retailers offering their apologies. In the kitchen was a large chest freezer full of various joints of meat and chickens.

We took possession of the paperwork and informed the man he would have to be taken into custody on suspicion of criminal deception. He insisted putting paper in the C.I.D. car before getting inside and being taken to the police station. He was placed into custody with clean paper provided for him in the cells. As a precaution a Police Surgeon attended and examined him to ensure he was fit to be interviewed.

He admitted it started off quite innocently as a genuine complaint, but it put the idea in his head how to make money. In the end majority of his complaints were fictitious and he had written to stores he in actual fact had never visited so obviously he had committed criminal deception. He was charged and eventually at court he received probation and was offered help to try and sort out his problems. In some respects you could not help but feel sorry for him and I am positive he never re-offended.

In addition to this, nearly every day prisoners were left in the cells overnight for interview which I found was extremely interesting and completely different to my normal role. Gone were all the normal everyday contacts in walking the beat this new role was in complete contrast to anything I had ever done. Having my own crimes to investigate on a continual basis being organised and utilising every talent I had in clearing crime was a tremendous challenge and my previous dealings with criminals of all kinds whilst walking the beat seemed like a natural progression, especially working in a completely new environment.

Part of the secondment involved a two week visit to Force Headquarters where I familiarised myself with various CID departments dealing with unique areas of police work, all tools necessary for a criminal investigation. This included the Photographic Department where photo fits and drawings of suspected offenders were produced, whereas today majority of this kind of work is all computerised. With visits to the Stolen Cheque Squad and one of the most interesting aspects of police work a two day visit to the Regional Forensic Science Laboratory. This was such a fantastic experience and extremely interesting of what could be done even back then in the fight against crime and that was without the concept of DNA not even being in place. I would have loved a return visit towards the end of my service as the amazing improvements in all areas of scientific research were out of this world. Sadly this did not materialise.

In my view in whatever police enquiry that was taking place during my service, especially dealing with crime and working in CID there was never any criticism in being completely thorough in your investigations. This is especially true when interviewing all witnesses and obtaining written statements, whether at the time they are significant to the enquiry or not. In addition seizing anything you suspect may be an item connected with the enquiry as you normally only ever get one chance, which then can be examined forensically and possibly become an exhibit.

After all the issue of police work is just not solely to prosecute an offender, but also if evidence come to light to the contrary which may eliminate the suspect as being involved, this is just as important. More crucial than anything it is the duty of the police to establish the truth of what took place and any evidence obtained whether useful or not to the prosecution must always be disclosed to the defence. As I discovered during my career this philosophy was perfectly true, especially in any complex investigation such as murder, manslaughter, sexual offences, acts of violence fraud or arson. Evidence sometimes gathered may appear to be irreverent at the time, but can turn out crucial later in any enquiry especially when corroborated by other evidence.

Another interesting case I dealt with involved a young lady who was in her early twenties. This time it involved a cheque book, where she had gone berserk en-cashing a series of cheques with various store keepers. Apart from there not being any funds in the account she had been told in person by her bank Manager her account was closed and she was to return cheque books and bankers cards. We had no choice but to investigate and the young lady was arrested. She admitted responsibility and could not give any real explanation for her behaviour other than it was grossly stupid, realising she would be accountable for her actions. She was not in any position to repay anyone as the total amount of goods obtained came to over a £1000. Being an adult, she had to face proceedings and was subsequently charged.

At the time she was not working and I also offered this lady advice in how to change her life round and if she went for any job interview come clean and tell the truth and to learn from this costly and stupid mistake. This had the totally opposite effect in that she failed to appear at court and a warrant was issued for her arrest. I made enquiries at her home address which was a council flat and established it had been vacated. A couple of weeks went by and I established someone had moved into the address soon after.

I thought to myself this was a little too quick and had a haunch what this absconder from justice had possibly done. I checked with Housing department of the local council and discovered the new tenant had moved from an address some 80 miles away. Checking the previous address with the police that covered the area, I sent photocopies of all my dealings, together with a photograph of the young lady still wanted.

Within a couple of days I received the phone call that both council tenants had swapped addresses indefinitely. They made a visit to the new address resulting in the wanted person being arrested. She was an extremely silly girl and on being returned to our station, she was remanded into custody by the court. Just the difference between some people, some take advice others just do not want to know. You cannot win them all and I am sure she realised this when she was given 6 months in custody.

I regularly cleared burglaries, robbery and thefts of every kind together with major incidents of violence resulting in serious hospitalisation of victims and the obtaining of evidence for forensic examination. In addition I assisted in many enquiries involving indecency, a completely new area for me and realised I had a talent in getting to the truth in these matters. No murder enquiry yet but you never knew what to expect from day to day, in any case I had my whole future in front of me. You just did not ever stop learning. I was soon accepted by my colleagues and upon completion of my six months period, I was recommended for permanent attachment to C.I.D. So it was back to the beat and for Monty to take his turn. All I knew was that I was promised the next vacancy in C.I.D and I could look forward to a challenging and promising career improvement for which I personally had worked very hard to achieve.

Printed in Great Britain
by Amazon